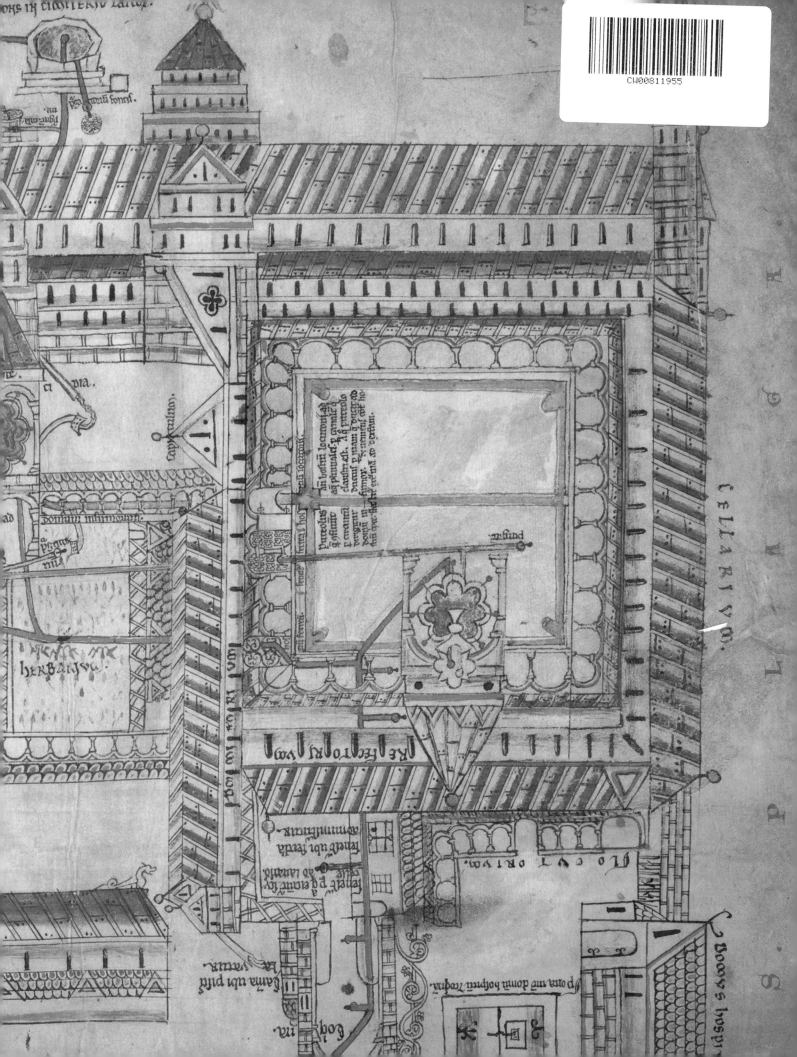
CW00811955

Canterbury Cathedral Priory
in the Age of Becket

Peter Fergusson

CANTERBURY
CATHEDRAL PRIORY
IN THE AGE OF BECKET

Published for the Paul Mellon Centre for Studies in British Art by

Yale University Press ❖ New Haven and London

Copyright © 2011 by Peter Fergusson

All rights reserved.
This book may not be reproduced, in whole or in part,
in any form (beyond that copying permitted by
Sections 107 and 108 of the U.S. Copyright Law
and except by reviewers for the public press),
without written permission from the publishers.

Designed by Emily Lees

Printed in China

Library of Congress Cataloging-in-Publication Data

Fergusson, Peter, 1934–
Canterbury Cathedral Priory in the age of Becket / Peter Fergusson.
p. cm.
Includes bibliographical references and index.
ISBN 978–0–300–17569–1 (cloth : alk. paper)
1. Christ Church Priory (Canterbury, England)
2. Church architecture–England–Canterbury–History–To 1500.
3. Architecture and society–England–Canterbury–History–To 1500.
4. Wibert, Prior, d.1167–Art patronage. I. Title.
NA5471.C25F47 2011
726'.70942234–dc23
2011022849

A catalogue record for this book is available from The British Library

Endpapers: Eadwine Psalter, MS R. 17. 1, fol. 284v, Trinity College, Cambridge (detail of fig. 3).
Frontispiece: Canterbury Cathedral Priory, Water Tower, view from north (detail of fig. 133).
Image on p. vi: Canterbury Cathedral, view over the Great Cloister © Cathedral Enterprises Ltd.

For Ruth Fergusson

Contents

Acknowledgments

My father introduced me to Canterbury, our visit beginning with him telling me that it was the most beautiful cathedral in England. A different introduction occurred many years later when I accompanied Peter Draper and the late Katherine Galbraith to look at the remains of Archbishop Lanfranc's 1070 rebuilding which had been identified by the then cathedral archaeologist, Tim Tatton-Brown. We spent a morning with him studying a small area of the crypt while he read out its history through a series of informed deductions based on the evidence of stonework and phasing. Teacher that he is, the building began to be revealed as a treasure trove of scholarly delights and puzzles. It was he who introduced me to the name of Prior Wibert.

The Precinct was harder for me to understand. I could follow the history from John Newman's lucid *Buildings of England: North East and East Kent* volume, but making sense of the buildings' uses remained a mystery, as, too, did their development through time. Clarity came slowly and then from experience at other sites. Working on an English Heritage guide at Roche Abbey (Yorkshire), I needed help to recognize its sparse precinct remains and turned to Glyn Coppack, an early pioneer of the study

of inner and outer courts. Some years later he came to my aid again, unraveling the suppression inventories at Rievaulx Abbey in the North York Moors with their wealth of information about the precinct and its buildings. Adapting these experiences to Canterbury involved breaking down the Precinct into separate problems. Over time they became the subjects of professional papers. A beginning came with the prior's Green Court Gatehouse for the *festschrift* volume offered to Eduard Sekler in 1994, one of my most influential teachers at Harvard. Another looked at the sacrist's need for vestment and reliquary storage in the Treasury and started as a paper for the conference celebrating the publication of Eric Fernie's *The Architecture of Norman England* (2000) (and appeared in the *Journal of the Society of Architectural Historians* for 2006). In turn, this stimulated a study of the fountain houses constructed by Prior Wibert, a contribution to Madeline Caviness's *festschrift* (2009). A last paper examined the Priory's entry complex and its relation to the revival of jurisprudence, published for the British Archaeological Association's *Transactions* series (2012). Each paper prompted further questions – and the idea for the present book began to form. Diverting progress was a developing interest in twelfth-century patrons. The subject caught my attention while working on Rievaulx Abbey (1999) and the role played in its architecture by the community's third abbot, and saint, Ailred (1147–67). It continued with Bury St. Edmunds, whose famous church gate constructed by Abbot Anselm (1121–48) became a *festschrift* paper in honor of Paul Crossley (2011). Together, these studies encouraged me to think that a history of Canterbury Cathedral Priory could benefit from an attempt to piece together Prior Wibert's patronage. Thus, my interest in patrons converged with the precinct interests and led to the present study.

In the course of my work I have accumulated debts to colleagues and friends. Their forbearance as they listened to accounts of what I was doing, their suggestions and ideas, and their interest helped and encouraged me. I want to thank Jonathan Alexander, Katherine Baker, Paul Bennett, John and Mary Berg, Thomas Bisson, Sheila Bonde, Father Laurence Bourget OCSO, Caroline Bruzelius, Alexandrina Buchanan, John Burton, Suzie Butters, Walter Cahn, Mary Carruthers, Lady Frances Clarke, Nicola Coldstream, Thomas Coomans, Glyn Coppack, Paul Crossley, Charles Donahue, John Doran, Peter Draper, Valija Evalds, Paul Everson, Richard Fawcett, Julian Gardner, Alexandra Gajewski, Richard Gameson, Richard Gem, Dorothy Glass, Lindy Grant, Erik Gustafson, Jacki Hall, Jeffrey Hamburger, Barbara Harvey, Sandy Heslop, Rachel Jacoff, Emilia Jamroziak, Michael Kauffmann, Peter Kidson, Terryl Kinder, Susan L'Engel, Carla Lord, Charles McClendon, Clark Maines, Richard Morris, Stephen Murray, Ursula Nilgen, Christopher Norton, David Park, Mary Pedley, Nicolas Pickwoad, Nigel Ramsay, Valerie Ramseyer, Lilian Randall, Lisa Reilly, David Robinson, Brian Rose, Jens Rüffer, Gyde Shepherd, David Stocker, Neil Stratford, Malcolm Thurlby, Giovanna Valenzano, Lady Cristabel Watson, and Teresa Webber. The chance to finish my work I owe solely to the emergency skills of Dr. David Brull who saved my life on January 8, 2009.

Generous financial help has come from Wellesley College. I gratefully acknowledge financial support for my attendance at the seminar in 2008 on York Minster (a contemporary undertaking to Prior Wibert's work at Canterbury) organized by Professor Christopher Norton and Mr. Stuart Harrison. Again in 2010 the college covered the costs for the construction of two digital models of the Guesthouse and the *Aula Nova*. Both are critical to an understanding of the subject of this book. Seeing them whole rather than in their standing fragmentary condition is central to two of the chapters in the book. The models were kindly prepared by Mr. Stuart Harrison, who produced six images from their rotation.

Over many years discussion with colleagues at Wellesley College has played a central role in my still evolving education in architecture. I am particularly indebted to Lilian Armstrong, Rebecca Bedell, Heping Liu, Miranda Marvin, James O'Gorman, James Oles, and John Rhodes. When the manuscript came together, Meredith Martin offered her services as a reader despite the pressures of the early years of teaching. Her many suggestions and clarifications are gratefully acknowledged. At the same time, staff members rescued me as I struggled with the major technological shifts of the last twenty years. Tolerating my tantrums and deftly moving me toward skill acquisition, they shepherded me from carbon paper and manual typewriters to electric typewriters and then to computers, from film-based images to digitization, from single-box Princeton-method slide arrangements to PowerPoint. The loyalty and kindness of Nancy Bowman, Maggie DeVries, Nancy Gunn, Jeanne Hablanian, Lisa Priest, and Pam Rogers mean a huge amount to me.

Professional colleagues generously read early drafts of chapters, and I have benefited from their criticisms and restructuring suggestions. At various stages this burden was taken on by Caroline Bruzelius, John McNeill, Kristin Mortimer, Margaret Sparks, Tim Tatton-Brown, Jeffrey West, and Christopher Wilson. They helped me with organizing the text, supplied further bibliography, and offered ideas. Eric Fernie provided generous and continuing support of my work, for which I am greatly indebted. The three anonymous reviewers of my manuscript at Yale University Press in London encouraged me with suggestions for development of further work, and I remain heavily indebted to them.

At Canterbury I have to admit to my unpreparedness for the rigors of dealing with the half-dozen jurisdictions which control access to the Precinct's buildings, many the consequence of its status as a World Heritage Site. At the start of my work the cathedral historian, Margaret Sparks, provided patient and generous help and introductions. Her beautiful handwritten letters are prized possessions. She saved me from many errors, generously answered questions, and, not least, steered me through the intricacies of the cathedral archives. Similarly, the master mason at the Cathedral, Heather Newton, extended every possible kindness and shared her wealth of knowledge with me. She accompanied me on a number of site visits, opened locked doors, climbed scaffolding to look at stonework, furnished escorts for building visits and for access to the Dean and Chapter's lapidarium at Sturry to the north of Canterbury. The Receiver General, Brigadier Meardon, kindly facilitated my work when stumbling blocks arose. The consulting architect to the Cathedral, John Burton, kept me informed on the matter of medieval mortars. At King's School, the surveyor, Gavin Merryweather, generously escorted me on two visits to look at twelfth-century buildings on the north side of the Green Court. The school's regimental sergeant major opened the Armory for me with its bounty of surviving material from the *Aula Nova* undercroft.

As ideas came into focus, I benefited from invitations to try them out in lectures or seminars. Audience comments and suggestions proved invaluable. My thanks go to Stephen Murray at Columbia University (through the Branner Forum), Jonathan Alexander at New York University's Institute of Fine Arts, Valija Evalds at Smith College, Lindy Grant at Reading University, Barry Singleton at Morley College, Thomas Bisson at Harvard College, Jane Loeffler in Washington, Charlotte Grey at Harvard University, and Alixe Bovey at the British Archaeological Association.

Scholars who work directly on Canterbury Cathedral gave generously of their time. Their diplomatic suggestions that I might find it "of interest" to consult such and such an author resulted in the correction of my wilder ideas. They also read and helped me with chapter drafts. I owe special thanks to Paul Bennett, Madeline Caviness, Peter Draper, Sandy Heslop, Deborah Kahn, John McNeill, Nigel Ramsay, Tim Tatton-Brown, Christopher Wilson, and Frank Woodman. Their publications stand as models of clear writing and thinking about twelfth-century Canterbury. Particularly generous has been Jeffrey West. He helped me with the sculpture, critiqued drafts of three chapters, recommended bibliography, and came with me on a visit to Canterbury to look at stone cleaning and conservation at the Green Court Gatehouse in 2010.

I am particularly grateful to the authors of Appendix A and C: Mary Pedley for her transcription and translation of Prior Wibert's 1167 *Obit* and Christopher Wilson for his solution to the long-lasting problem of the identification and source of semi-precious stones used in a number of buildings discussed in the text.

Librarians have been central to my work. At Cambridge, my visits to Trinity College to study the Eadwine Psalter stand out as memorable. They merged the beauty of the college and the luminous space of the Wren Library with the privilege of handling the Eadwine Psalter, the most valuable surviving Canterbury manuscript from the period covered by this book and a central monument of English Romanesque art. For making this possible I am most grateful for the help and interest of the librarian, Professor David McKitterick. At Lambeth Palace, Giles Mandelbrot kindly helped me with the *obit* of Prior Wibert recorded in MS 20. He also accompanied me to look at the Morton Gatehouse. The Society of Antiquaries library remains the most valued resource for someone with my interests. Working there has been a decades'-long pleasure, one mightily helped by Adrian James, the assistant librarian, who answered my questions, tracked down books, made xeroxes, and secured permissions. At the Warburg Institute, Jill Kraye and her staff were models of helpfulness. At Wellesley College I owe special thanks to the art librarian, Brooke Henderson, and the amazingly patient assistant librarian, Jeanne Hablanian.

At Yale University Press the transformation from manuscript to book would not have taken place without the support of Gillian Malpass. Her judgment and encouragement are deeply valued. It has been a privelege to work with her. Furthermore, she provided me with the invaluable help of Nancy Marten as copy editor. Her meticulousness and concentration winnowed out numerous errors and duplications. For the book's design I am much indebted to the labors and skill of Emily Lees. Her courtesy and forbearance made a pleasure of the last stages of the book's production.

Longer than anyone, my wife, Lilian Armstrong, has endured my interest in Canterbury with loving patience. As the study developed and changes and U-turns multiplied, she remained a center of calm and order. Her reading of the entire manuscript resulted in many improvements in organization. Throughout, I have benefited from her common sense, good judgment, scholarly example, and loyal support. Without her generosity of mind and spirit this study would not have been completed.

Lastly, I acknowledge an overarching debt to Stuart Harrison. As early as 2002, he came down from North Yorkshire to help me look at the Treasury when I got stuck reading its confusing fabric. In 2007, and again in 2008, we spent several days examining problem areas in the Precinct, benefiting from cold spring weather to see areas otherwise obscured by the growth of plants and trees. Throughout this period I drew freely on his skills in the analysis of *in situ* remains and loose stonework. Just as important he listened to my ideas, qualified some, changed many, and proved repeatedly a generous sharing colleague. Equally, I have profited from his photographic and modeling skills. Thirty of the images in the book are his.

Introduction

The extensive architectural renewal carried out in the mid-twelfth century at Canterbury Cathedral Priory is the subject of this study. During these years the monks faced serious challenges in central areas of monastic life. As the premier Benedictine monastery in the British Isles whose titular abbot was the archbishop, the Primate of All England, the Priory was called on to provide for increased numbers of visitors expecting hospitality, for higher standards of hygiene, for improved health care, for law reforms, and for changes to the Cathedral concerning liturgy, rituals, and circulation. To address these challenges the monks took bold actions. They determined to increase the size of their precinct, raise new buildings and enlarge old ones, install a state-of-the-art piped pressurized water system, and create improved spaces for the conduct of judicial business – all the while maintaining their time-honored responsibilities for the "Opus Dei," the daunting daily cycle of services in the Cathedral directed to the praise of God. The renewal entailed the adoption of building types not seen before in England, utilized up-to-date technology, and employed an architectural style distinct in its own terms, different from Romanesque and with few anticipations of Gothic. Although the types and technology remained largely discrete to the Priory, thereby underlining and defining the immediacy of their references, the style appeared elsewhere in southeast England and even as far away as the north of England, and was overshadowed only by the arrival of Gothic.

Analysis of this body of work (figs. 1 and 2) – outlining its development, tracing its sources, assessing its intentions, and evaluating its importance – forms the core of the study. To organize discussion in the following chapters, the architectural history is embedded in five broad subject headings which define the major concerns faced by the Priory in these years. Thus, hygiene becomes the means to examine the new water system and the buildings which it made possible, such as the Bath Building, the *Necessarium*, the *Piscina*, the five laving fountains, and the service functions in the Precinct. Similarly, hospitality addresses the expanded facilities of the Guesthouse and Common Hall, the revival of jurisprudence shapes the assembly of the entry buildings at the Green Court gate, the care of the sick and old underlies the expansion of the Infirmary

1   Canterbury Cathedral Priory, aerial view from the south showing the overall Precinct (photograph courtesy Countrywide Photographic).

The ovoid shape of the overall Precinct with the Cathedral at the center is formed at the top (or north) by the old Roman City wall which curves around to the east of the Church with Broad Street framing it beyond. The road to the north leads to Horsefold, the source of the water system. On the south and west side of the Cathedral the light-struck facades of Burgate Street lead to the Christ Church gate, the public entry to the Precinct. The buildings to the west, within the north-curving contour of Palace Street, are those of the Archbishop's Palace.

The west-to-east view of the Cathedral provides an orientation for the Priory buildings. Immediately adjacent to the west end may be seen the Great Cloister with the remains of Lanfranc's dormitory on its east boundary. To the north of the Cloister lies the garden of the Archdeacon, formerly the site of the Kitchen with the Archdeacon's house lying over the east range of the Cellarer's Court. Above and at the edge of the image is the Green Court Gatehouse, the medieval entry to the Priory. Extending west-to-east from it are the buildings containing the remains of the Bakehouse, Brewhouse, and Granary. Perpendicular to the south is the Dean's House built over the Un-named Building and the Bath House. The remains of the Infirmary Hall and Infirmary Chapel lie next to the east termination of the Cathedral. To the south is the re-located Cemetery Arch leading to the Memorial Garden; the Piscina (fishpond) would have lain more or less in front of and to the south of it. Opposite the east transepts the roughly circular, parched grass area marks the position of the free-standing Campanile.

and the establishment of the Almonry, and liturgical developments elucidate the additions undertaken to the Cathedral.

Architecture, as well as conveying physical presence and period style, carries the imprint of human agency. The literature variously credits the renewal at the Priory to either Archbishop Theobald (1139–61), the major spokesman for the church in England at this period, or Prior Wibert (ca. 1153–67), the far less well-known head of the Benedictine community of monks.[1] Establishing which of the two men was responsible is important because they each represent different orientations, Theobald the world of politics and ecclesiastical statecraft, Wibert that of monasticism. Early on, their relations were vexed. In 1154 disputes over the Priory's autonomy led Theobald to arrest and imprison Prior Wibert along with two of his monks who were preparing to travel to Rome to enlist the pope's support for the convent's cause (Searle 1980, 22). In the coming pages I argue that there is sufficient evidence to credit Wibert with the renewal and enough to allow for a study of his patronage.[2] Following Wibert's release from prison, the archbishop proved a generous benefactor. Around 1155 he gave the Priory the bountiful springs of fresh water outside the Precinct to make possible the new water system, and donated land from his palace grounds for the construction of the new Guesthouse. On one occasion he was moved to generalize: "it is not the community that should build for the archbishops but the archbishops for the community."[3]

The case for believing the prior initiated the changes is supported by visual, documentary, and archaeological evidence. The visual evidence is the unique, color-washed drawing of the overall Precinct, its buildings, cloisters, water system, and huge Cathedral. It appears on a bifolium (fols. 284v and 285r) at the end of the Eadwine Psalter, now in Trinity College, Cambridge, MS R. 17. 1, and is referred to hereafter throughout this study as *Drawing I* (fig. 3).[4] The image represents, at least in part, Wibert's building accomplishments as prior. It

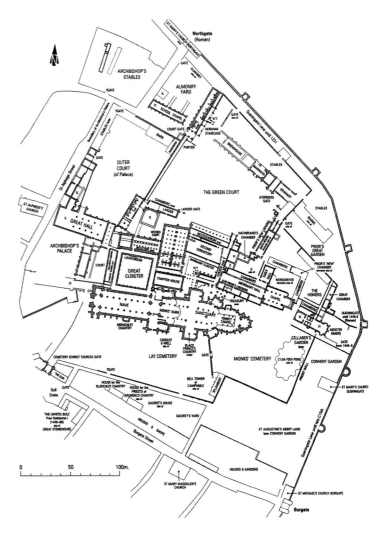

2   Canterbury Cathedral Priory, reconstruction plan of the medieval Precinct (courtesy Dean and Chapter).

includes detailed representation of his buildings and the water system explicitly credited to him in the *obit* composed for the Priory's Chapter at his death in 1167 (see Appendix A). Contemporaries such as Gervase, his fellow monk and later sacrist of the Cathedral, described

(Following page) 3   Eadwine Psalter, MS R. 17. 1, fols. 284v and 285r (*Drawing I*), Trinity College, Cambridge (courtesy the Master and Fellows, Trinity College, Cambridge). As illustrated on the following spread, the folios are rotated 180 degrees so as to conform to their likely original arrangement (see the collation plan on p. 29).

The bifolium in its present position in the manuscript was bound in upside down, probably in the early seventeenth century. East is at the top as indicated by the words *orientalis plaga*. On the left page the artist shows the source of the water system outside the Precinct and the Green Court. The right page shows the strict enclosure with the Great Cloister and the Infirmary Cloister and the Cathedral. The drawing includes the pipework of Prior Wibert's water system in red, green, and orange.

3

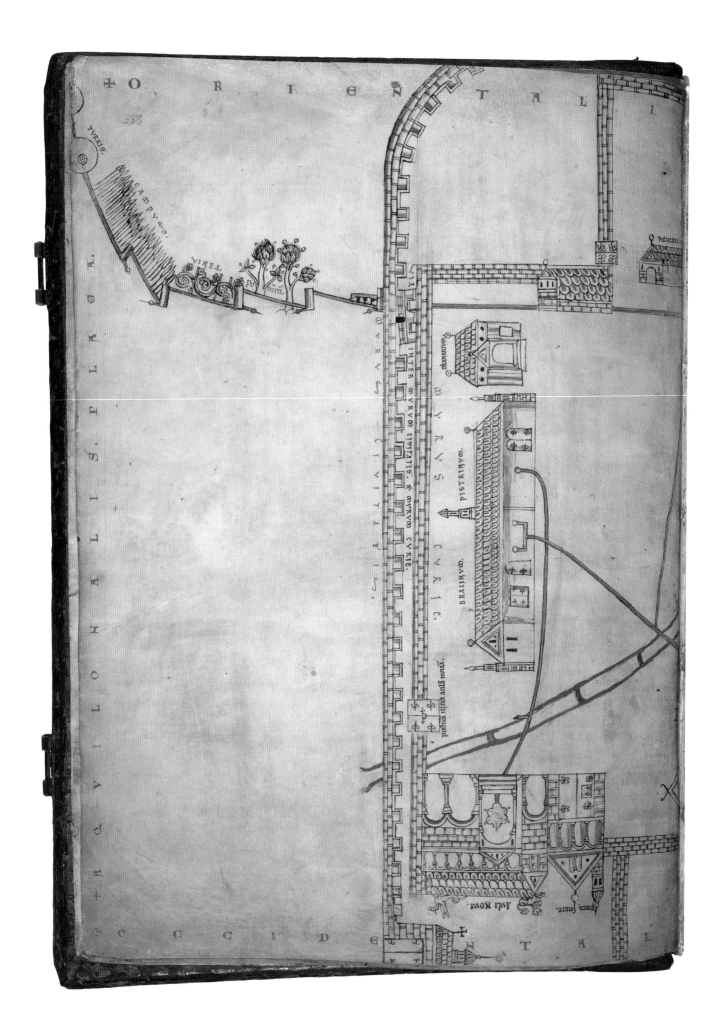

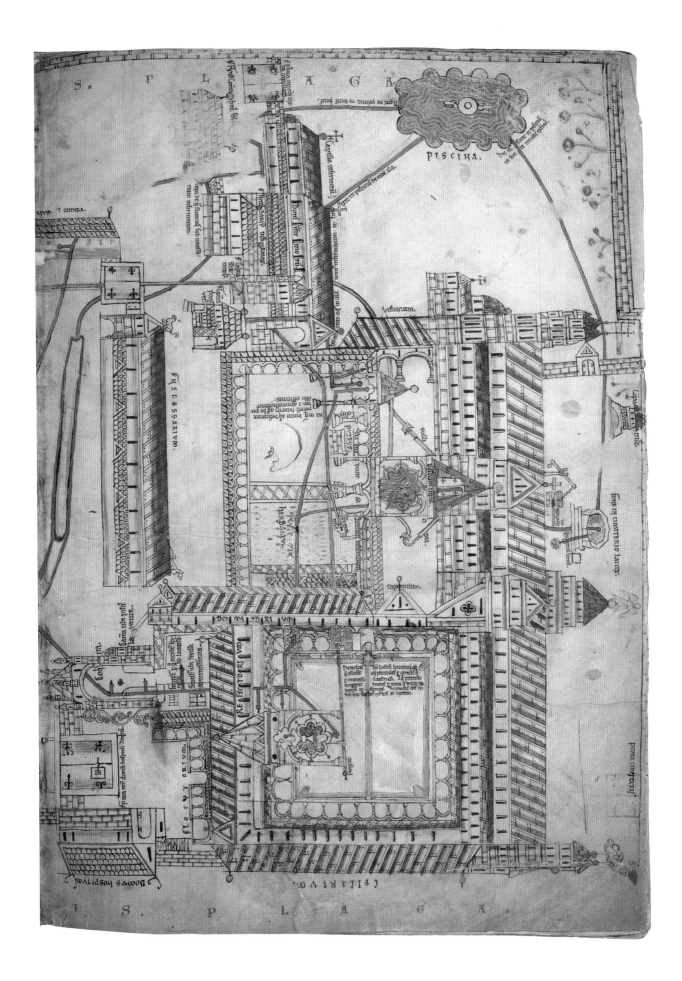

him around 1190 as "virum commendabilem et in operibus bonis mirabilem" (Stubbs 1879, vol. I, 146).

Documentary evidence further supports the notion of Wibert as patron. The acquisition of land adjacent to the Priory, over which the new water system and the buildings related to it were laid out, is recorded as being purchased by Wibert in *Rental A*, compiled between 1153 and 1167 and the earliest of the Priory's Rental Rolls (Urry 1959, 583; Urry 1967, 221–25). Lastly, archaeological evidence links the renewal to the 1150s and 1160s when Wibert was prior. Work conducted by the Canterbury Archaeological Trust on sites and buildings within the Precinct, analysis of the still-standing physical remains, and the evidence of loose stonework all support a dating during the years of his rule.

Beyond the attribution of the work lies a broader issue of patronage. Although little is known about Wibert from personal or documentary sources, the outline of his interests and a profile of his character can be inferred from his varied undertakings. In turn, these reveal the human side of his years in office and the intentions behind the monumental achievements of the age. They also provide clues about the process of generation. For instance, the prior's reshaping of space consequent on the expansion of the Precinct on its northern and eastern boundaries reveals much about the planning phase of the renewal. Likewise, Wibert's placement of buildings to form the Green Court tells a clear story of his penchant for order and unity, as also does the demarcation of circulation established by the gatehouses, or the improved amenities consequent on the water system and infrastructure (and the elimination of open-drainage channels). Further clues to Wibert's varied roles in the Priory's renewal can be traced from his concepts of human environments, concerns for the well-being of the community, ideas about status, and commitment to architecture's role as a carrier of symbolic association.

The focus of the study thus differs from standard medieval architectural histories. The goal is to reconstruct a single discrete period *across* time, a horizontal or lateral history, rather than to trace change extending *down* through time, a developmental history. This approach allows for the recovery of Prior Wibert's renewal and provides a glimpse of the person responsible for it. A fresh picture emerges of monastic life during a period of rapid change, when long-standing institutions like the Priory adjusted to the self-confident challenges of the new reform orders during their most rapid period of expansion across England. The thrust of expansion and the response to it by the established monastic orders took the form of consolidation and renewal and set up a creative tension that marks out the period. Far from being an inert hiatus between the end of Romanesque and the start of Gothic, the years from the accession of Henry II in 1154 to the great fire at the Cathedral of 1174 need to be seen as alive with new ideas, receptive to outside influences, and open to technological innovation.

The confusion in the literature between the roles of the archbishop and the prior as patron mentioned above has an important history. Its origins extend back to the distinctive English tradition of aligning episcopal and monastic rule, a tradition dating from the ecclesiastical reforms of King Edgar (959–75). Bishops were to serve as the abbot of the monks, although given their broader diocesan responsibilities the day-to-day running of the monastery was delegated to the prior (Knowles 1971, 21; Lawrence 1989, 138). A second wave of church reform followed Duke William's conquest of England in 1066 and incorporated many of Edgar's reforms. Led by Archbishop Lanfranc, whom William moved to Canterbury in 1070 from his own church of St.-Etienne in Caen (in Normandy), the Normans brought liturgical observance and monastic custom into line with Benedictine practice on the Continent.

Further changes came from Lanfranc's appointment of Henry, another Norman from the abbey of Bec, as prior at Canterbury. These included increasing the size of the community to around 100 by importing Norman monks to outnumber and outvote the conservative Saxons.[5] The archbishop retained, however, close control of the Priory's affairs. He undertook the construction of the new Cathedral (1070–77) and raised buildings for the expanded community, both based on Norman models. He also wrote in 1077 a customary for the monks, the *Constitutions*, detailing their liturgical responsibilities, also reflecting continental practice (Knowles and Brooke 2002, xxxi–xxxiv). Under his successor, Archbishop Anselm (1093–1109), a shift in responsibilities can be discerned with the monks assuming greater control of their own affairs. It was they (rather than the archbishop) who completed in 1130 the large-scale east extension of the Cathedral which Anselm had begun. The relation of community and episcopate remained close. Anselm lived with the community for periods of time and engaged with them in spiritual conversations, a custom continued fifty years later by Archbishop Thomas Becket (1162–70). The monks elected the archbishop (at least in theory), and they regarded him as their titular abbot.

Were more known about the monastic buildings which Wibert inherited from Archbishops Lanfranc and Anselm, the assessment of his work would be easier. Nearly all trace of them has disappeared, and only limited information comes from sparse archaeological and documentary sources (Rule 1884, 12–13; see also Chapter 4). The one standing building, the Dormitory, poses unexpected puzzles. A standard form based on Norman precedents might have been expected. Instead, the Dormitory was unusually massive, a six-aisled, two-story building of which parts of the undercroft remain. Vaulted with seventy-two groin vaults, the undercroft provided space for a number of purposes such as the monks' day room, parlor, and warming room. But these would have accounted for only about half the floor area, and the use of the remaining parts is unclear. It is likely they served ancillary offices for the Infirmary such as the infirmary master's residence. On the first floor lay the Dormitory. Outside the monastic enclosure all that is known of the buildings listed by Lanfranc is their mention in his *Constitutions*, but it is impossible from this source to know details of their placement, adjacency, scale, or form. Further uncertainty surrounds the work of his successor, Archbishop Anselm. His huge eastern extension of the Cathedral nearly doubled the size of the building and can be understood in the context of great church building in Europe, but his conventual buildings are far from clear. Lacking remains, scholars assume some buildings on the eastern and northeastern side of the church. Only archaeology could provide information about them.

The extent of Prior Wibert's renewal can be established thanks to the unique survival of the contemporary image of the Precinct, *Drawing I*. Made in the late 1150s in the Priory's scriptorium, it shows the huge Cathedral constructed by Archbishops Lanfranc and Anselm, the new water system with its pipes and infrastructure, and thirty buildings for the Priory's monks to fulfill their responsibilities for the services, shrines, altars, and

administration of the institution (see Chapter 3). Three of these buildings remain reasonably complete into the present day: the Green Court Gatehouse, the Water Tower, and the Treasury (the only one to retain some of its original uses). But eleven more survive in part, thereby allowing for varying degrees of reconstruction: the Great Cloister and its Fountain House (see Chapter 4), the Guesthouse and Great Kitchen in the Cellarer's Court (see Chapter 5), the *Aula Nova* for the prior's courtroom with its formal entry known as the Norman Staircase (see Chapter 6), the *Necessarium* (or Toilet Building), the Infirmary Cloister, Infirmary Hall, and Chapel (see Chapter 7), and the gateway into the monks' cemetery (now moved to the Memorial Garden) (see Chapter 8).[6] To these can be added at least two more buildings credited to Wibert which are known from archaeological analysis, the Pentice Gatehouse and the east guest range (extending from the Pentice Gatehouse to the Larder Gate), both in the Cellarer's Court (see Chapter 5), and further projects on the Cathedral carried out after *Drawing I*'s completion, such as the heightening of the east transept towers, the large-scale renovations of the chapels of St. Andrew and St. Anselm and their added upper chambers, the improved entrances to Anselm's crypt, and the added height of the Treasury (see Chapter 8). About half of Wibert's mid-twelfth-century buildings are, therefore, known in greater or lesser degree.

More than 850 years separate us from the renewal of the 1150s and 1160s. Rebuildings undertaken by Wibert's successor priors, and others resulting from the transformations following Henry VIII's suppression in 1540 when secular clergy replaced the Benedictine monks, present formidable problems for an understanding of the period. Discoveries over the past thirty years, however, make it possible to study Prior Wibert's renewal. A firmer estimate of its extent and a better knowledge of the forms chosen permit an interpretation which allows insights into one of the most interesting periods in Canterbury's long history.

I

ESTABLISHING THE EXTENT
OF PRIOR WIBERT'S RENEWAL

To make credible the claims for the mid-twelfth-century work undertaken by Prior Wibert in the following pages, it is necessary first to disentangle the buildings raised by him from those of his monastic successors in the Middle Ages and then from those of deans and chapters in the post-suppression centuries. The Precinct was not infrequently a construction site. Within the first decade of Norman rule, Eadmer recorded Archbishop Lanfranc's reconstruction of the Saxon monastery. In turn, Lanfranc's buildings were demolished or changed by Prior Wibert beginning in the 1150s. Fifty years after Wibert, Prior John of Sittingbourne (1222–32) reconstructed the northern side of the Great Cloister, including a new Refectory, and rebuilt the entry door into the northwest transept. In the fourteenth century three formidable priors – Henry of Eastry (1285–1331), Robert Hathbrand (1338–70), and Thomas Chillenden (1391–1411) – embarked on a series of major changes: Eastry added the Checker in the northeast part of the Infirmary Cloister (1288–90), Hathbrand altered the Infirmary Hall and Chapel and their ancillary structures, and Chillenden rebuilt the Great Cloister, Chapter House, Refectory laver,

Cellarer's Court Gatehouse, Green Court Gatehouse, Water Tower, and Infirmary Hall, as well as the nave of the Cathedral. In the late 1400s Prior Goldstone remodeled the Bath House and parts of the water system. These undertakings were mostly makeovers, and it is possible to trace earlier work. Rebuildings resulted from shifts in monastic culture and amounted to attempts to provide for new needs. In the Infirmary Hall, for example, the transformation from a single, unitary space to divisioned rooms, and then in the fifteenth century the insertion of the sub-prior's residence in the southwest bays, need to be understood in terms of shifts in monastic numbers and the endowment income to support them as well as different expectations of medical treatment.

Further obscuring Prior Wibert's work were changes following Henry VIII's suppression (1540) and the expulsion of the monks. In their place the king established the New Foundation in 1541 with a staff consisting of a dean, twelve canons, minor canons, six preachers, lay clerks, porters, masters and pupils of the school. To accommodate them necessitated substantial changes in which the monks' two-story halls were transformed into

4 Canterbury Cathedral Priory, Infirmary Hall (detail), watercolour by L. L. Razé, 1865 (courtesy King's School Library).

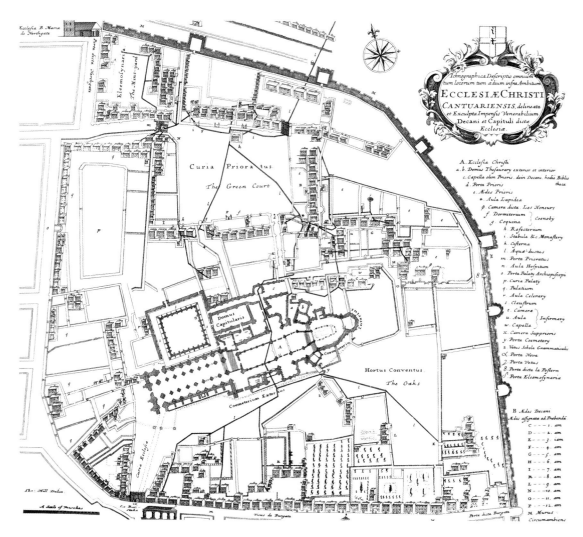

5   Canterbury Cathedral Priory, Precinct plan by Thomas Hill, ca. 1680 (courtesy Dean and Chapter).

The Precinct is shown a century and a half after the suppression. Many of the medieval buildings have been broken into smaller residences, particularly those surrounding the Green Court and the Infirmary complex. The same applies to the archbishop's residence, vacated at this period.

domestic residences for the married clergy. A drastic restructuring of a number of the conventual buildings such as the Infirmary, Cellarer's Court, and Dormitory followed. The process can be seen over the span of 500 years if the 1150s *Drawing I* in the Eadwine Psalter (see fig. 3) is compared with the 1680s bird's-eye view of the Precinct made by Thomas Hill (fig. 5).

RECOVERY OF THE MONASTIC PAST

Knowledge of the changes and losses in the convent's buildings in the post-suppression years comes mainly from antiquarians. William Somner's *Antiquities of Canterbury* (1640), written a century after the suppression, drew on manuscripts and charters (some since lost) which the author had access to as auditor to the Dean and Chapter. Somner's volume appeared on the eve of the despoliations by the Commonwealth in 1642. A second edition in 1660 appeared after the Restoration and chronicled its changes, and a third edition published by N. Battely, *Cantuaria Sacra* (1703), added further material and included Thomas Hill's plan (originally commissioned as a guide to infrastructure).

Antiquarian publication makes it possible to follow the physical changes as different needs developed. A

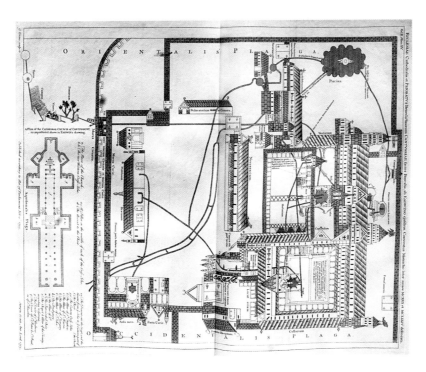

6 Canterbury Cathedral Priory, engraving by George Vertue, 1755, from *Vetusta Monumenta*, vol. 2, 1789 (courtesy The Society of Antiquaries of London).

A regularized rendering of *Drawing I*, oriented the way the bifolium appears in the manuscript of the Eadwine Psalter. To indicate the different colored washes of the original, Vertue used different shadings. To help the reader follow the text's argument, Vertue added a plan of the Cathedral in the space offered outside the Precinct on the northern side.

few buildings proved resistant to adaptation, such as the Great Kitchen and the Refectory, and were destroyed. More marginal buildings on the north edge of the Precinct were refitted to serve the king's promotion of education, one inherited from the monks. Housed first in the Almonry in 1573 with forty scholars, the King's School began occupying the former conventual buildings, a process which is still under way more than 400 years later (Sparks 2007, 92–93). From sixty-two scholars in the seventeenth century, the number increased to ninety in 1848 and to more than 800 today. Each expansion absorbed more of the buildings in Wibert's Green Court and then those to the east and north of the Infirmary Hall and Chapel. On the west side of the Precinct the archbishops appropriated some of the old monastic lands. They absorbed the Guesthouse back into their palace grounds (Archbishop Theobald had given land for this to Prior Wibert in the 1150s) and further enlarged them by appropriating the west range of the Great Cloister (leaving a blank wall to demarcate its western boundary) to increase the size of their palace garden. Clerical expansion further shrank the western parts of the Precinct, notably the insertion of residential gardens along the former boundary wall of the Green Court.

To meet the expanding interest in the past, city guides began appearing to supplement the antiquarian literature with its emphasis on documents. The guides were geared to site observation and included distinguishing one period's work from another. Interest in the mid-twelfth century as distinctive in Canterbury's long history began with Humphrey Wanley's recognition in 1705 of *Drawing I* as a twelfth-century image of the Precinct (see Wanley 1705). An engraved version of *Drawing I* (fig. 6) was first published in 1755 to illustrate a paper on the Cathedral authored by the Reverend Doctor Jeremiah Milles. The artist was George Vertue, and he engraved a second drawing from the Psalter that showed the scribe Eadwin. Milles titled his paper "An Account of Two Ancient Drawings, one Representing the Cathedral Church and Monastery at Canterbury and the other the Effigies of Eadwin the Monk," and it formed a stand-alone publication sent to subscribers by the Society of Antiquaries of London. Vertue spread the drawing of the Precinct over a bifolium, as in the original manuscript, but neatened it by straightening lines and typesetting the hand-lettered *tituli* (and reversing their position in relation to the buildings they identify). To reproduce the color washes of the original (fig. 8A), Vertue used generous areas of hatching (fig. 8B). On the left-hand folio where the twelfth-century artist depicted the passage of the water system across fields from its source to the Precinct, resulting in a blank area underneath (fig. 6), Vertue inserted a plan of the Cathedral to illustrate Milles's paper.

Milles dated both drawings between 1130 and 1174. He argued that the Cathedral in *Drawing I* was the building described by the monk historian, Gervase of Canterbury, in his eyewitness account of the reconstruction following the fire of 1174. Milles's argument was doomed since the image showed the eastern parts of Anselm's church of ca. 1100–30 rather than the rebuilding by William the Englishman and William of Sens of 1174–84 described by Gervase. Milles mentioned the precinct buildings only in passing and identified them as Lanfranc's work. As for the two drawings, Milles's sole comment was to note that the twelfth-century artist was "no master of perspective." Thirty-four years later, Milles's paper was gathered with others and published in volume II of the *Vetusta Monumenta* (1789), a series appearing at irregular intervals between 1747 and 1896.

While Milles's paper went mostly unremarked, Vertue's engraving enjoyed a century of further publication and copying. For the latter, none of the different artists attempted to correct Vertue's "improvements," as Willis pointedly remarked (1868, 5, n. 1). The engraving also became the source for an early controversy. A single architectural feature, Wibert's Water Tower in the former Infirmary Cloister, was identified by William Gostling in *A Walk in and about the City of Canterbury* (1774, 204–5) as the "old Baptistery." The attribution drew critics in the *Gentleman's Magazine* (vol. 44, 1774, 508–10), who questioned whether such a rite was undertaken in a monastery. The controversy continued into the next year's issue (vol. 45, 529–30). For the Dean and Chapter the idea of the Water Tower as the baptistery proved hard to resist. In 1787 they removed the font from the nave of the Cathedral and placed it in the Water Tower, at the same time changing the building's name to the baptistery. There it remained for over a century, despite

Denne's scholarly correction of Gostling's misattribution which appeared in 1794.[1]

Cathedral reform in the early nineteenth century initiated a new phase for the precinct buildings. Parliament ordained reductions in cathedral chapters in the so-called Dean and Chapter Acts of 1840. At Canterbury the reductions led to altered uses of some buildings and the restoration of others. The third edition of Gostling's volume (1825) contains valuable information about the condition of the Precinct immediately prior to restoration. The most radical idea was to reconstruct the *Aula Nova*, which had lain largely ruined after the various demolitions of 1730 and 1817. Prints and drawings from 1800 forwards show the building standing only up to the first stringcourse (above the arcades) (see fig. 79). Restored in a Romanesque style based on a study of the Treasury of the same date for the use of the King's School, the design came from the Cathedral's surveyor and architect, George Austin (1822–48), and was implemented in 1852–53 by his son and successor, H. G. Austin (1848–89).[2]

Some medieval buildings were destroyed during this period. Most notorious was the demolition in 1868 of the Checker on the east side of the Infirmary Cloister (Sparks 2007, 124–26; Willis 1868, 100–3). Elsewhere this phase in the former Priory's history was marked by the freeing of post-suppression insertions of residences within the Infirmary Hall, Infirmary Chapel (both Wibert buildings), and Dormitory, and the decision to present these buildings as medieval ruins (see fig. 4). The taste for ruins had originated a century earlier, although the concepts and settings had changed, moving from picturesque landscapes to domestic-scaled gardens. At the Priory the impulse to turn medieval remains into "Gothick" ruins also tempted the wives of several powerful deans to appropriate loose medieval stonework and construct "picturesque" compositions consisting of imitations and follies. Other chapter wives created rockeries in prebendal gardens using similar stonework where it remains unrecorded to this day in varying states of decay, a process accelerated in recent years by chemical fertilizers.

Another parliamentary contraction of cathedral clergy hastened the transfer of clerical residences to other functions in the early twentieth century. At the Priory these were mostly absorbed into the expanding King's School, particularly following World War I (Sparks 2007, 126–34). The fashion for presenting the Precinct partly as ruins has begun to wane. Rebuilding followed the damage done by World War II bombings, part of Hitler's Baedeker raids of 1940 and 1942. Although these destroyed the medieval Plumery on the south side of the Cathedral, the severely damaged library and archives were rebuilt along with the Deanery, and several buildings in the Green Court. More recently, new construction has met the needs of the King's School, and for the Dean and Chapter the Canterbury Cathedral Lodge and Conference Center on the town side of the Cathedral have reanimated the precinct function centered on the ancient tradition of hospitality and provided a welcome source of income.

THE RISE OF SCHOLARLY STUDY: ROBERT WILLIS (1800–1875)

A different impulse also in the 1840s can be identified: the appearance of scholarly study. George Austin's work on the Cathedral had drawn criticism on account of his demolition of Lanfranc's northwest tower and the misalignment of his Victorian Gothic replacement. A newly founded institution, the British Archaeological Association, chose Canterbury as the venue for its first conference in September 1844.[3] When the conference papers were published the following year, they provided an insight into the strong views that colored the restoration debate. The volume's editor, Alfred Dunkin, took the extraordinary liberty of adding footnotes of his own to the contributors' papers. In one of these he seized the opportunity to ridicule Austin for his "extreme vulgarity" in answering a question from the audience, observing that Austin's remarks were "received with peals of sneering laughter."[4]

The association's 1844 conference was divided into four sections with the one on architecture presided over by the Reverend Robert Willis. His presence was central to the success of the conference, and his publications from it remain major contributions into the present. Willis was the first scholar to publish *Drawing I* in detail, to sort out the complex sequences of work in the Precinct, and to set Canterbury's architectural history on an objective historical base. For all scholars of medieval architecture Willis is bedrock. His methods remain fundamental to the formation of the discipline.

Before the 1844 Canterbury conference, Willis was considered the leading figure in architectural history. He had already published books on Italian medieval architecture (1835) and architectural nomenclature (1844), and papers on medieval vaulting, Flamboyant architecture, medieval barns, and Hereford Cathedral (M. H. Thompson 1996, 163). Surprisingly, architectural history

was a side interest. His profession was mechanical engineering, a degree subject which he introduced at Cambridge University, where he held the Jacksonian Professorship of Applied and Experimental Philosophy for nearly forty years. In addition to his university teaching and writing, Willis designed machinery, took out patents, published widely on scientific matters, and eventually rose to become president of the Royal Society. Even by nineteenth-century standards he was an extraordinary polymath.

The paper Willis read at Canterbury in 1844 focused on Gervase's eyewitness account of the fire of 1174 and subsequent rebuilding of the east end of the Cathedral, the same topic as Milles's paper nearly 100 years earlier. Willis's stated goal was to demonstrate how the rebuilding "verified" Gervase's text (written ca. 1190) and also to delineate later changes and additions. It appeared lengthened into a monograph on the building in the following year. Willis then turned his interest to Canterbury's precinct buildings, on which much of his research was concentrated between 1847 and 1848 (Willis 1868, 134, n. 3). Like his work on the Cathedral, the paper posited *Drawing I* as a critical "text" capable of substantiation by the fabric remains. But he also had wider ambitions which he spelled out in the title of his paper: "The Architectural History of the Conventual Buildings of the Monastery of Christ Church, Canterbury considered in relation to the Monastic Life and Rules, and drawn up from Personal Surveys and Original Documentary Research." Nothing of this scholarly range had been attempted before. The importance of Willis's paper lay in its sequencing of work. He separated out the different architectural periods and devised a methodology to prove his argument. His interest lay in elucidating the complete history of work, medieval and postmedieval. Although he mentions Wibert's undertakings with some frequency, they were not the object of his study.

Twenty years were to elapse before Willis's paper appeared in print, the gap being explained to the reader as the result of the distraction of "other avocations" which denied him "the leisure to prepare the memoir for press" (Willis 1868, 1). How much of this we should take at face value can be debated. Willis had found time in the interim for numerous other publications in science as well as architectural history. Of the latter, his publications include "The Plan of St. Gall" (1848) and the Villard de Honnecourt "Album" (1859), both of which indicate his widening interest in medieval architectural drawing. There were also books on Greek

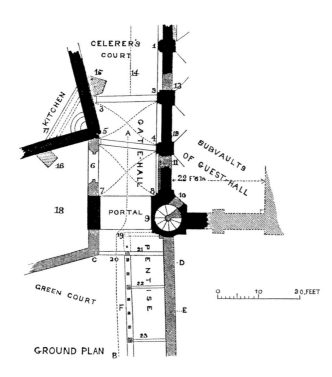

7 Canterbury Cathedral Priory, Pentice Gatehouse, plan
(Willis 1868, 127, fig. 21).

Willis's plan illustrates the ground floor of the Pentice
Gatehouse (now the archdeacon's private residence) and reveals
his strong didactic intention with arabic numbers and upper-
case and lower-case letters keyed to the accompanying text.

Orthodox architecture, York Minster, and Oxford and
Cambridge colleges (M. H. Thompson 1996, 164). When
Willis's study of the Precinct appeared in 1868, it was as
a 206-page paper in *Archaeologia Cantiana* (the publication of the Kent Archaeological Society). The following
year Willis published the same paper as a stand-alone
volume; the pagination is identical, and the additions
consist of an index and three large-scale precinct drawings tipped-in or included in a sleeve.

Willis phased the precinct buildings and placed them
in different historical periods. Before Willis it had proved
difficult to date securely a given wall or building, let
alone assign it to a particular prior. Willis proposed that
a physical fabric could be "read" as a "text" to reveal a
history of change over time. Devising an investigative
methodology, he demonstrated that masonry coursing
could be analyzed to distinguish building campaigns,
architectural detailing to establish dating sequences,
stonework to discern materials' preferences, and *in situ*
building fragments to provide clues to the three-

dimensional visualization of destroyed areas. To this day
it remains deeply instructive (and fascinating) to examine
the Priory's buildings with Willis's text in hand. One is
endlessly impressed by what might be called his lithic
forensics: that is, his meticulous grasp of physical evidence, the detailed range of his observations, and his
capacity to relate scarred or battered areas of masonry
to others more amenable to interpretation.

To help the reader Willis included a wealth of illustrative material. His text utilized thirty-three plans and
three large fold-out plates (an unparalleled luxury even
by present-day standards). Nearly all were his own drawings. Furthermore, figure and text were related through
his devised system of identifying keys using upper- and
lower case letters, Arabic and Roman numerals, dotted
and other connecting lines. Willis's plans convey a distinct, even at times a dense, diagrammatic quality. Sprin-
kled with information integral with the argument of the
text, they are uncompromisingly didactic (fig. 7). Their
value and that of Willis's observations are enhanced
because they preceded restoration, making parts of his
text important for their record of what is now lost.

To these analytical skills Willis added singular scholarly strengths. As his paper title promised, documentary
research confirmed building changes or additions using
primary material drawn from the Priory's sources in
Canterbury and Cambridge.[5] At Canterbury he discovered Prior Eastry's list of building works, then Chillenden's, and published both (Sparks 2007, 8). To explain
the use of buildings, he examined Archbishop Winchelsey's *Statutes* (1298), and pored through post-suppression
documents to track down later changes. Willis also
grasped the importance of information contained in
terminology, whether of buildings or forms (the subject
of his 1844 book), and what it conveyed about meanings
across centuries extending from Roman antiquity
through the Middle Ages. To elucidate historical contexts, he drew on his first-hand experience of medieval
architecture in Germany, France, Italy, and England, and
on scholarly study of them. Thompson could write
recently of Willis's "dazzling symbiosis between written
and material remains" (M. H. Thompson 1996, 158).

Fundamental to Willis's study of Canterbury's precinct buildings was *Drawing I*. Alert to the deficiencies
of Vertue's 1755 engraving, he persuaded the librarian
of Trinity College to allow him in 1867 to make a
tracing. Clear and easy to use, and economical to publish
his black and white line drawing has been constantly
reproduced ever since. Yet the tracing is not quite
the exact copy Willis intended. Inevitably, it involved

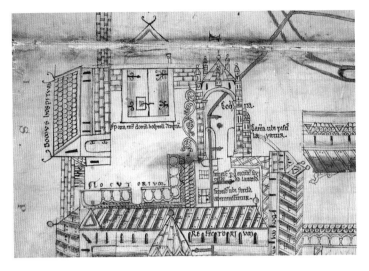

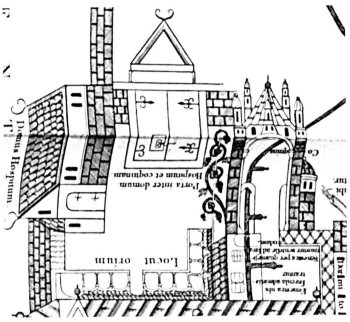

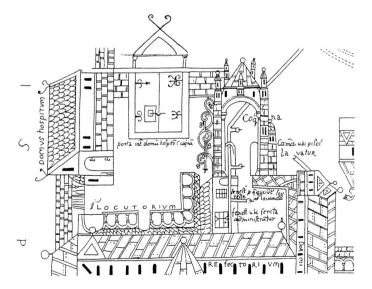

choices. Even line work replaced the medieval artist's hand-drawn pen work. Willis omits certain details, most obviously the artist's use of color washes which gives volume to the original.[6] The different effects of each emerge in a comparison of the Cellarer's Court in the original (fig. 8A) with Vertue's rendering (fig. 8B) and with Willis's tracing (fig. 8C). They range from the representational character of the original with its even-handed interest in the Precinct and its buildings to the diagrammatic character of Willis's tracing with its emphasis on the water system. On occasion Willis could not resist adding improvements. He joined up incomplete pipework or eliminated details which he deemed superfluous, such as the strigillated surface of the laver in the Water Tower for hand-washing (figs. 9A and B), the *Piscina*, and the prior's *cupa* (bath). The omission loses in consequence the artist's communication of the surface animation of the water (an apt contrast to the mirror-still reflection of the well-drawn water which had preceded the new system).

In his study of *Drawing I* Willis referred to the artist's projection as a bird's-eye view. In fact, the artist employed multiple viewpoints. He showed all four sides of the Great Cloister as if each was seen straight on. Elsewhere, he drew parts of the complex upside down, others flat. Later in his text Willis modified his characterization of the projection as bird's-eye and observed that the artist's methods recalled those used "on seals or monuments of the middle ages and earlier" (Willis 1868, 179). At times the exasperation of the nineteenth-century engineer got the better of him, as when he characterized the medieval artist's drawing skills in depicting the entry gate to the Cellarer's Court as "preposterously exaggerated" (Willis 1868, 126).

Willis had no doubts about the reasons for the making of *Drawing I*. It was the product of the "hydraulic engineers who carried out much of the mechanism and system of the water supply" (Willis 1868, 6). The detail with which the system's parts were shown and their extensive representation proved to him that "the buildings of the convent were inserted solely to receive the

8   Canterbury Cathedral Priory, Cellarer's Court. Three versions of the Cellarer's Court illustrate the different effects of (top: A) the painted original from the Eadwine Psalter, ca. 1158 (courtesy the Master and Fellows, Trinity College, Cambridge); (middle: B) the engraved version by George Vertue, 1755 (courtesy The Society of Antiquaries of London); and (bottom: C) the tracing by Robert Willis, 1868 (Willis 1868, pl. I).

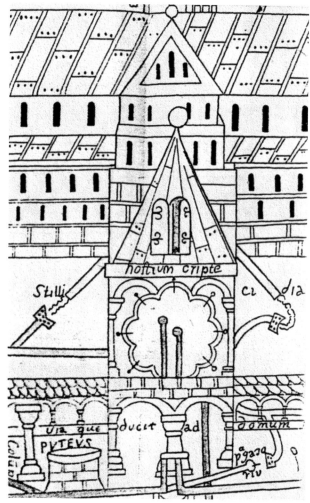

9A Eadwine Psalter, *Drawing I*, detail of the Water Tower, Trinity College, Cambridge (courtesy the Master and Fellows, Trinity College, Cambridge)

9B Willis's tracing showing detail of the Water Tower (Willis 1868, pl. 1).

Willis's tracing contained an element of simplification, as in the omission of the strigillated patterns on the laver's basin. It also hardens the color-washed original and conveys a more diagrammatic accent fitting his view of the artist's intention to create a "waterworks" drawing.

plan of the pipes, receptacles and sewers." Willis's claim was backed by careful scholarly argument. He devoted all of Chapter X of his study to explain his reasons, and provided thirty pages of valuable analysis. The chapter begins with a clear summary: "[*Drawing I* is] a most valuable record of the state of hydraulic practice in the twelfth century and a monument of the care with which the monks studied practical science" (Willis 1868, 158). He also believed that the image had no connection to the manuscript (but offered no explanation for its inclusion). For these reasons Willis used "water-works" as a

modifier, and his text frequently refers to "the Waterworks Drawings," a designation that continues into the present (see Woodman 1992, 168). It is one not adopted in this study, however. In Chapter 3 I set out the case for an alternative way of looking at *Drawing I*. My intention is to broaden understanding of the image and to integrate it with the overall purpose of the Eadwine Psalter. Both are critical to dating Wibert's work and to its interpretation.

Turning to other features of Willis's text, not every matter caught his wide interests. Woodman faults his preference for twelfth- and thirteenth-century work to the exclusion of later periods (Woodman 1981, xvi). On restoration, Willis's reticence to take a position on work under way at Canterbury which he witnessed during a twenty-five-year period (1844–68) is puzzling. At the start of his study he promised the reader "to develop the successive changes the [buildings] have undergone through the periods of reverent care and improvement during the middle ages, of the neglect, destruction, and cupidity of the Reformation and Rebellion, and of the meddling ignorance and indifference of the times approaching our own" (Willis 1868, 16). For the last, Willis's intention soon faded. Of Austin's extensive changes to the *Aula Nova* in 1853 amounting to a virtual rebuilding, Willis penned only a single anodyne sentence: "Mr. Austin raised a modern Norman façade of stone above the old arches which still remain" (Willis 1868, 146). More often Willis is mute. He has nothing to say about the restoration of the Gatehouse or the Guesthouse, or the destruction of the Checker or the sub-prior's residence, which he thought "a beautiful example of domestic architecture" (Willis 1868, 58). His ire was stirred only in his discussion of the Deanery:

> [The changes to the building and its surroundings had been initiated] to please Lady Harriet Bagot, the wife of the Dean at that time, who happened to have a taste for ruins in landscape gardening, according to the fashion of that period, the effects of which may be seen in many parts of the Deanery and other gardens, where genuine old doorways, archways, and windows (obtained by the destruction of the remains of monastic offices, where, if left, they would have told their tale of the real use of these buildings), are now to be seen in impossible positions, inserted into walls and corners, where no buildings ever existed (Willis 1868, 112).

These details aside, Willis's contributions to Canterbury remain monumental. His broad definition of building phases stands largely intact. For his analytical passages, only the occasional adjustment is needed at the space of 150 years. Ironically, Willis's brilliance had the effect of paralyzing further investigation. His comprehensive paper dried up Precinct studies. His dissection of building sequences seemed to have answered all the questions. In fact, they had not, as work at other sites has shown. Architectural history in its present form begins with phasing but progresses well beyond it to address such issues as the source of forms and ornament, patronage, building typology, iconography, material culture, and the correlation of architecture with economic and social history. Few of these matters have been taken up at Canterbury. By contrast, Willis's documentary work prompted followers. Scholars such as R. C. Hussey and C. E. Woodruff used the cathedral archives to expand the understanding of building activities, their papers appearing in *Archaeologia Cantiana*.

TWENTIETH-CENTURY HISTORIOGRAPHY

Although interest in the incomparable Cathedral has long overshadowed that in the precinct buildings, their importance is nonetheless considerable.[7] More recently they have begun to attract greater attention. Among the different periods, the renewal undertaken by Prior Wibert has attracted interest as its extent has become more fully understood. The broadening of perspectives derives in part from architectural history. At the same time, the new perspectives depend heavily on related disciplines such as archaeology, the study of loose stonework, and research into monastic and cathedral precincts. Some outline of each of these is important in order to understand the unfolding modern scholarship carried out on the Precinct and its history.

New primary material has emerged over the past thirty years from archaeology. The founding of the Canterbury Archaeological Trust in 1976 brought about major discoveries as well as a revolution in fabric recording. The trust's work relevant to this study represents a tiny proportion of its annual undertakings, which extend throughout Kent and southern England. For the Priory, the major contributions have been to knowledge about Meister Omers, Linacre Garden, St. Gabriel's Chapel, the *Aula Nova*, the Almonry Chapel, Dormitory, and nave of the Cathedral. Extensive publication has meant the swift release of material.[8] In addition, the trust conducts *ad hoc* archaeology or watching briefs related to emergency work necessitated by storm damage, the installation of power cables, drainage, floodlights, and so forth.[9]

A less well-known discipline has centered around the study of loose stonework. It appeared as an analytical tool in the 1970s. Unanticipated discoveries soon followed, some from medieval builders' tradition of incorporating torn-down material in new construction. At Canterbury such evidence emerged from the Great Cloister restorations of the late 1960s and 1970s. The recovery of reused mid-twelfth-century material made it possible to reconstruct Prior Wibert's Great Cloister despite its disappearance 600 years ago. When Prior Chillenden replaced it, his masons smashed Wibert's arcades and fountain house and reused the pieces as masonry fill. Tim Tatton-Brown was among the first archaeologists to grasp the importance of this evidence. Using the recovered pieces of smashed masonry, he reconstructed the radii of Wibert's cloister arcades and much of the architectural detailing of bases, capitals, and moldings (Tatton-Brown 2006). To add to this, Jeffrey West (2012) used the same technique to reconstruct the laver at the entrance to the Refectory and its sculptural program. His work was likewise based on recovered fragments found in the early 1970s. Both discoveries have resulted in information which had previously been accepted as irretrievably lost and allowed for the development of new ideas about the nature of Prior Wibert's renewal.

A further expansion of knowledge has come from the study of precincts as a distinct branch of monastic history.[10] Led again by archaeologists working on ruined monastic sites and utilizing noninvasive tools such as resistivity surveying, ground radar, magnetometry, photogrametric recording, and flotation tanks, precinct studies have progressively broadened to include cathedrals, castles, and palace sites. It is no longer satisfactory to see an individual building, or clusters of buildings, as unrelated phenomena. Consideration has to be given to the building's relationship to the overall precinct and to take account of the community (religious and lay) who inhabited it as well as the complex mix of lands, rights, and privileges assembled to sustain it (Coppack 2006,

27–36; Fergusson and Harrison 1999, 177–86). Roberta Gilchrist's monograph on Norwich Cathedral (2005) and her many earlier papers, and Anne Holton-Krayenbuhl's papers on Ely (1997, 1999), have contributed to an understanding of precincts with close bearing on Wibert's work at the Priory.

To this work has to be added the notable contributions by historians to twelfth-century Canterbury. Indispensable studies of Archbishop Theobald (Saltman 1956), the Angevin kings (Urry 1967), and Becket (Barlow 1976; Duggan 2007) provide the basis of present work, along with site-specific surveys (Collinson, Ramsay, and Sparks 1995) and the invaluable focused history of the precincts across time (Sparks 2007). At Benedictine Westminster Abbey, Barbara Harvey's *Living and Dying in England, 1100–1540: The Monastic Experience* (1993) revealed in absorbing detail how great institutions functioned and the life of those who served them.

Despite the welcome accumulation of knowledge about Prior Wibert's work over the past thirty years, there has been no book or professional paper devoted to it. Equally missing have been studies of the architecture, the adoption of new architectural types, iconography, or the prior's patronage. Over time, archaeology can be expected to reveal more primary material, even in areas critical to the water system such as the east range of the Infirmary Cloister. Nonetheless, given the advances that have been made, the time seems right to set in motion discussion about the "state of the question" of the renewal and to begin to credit Prior Wibert for his role in it.

2

PRIOR WIBERT

Powerful political and social movements in the 1150s formed the background for the Priory's renewal and for the role played by Prior Wibert in its planning and construction. Following the disruption and civil war during the reign of King Stephen (1135–53), the accession of the twenty-two-year-old Duke of Normandy and Count of Anjou as King Henry II (1154–89) and his queen, Eleanor of Acquitaine, prompted a surge of optimism throughout England. Expectations of peace and economic recovery set the stage for change. Contempories clearly grasped the shift in power. Ailred of Rievaulx in his *Genealogia regum anglorum* (1153–54) recorded the divisions of the Anarchy pitting Normans against Saxons and presents the new Angevin rulers as the "cornerstone" uniting the two fighting parties (*Pat. Lat.*, v.195, col. 738–8). Adding to the sense of a new dawn was the election in Rome, a week or so before Henry's accession, of Nicholas Breakspear as Pope Adrian IV (1154–59), the only Englishman to sit on the throne of St. Peter. In the context of monasticism, a further factor needs to be added to those just mentioned. Older monastic institutions such as the Benedictines faced the accelerating success of the emerging reform orders such as the Carthusians, Augustinians, Cistercians, Gilbertines, Premonstratensians, and others. Attempts to address this challenge can be seen as early as the late 1120s and 1130s

in programs of modernization and expansion at prominent abbeys such as Cluny III in Burgundy (Stratford 2010, 246–61), Bury St. Edmunds in Suffolk (Fergusson 2011, 25–34), and St.-Denis outside Paris (Grant 1998, 241). As a response to the pressures of reform, the Priory's renewal begun in the mid-1150s asserted Benedictine vitality and innovation. Just as important, it signaled the emergence of a highly skilled administrator and energetic leader, Prior Wibert.

Throughout this period Canterbury played a central role in national life. Archbishop Theobald's authority ensured him a prominent place in political and ecclesiastical affairs. Determined to influence the young king, Theobald ordered the immediate return from law study in Italy and France of one of his most able clerks, Thomas Becket. Appointed to serve the king as his advisor on church matters, Becket's rapid friendship with the new monarch culminated in his promotion to royal chancellor of England before the year 1154 had ended.[1] Theobald's far-ranging exercise of power was complemented by intellectual interests. He filled his curia or household with clerks and clergy of high caliber which included six future bishops and three archbishops, among them Roger Pont L'Evêque (York), Thomas Becket (Canterbury), and John of Salisbury (Chartres), as well as scientists, poets, theologians,

19

philosophers, and lawyers. Among the last were two famous scholars from the school of law in Bologna, Master Vacarius and Master Lombard of Piacenza, who assumed central roles in the development of jurisprudence in England, a particular interest at Canterbury and of the new monarch and his court.

The cosmopolitanism of Theobald's curia extended beyond Canterbury. The king and queen's first-hand acquaintance with the Mediterranean world and the range of their continental domains reaching from the Channel to the Pyrenees meant a court culture wider than that of their Norman predecessors. In addition, close ecclesiastical connections linked Canterbury with church centers in the Lowlands, the Rhineland, and Italy, particularly Rome. Even before the election of Adrian IV, the Lateran Palace hosted visits from Theobald accompanied by Thomas Becket and John of Salisbury in 1144 and 1152. The latter had made ten such trips to Rome before 1159.

Prior Wibert's career ran in parallel to these events. Although the place and date of his birth are unknown and likewise the year when he entered the Christ Church community, it can be assumed that he was rising through the monastic hierarchy at Canterbury during Stephen's reign.[2] Elected sub-prior in 1148, Wibert held this office for five or so years. His elevation to prior is variously noted as 1150, 1152 (following the return from exile of Archbishop Theobald and his curia), 1153, or 1154.[3] Wibert had thus been in office for only a brief period before the accession of Henry II. Few documented references mark his years as prior. His imprisonment in 1154 over the dispute with Theobald regarding the autonomy of the Priory has already been mentioned. He was the recipient of letters from John of Salisbury and Pope Alexander III in 1163 (Greatrex 1997, 319). Apart from these references, the only other secure date is that of his death on September 27, 1167.

The lack of documented references deprives us of biographical detail about Wibert. Unlike his monastic builder contemporaries and fellow abbot patrons such as Anselm of Bury St. Edmunds (1121–48), Ailred of Rievaulx (1147–67), and Suger of St.-Denis (1122–51), nothing is known of his family background or personal appearance. Access to his role as patron comes from his interests as gleaned from documents, from what happened in his years as prior, and from his buildings. They provide clues to his tastes and design preferences. Strong leadership abilities emerge from Wibert's rise from monk to sub-prior and then to prior and his courageous confrontation in 1154 with Archbishop Theobald, one of the most powerful men in England. Shrewd business skills are evident from his expansion of the Precinct, enlargement of the endowment, orchestration of building programs, and financial reforms. Urbanity may be presumed; every medieval prior or abbot traveled widely and was required to entertain visitors of high social rank, responsibilities particularly necessary at Canterbury, the Benedictines' leading institution in England. Bibliophile interests are apparent from his ownership of manuscripts inventoried at his death, as well as from his support of an active and intellectually vigorous scriptorium (James 1903, 143–45). Care of the sick and old is known from his construction of the vast Infirmary Hall for his monks and the Almonry and Chapel outside the Priory's Green Court Gatehouse for the city's sick and for pilgrims. By no means least, Wibert's passion for the arts is evident in manuscript painting from the commissioning of the sumptuous Eadwine Psalter, in the promotion of fresco painting in the Cathedral, in the wide use of sculpture on buildings – and, above all, in the architecture employed for the renewal with the use of expensive building materials such as marbles and polished limestones, the adoption of new building types and up-to-date styles, and the iconographical references to architectural archetypes.[4]

Such qualities of mind reveal a person with wide-ranging interests extending from England to Europe, and to the Holy Land. Furthermore, a broad curiosity, strong tastes, administrative and financial skills, and knowledge of the arts suggest an engaging and cultivated personality. These lift a corner of the veil of invisibility that shrouds Wibert, although they tell us nothing of his personal appearance, temperament, or habits, such as are recorded for Thomas Becket, his contemporary and clerical colleague. Further information comes from Wibert's role as patron of the renewal. His building undertakings reveal an involvement with programming, typology, design, style, technology, and iconography, the information often dovetailing with the interests just mentioned. These concerns determined the renewal of the Priory and are recoverable from *Drawing I*. They will be taken up in separate chapters below. An outline of them in this chapter serves to establish a profile of Wibert as a patron.

His first concern centered on the need for a reliable water supply for general hygiene and for the provision of buildings related to it such as the Bath House, *Necessarium*, and Fountain Houses. In its earlier history the Priory had depended on hand-drawn water from wells, but as the monastery grew in size, the shortcomings of this arrangement became increasingly apparent. To solve them Prior Wibert installed the new pressure-fed, piped water system celebrated in the Eadwine Psalter's *Drawing I* and in the *obit* written at his death in 1167. It remains the most widely recognized accomplishment at the Priory in this period (Grewe 1991a, 229–36). Contemporaries saw the water system not in terms of amenity (as we might today) but as a miracle for the means by which water was brought to the monastery and distributed to different buildings. The prior's *obit* highlighted both: "[among the] many other useful things Prior Wiburt as a good pastor contributed to this church, . . . [he built] a watercourse with its ponds, conduits, and fish pools, which water it carried nearly a mile from the town into the precinct, and thus miraculously through all the offices of the very precinct itself" (see Appendix A). The emphasis on conveyance and distribution can be understood as a contrast to the Priory's earlier static, hand-drawn well water. The water system also transformed many aspects of health and hygiene in monastic life and culture.

A second concern driving Wibert's renewal focused on hospitality. This monastic obligation extended back to apostolic times. Met in different ways in preceding centuries, hospitality was accommodated in the 1070s in Archbishop Lanfranc's Priory by a single building, the 100-foot-long west range of the Great Cloister. Eighty years later, this building was deemed inadequate to serve the needs of mid-twelfth-century visitors and was replaced with four new ones by Wibert. Each new building served a different social class of visitor and its expectations for hospitality. The Priory's facilities thus say much about social segregation in the early Angevin period and the monastery's efforts to meet the standards of comfort and security demanded by its guests. At the same time, the new accommodations offered compelling contrasts to the more austere quarters and plain provisions of the reform orders.

For the top social rank of visitor such as royalty or high aristocracy, the prior's *Nova Camera*, a two-story hall, provided a spacious day room and sleeping accommodation above. The guests accessed the new adjacent large-scale Infirmary by an enclosed passage for food, toilets, and medical needs. They also had use of generous grounds in the northeast of the Precinct where they enjoyed a separate bath, apparently open to the sky like a pool, reserved exclusively for them, even though the large communal Bath House lay only a few dozen feet away.

For visitors of lesser rank such as gentry or lower noble ranks, Prior Wibert provided a particularly notable Guesthouse whose architectural elegance and range of amenities exceeded any known elsewhere in England. Approached through its own gatehouse, the Guesthouse offered a rib-vaulted ground-floor hall with sleeping space above and a rib-vaulted parlor for discussions with the monks and for certain rites such as the *mandatum hospitum* (the ceremonial washing of the feet of guests). Fronted by arcaded walkways and entered under a doorway with piggybacked sculpted tympana, the building was generously furnished and provided with fireplaces and running water. An appointed secular staff looked after the visitors. For pilgrims or middle class visitors, the Common Hall provided lodging. Located in the *Aula Nova* adjacent to the Green Court Gatehouse, it took the form of a well-lit and flexibly furnished twin-aisled hall of generous dimensions over a groin-vaulted undercroft. For the servants, grooms, and cooks who accompanied the upper class of visitor, their needs for sleep and food were met in the Servants' Hall in the most northerly part of the *Aula Nova* at the furthest distance from the Cathedral.

A third concern of Prior Wibert was directed to the care of the community's sick and aged. The huge Infirmary Hall, the largest such facility in the country, served both groups as well as those recovering from bloodletting, an ordeal for Benedictine monks ordained six times a year as essential for good health and the curbing of sexual appetite. The Infirmary's services and forms reflected changes within monasticism as well as outside it. In addition, Wibert's construction of the Almonry on the west or city side of the Green Court Gatehouse and of hospitals within the city itself extended Lanfranc's earlier concerns for health to the urban population. Both point to improved standards in care and medicine notable around 1150 elsewhere in the south and north of England. To administer care, the Priory appointed secular physicians who are documented in service in the 1150s and 1160s.

A fourth concern of the prior took account of the revival of Roman-based jurisprudence and the establishment of canon law. These new disciplines sweeping through European life at mid-century were centered in the famous law school in Bologna, then among the largest cities in Europe. One of the school's distinguished magisters, Vacarius, had joined Archbishop Theobald's curia in 1143. Vigorous support for the new legal innovations came from Henry II, who viewed them as a means of loosening ties to feudal institutions. Advances in jurisprudence were linked to several social factors, including the rise of the communal movement in Italy and France to resist imperial ambitions. To meet these needs at Canterbury, the Priory acquired additional land on which to construct the prior's Court Hall as part of the *Aula Nova* and related buildings around the Green Court Gatehouse.

A fifth concern focused on the needs of the Cathedral. Although Archbishop Anselm's "glorious choir," as contemporaries called it, had been finished only twenty years earlier, Prior Wibert clearly sought to remedy what use had shown to be inadequacies. Several can be reconstructed and indicate changes in practice. They included a building for the laving ritual performed by the monks as they entered their choir for the night office at 2:30 a.m. each day, a treasury for vessel and vestment safe keeping (in the upper story) and for the liturgy of burial (in the lower story), heightened towers to facilitate access to the choir galleries, added stories to the chapels of St. Andrew and St. Anselm necessitating new vaults, improved entrances to the crypt, and sculptural enrichment of the exterior.

The shaping of these concerns and the manner in which architecture addressed them reveal Prior Wibert's determination as patron to create human environments adjusted to new expectations for hygiene, health, hospitality, law, and worship. They also reveal his leaning toward unusual as well as standard features of architecture. One of the unusual features was Wibert's fascination with technology. This is evidenced in the construction of the water system with its array of valves, cisterns, and filtration mechanisms, in the on-site casting of the massive bell for the free-standing campanile on the south side of the Cathedral (with the demanding control of high temperatures for the metal and the cold-chasing for the bell's tuning), and in the metallurgy for the water system's faucets, gratings, and cisterns, as well as the more than forty metal finials shown on *Drawing I* which embellished the rooftops of the Precinct.

Similarly, Wibert's involvement with the renewal embraced all phases of work extending from the program to its completion. Everything known about the prior supports the notion of involvement. All the projects lay on his very doorstep, within sight and hearing, rather than at some distance. It is inconceivable that the love of such details as the rich building materials and the obsession with high gloss finishes manifest in the Great Cloister, the Water Tower, the *Aula Nova*, and elsewhere were anything other than the direct reflection of personal tastes.

In the context of the competition with the reform orders already mentioned, Wibert's work as patron visibly reset the standards and expectations of monastic visitors, postulants, patrons, and the community of monks. Viewed as a direct response – a challenge even – to counter the pulse of reform, the renewal paraded the prior's accomplishments as patron. The *obit* composed for the Chapter at his death in 1167 made mention of the marvel of contemporaries about the water system and the improvements to the Cathedral. Such admiration illuminates the context in which contemporaries received them, and doubtless reflected the intent that underlay them – and they bring into focus our understanding of the man responsible for them.

THE SOURCES FOR PRIOR WIBERT'S RENEWAL

For a number of buildings linked to the renewal, Prior Wibert utilized new architectural types. Their adoption raises the question of their source. Did they derive from Wibert's wide tastes and travels? Should they be explained by general period trends? Or did they originate with persons outside the community but with distinct connections to it such as Vacarius, Thomas Becket, John of Salisbury, or other members of the archbishop's household?

Within the constraints of monastic tradition, it remains to be shown whether a single individual, even a figure like Abbot Suger of St.-Denis, could engineer innovation on the scale involved at Canterbury. In general, Benedictine communities in the twelfth century were more open to new ideas than the reform orders such as the Cistercians, where change was monitored by annual visits from the abbots of founding houses and the annual meetings of the General Chapter. Yet within Cistercian communities, patrons such as Ailred of Rievaulx, Wibert's contemporary, sponsored architecture with a surprising range of new forms without incurring censure or demolition in some cases (Fergusson and Harrison 1999, 83–99).

Wibert's travels, and general curiosity could have provided ideas about new building types. Likewise, period trends, such as the cosmopolitan composition of the court and the archbishop's curia at Canterbury, provided access to information about them. The case for the involvement of an individual, notably Thomas Becket, with close connections to the Priory and the prior also needs to be examined. Becket had joined Theobald's household in 1144. Although his first duties are undocumented, early on he would have encountered Vacarius, the Bolognese law magister. The suggestion has been made that Vacarius had begun training clerks and others in what amounted to an incipient school of law. This circle almost certainly included Becket and also possibly Wibert. Both were clearly marked out for advancement.[5] Becket spent 1148–52 in exile with Archbishop Theobald at St.-Bertin at St.-Omer (Pas-de-Calais), where he would have been exposed to Channel School ideas in a wide area of northeast France and the Lowlands. Between 1151 and 1153 he was studying canon law and Roman law for a year at Bologna with continued studies at Auxerre (Duggan 2007, 10–11) and again at Paris. In Auxerre he would have known the young Cistercian mother house at Pontigny, twelve miles away, and was to return there to spend two years of his exile (1164–66). On the command of Archbishop Theobald, he returned to Canterbury in 1154 to take up the position of ecclesiastical advisor to Henry II.

Wibert's appointment as prior preceded Becket's return. There is no way of knowing what prompted the archbishop to imprison Wibert except that the dispute turned on the Priory's autonomy. Could one factor have been the grandiose plans for the renewal launched by the prior? Becket was certainly around when the ideas for the renewal were in discussion, albeit briefly before his elevation as royal chancellor, an office which necessitated his constant attendance of the king and his court, took him away from Canterbury. On the other hand, Canterbury lay on the road between London and Dover and would have been one of the stops en route. Becket's sophisticated taste in clothes, liveries, luxury goods, and collecting indicates strong interests in visual matters, as Nilgen has shown (1986, 145–58). His role in the introduction of the Channel School style in manuscript production suggested by Cahn and others indicates his influence on at least one of the arts (Cahn 1975a, 47–59). Becket's sporadic contacts with the community at the Priory in the 1150s are known from the criticism of his penchant for wearing colorful court dress in the cloister. Later, as archbishop, he lived for periods with the monks, joining them on occasion for the offices in choir.

At a minimum, Becket was informed about the work and supported the prior's renewal. The case for a more active role is based on Becket's artistic interests, wide travels, and direct knowledge about developments in Italy and France at mid-century. Particularly relevant was his knowledge about the revival of jurisprudence in the 1140s and 1150s. This would have included the physical settings of law courts, their placements, and ancillary spaces. He would have known early examples

of the *palazzo comunale* type in Italy and committal halls in France. Yet such ideas could have come as readily from the Bolognese law magisters who were in Archbishop Theobald's household in these years. Other features of the Priory's renewal, such as the sizable Bath House or the piggybacked sculpted tympana at the entrance to the Guesthouse or the Bath House, also suggest Italian influence. Narrowing this influence to individuals again points to either Becket or the Bologna law magisters. For the Bath House and the bath (*cupa*) in the prior's *Nova Camera* or residence, the evidence suggests a motivation linked to the curative properties of baths. Contemporaries record Becket's chronic stomach ailments, which caused him continuous discomfort and made him short-tempered (Barlow 1976, 25–26, and n. 2). Becket's knowledge of contemporary treatment for such illnesses could plausibly have been gained from his travels to Italy, and more precisely from his awareness of papal interest in baths at the Lateran Palace during the rule of the English pope Adrian IV (see Chapter 6). None of the examples just mentioned proves Becket's involvement in the Priory's renewal. But they make the case for his discernment in matters artistic and his intense interest in them as well as his known habit of forcefully expressing his views.

The same question underlies some of the prior's other projects such as the ceremonial Norman Staircase, the *Aula Nova*, the five fountains, and the Treasury and Burial Gate. Someone with knowledge of models must have been at hand with a personal link to the community. How ideas, types, and forms previously unknown (or unrecorded) in England surfaced in Kent remains a central issue. Some features at the Priory were matched elsewhere. Wibert's contemporary, Henry of Blois, bishop of Winchester and abbot of Glastonbury, is credited by Giraldus Cambrensis with the construction of piped pressure-fed water systems; he traveled to Italy and collected classical sculpture in Rome (West 2008, 213–30). Unfortunately, not enough is known in detail about the Winchester system to make a comparison with Canterbury possible. Furthermore, the intense antipathy between the two curias casts doubts about cross-influence.

For Becket's input on the Priory's renewal to have counted, it would have needed to occur during his flamboyant years as royal chancellor (1154–62). During this period he was sporadically in Canterbury, although the length of stays mattered less than the contribution of ideas. By the time Becket assumed the archbishopric in 1162 and the subsequent dramatic change in his tastes and manner of life, the Priory's renewal was completed or in its late stages. It is the preceding period when he was closely allied to the Angevin court that is critical. Positing Becket's role in the Priory's renewal is merited when account needs to be taken of sudden and unexplained changes in architectural types or technical innovations. How such innovations came to the attention of the prior and how they were implemented by him are legitimate concerns. Becket had the artistic interests, the contacts and connections, the knowledge gained from wide travel, and the resources to be considered as a plausible advisor and supporter of the renewal.

Consideration of Becket's role as a potential outside source has to be played off against the fierce sense of autonomy prevailing within the Priory in these years, as manifested in the ugly quarrel with Archbishop Theobald in 1154. In the aftermath there is no evidence to support an inward-turning mood bent on protecting the Priory's rights and privileges to the exclusion of outside influences. Rather, the balance of evidence favors an assessment of Wibert as a gatherer and collector of ideas, as someone in touch with top figures within Benedictine monasticism as well as churchmen in London and Rochester with active building programs in hand. Everything about Wibert suggests a pragmatic leader, curious, open to ideas for the benefit of the community, and earning thereby its respect and affection.

The regard with which Wibert was held by his contemporaries at Canterbury is best gauged at his death by the *obit* commissioned by the Chapter. Although the circumstances of his death are unknown, the decision to bury him in the Chapter House was a mark of distinction accorded to only two other priors in the twelfth century. Further, Wibert was granted a special tomb, probably the "monumentum" mentioned in the late thirteenth-century *Instructio Noviciorum* (Knowles and Brooke 2002, 215; Wilson 1995, 489, n. 169). Located just inside the entry to the building, the tomb took the unusual form of a chest raised above floor level. Particular care was taken in the preparation of Wilbert's body for burial, as may be inferred from the inhumation carried out in 1404 by Prior Chillenden and the discovery of its incorruption after nearly 250 years of burial. The inscription in brass on the grave, "here lies Wibert, formerly prior of this church," noted in 1640 by William Somner, the Canterbury antiquary and keeper of the cathedral archives, probably dates from the reburial (Somner 1640, 111).

Proof of Wibert's reputation rests equally on the *obit* (see Appendix A). It comes down to us from a ca. 1500 compilation at Canterbury drawing together earlier material. The list of his accomplishments is highly selective. Pride of place is given to the vestments and fabrics he donated to the Cathedral, all of which have vanished. No buildings are mentioned and the only hint of them is the unspecific reference to the "many more such things as [he made] happen . . . as a good pastor [*bonus pastor*] . . . to this church." His achievements as builder of the water system are admiringly hailed, and reference made to his plans "for the making of a chapel" which was unrealized.

Both sources confirm the esteem in which Wibert was held. That his anniversary on September 27 each year was kept complete with the ringing of the great bells, a Mass with two cantors, a feast following for the community, and the prominence given to his raised tomb at the entrance to the Chapter House attests to the high reputation of one of Canterbury's great builder priors.

3

THE EADWINE PSALTER
DRAWINGS OF THE PRECINCT

Drawing I (see fig. 3) depicts the Priory at the height of Prior Wibert's rule. Spread over a bifolium in the last gathering of the Eadwine Psalter (Trinity College, Cambridge, MS R. 17. 1, fols. 284v and 285r), the artist combined into a coherent image the overall Precinct, the huge Cathedral, thirty of the buildings used by the community, the cloisters and open courts, water system, ornate fishpond, drainage channels, and sewer lines.[1] The image is without peer anywhere in twelfth-century Europe. Modern authors hail its survival as "almost miraculous" and draw attention to its unique importance to the topographer, engineer, hydraulics specialist, cartographer, and architectural historian (M. W. Thompson 1998, 158; Woodman 1992, 168).

Given this range of interests, *Drawing I* is subject to different interpretations. Most authors agree, however, that it shows a contemporary image of the Priory and its buildings, a time capsule freeze-framing, as it were, a settled picture of building achievements carried out under Prior Wibert. In this documentary or chronicle role, part of the image's fascination comes from hindsight. The artist depicts the physical layout of the country's major Benedictine monastery on the brink of

dramatic change. Within twenty years three major events were to transform Canterbury's history. In 1170, four armed knights pursued Archbishop Thomas Becket through the seldom used southwest cloister door linking the Archbishop's Palace and the Cloister, traversed the south alley of the Great Cloister, entered the Cathedral through the northwest transept portal (all represented on the drawing), and hacked him to death in front of that transept's southern altar.[2] The murder in the late afternoon of December 29, 1170 transformed Becket the man – contentious, brilliant, principled, difficult – into Becket the "holy blissful martyr," and transformed the Cathedral from an important national shrine into one of medieval Europe's major international sites of pilgrimage. Three years later, fire destroyed much of Archbishop Anselm's celebrated choir and east end of the Cathedral shown on *Drawing I*. Rebuilding and the Cathedral's further extension eastwards followed (1174–84), although no part of either appears in the image. A third crisis of national dimensions occurred in the late 1180s when Archbishop Baldwin attempted to outflank the Priory through the establishment of a secular college at Hackington just outside Canterbury. By then, dissension between the archbishop and the Priory and between both and the king ushered in a period of turmoil in the internal workings of Christ Church and climaxed in Archbishop Langton's exile to St.-Bertin at St.-Omer from 1207 to 1213. All this lay in a quarrelsome and disruptive future just beyond the stable conditions represented on *Drawing I.*

Less well known is a second drawing, hereafter referred to as *Drawing II*, which appears on the following folio of the Eadwine Psalter, folio 286 (fig. 10).[3] Once also a bifolium although only one-half survives, the other having been lost or stolen 400 years ago, the image similarly depicts the Priory's water supply but pays little attention to the buildings, which are shown in abbreviated form, and none at all to the divisions and spaces of the Priory or to its circumscribing wall.

For many scholars the drawings present images unrelated to the preceding texts and were made at a later date than the manuscript. Were these claims provable, they would compound the mystery surrounding their inclusion in the most important manuscript produced in Romanesque England. For Willis, as seen, the two architectural drawings were "waterworks drawings" inserted in the manuscript some years after its completion. The view of them as "waterworks drawings" continues unquestioned into the present (Woodman 1992, 168–77). Willis's characterization of *Drawing I* is open to discussion, however, as also is his suggestion that the drawings lack connection to the manuscript and are later insertions. In this chapter I outline an alternative explanation.

THE EADWINE PSALTER

Knowledge about the Eadwine Psalter expanded hugely with the ground-breaking 1992 publication, *The Eadwine Psalter: Text, Image, and Monastic Culture in Twelfth-Century Canterbury.* The editors – Margaret Gibson, T. A. Heslop, and Richard Pfaff – joined ten other scholars to address central matters related to the Psalter such as codicology and paleography, decoration and illustration, the calendar, *tituli*, Latin apparatus, English and Anglo-Norman versions, the comet, prognostications, waterworks drawings, the *Scribal Portrait*, the manuscript's relation to the Paris Psalter (Paris, BN, MS lat. 8846), and the book's later history. No better tribute could be paid to the authors than the new questions prompted by their 1992 publication. They have moved enquiry in different directions. At the same time they have accentuated the

most basic questions about the manuscript, such as the reasons why it was made, who its patron was, and how the different parts of the Psalter (which contained much more material than the Psalms) relate to each other, all of which remain unresolved.

Thanks to the book's pioneering scholarship there is general agreement that the text and illustrations of the Eadwine Psalter were produced in the scriptorium of the Priory around 1155–60.[4] No other undertaking compares with its scale, compositional complexity, scholarly apparatus, lavish illumination, and expense. The Psalter contains Jerome's three Latin translations of the Psalms: the *Gallicanum*, the standard text used in the Divine Office; the *Romanum*, his original translation; and the *Hebraicum*, his Latin translation from the Hebrew (Gibson 1992a, 113–15). Each version incorporates interlinear commentary: Latin for the *Gallicanum*, Anglo-Saxon for the *Romanum*, and Anglo-Norman French for the *Hebraicum*. Flanking each psalm is a marginal Latin commentary and a prologue, collect, and *titulus*. To bring clarity to this material posed an extreme design challenge to the scriptorium. Each page required ten columns and ten sizes of script in different formats. Paleographers have identified the hands of a dozen different scribes. Like other medieval psalters, the Psalms are preceded by a six-folio calendar, and followed by a series of canticles and creeds. Far less usual are two sets of prognostications (divinatory texts) and of comet commentary (Webber 2005, 90).

The written texts were enriched with lavish illumination. Five hundred initials in silver and gold adorn the different psalm openings or serve as headings. In addition, 167 drawings in colored inks filled with figures,

(Facing page) 10   Eadwine Psalter, *Drawing II*, fol. 286, Trinity College, Cambridge (courtesy the Masters and Fellows, Trinity College, Cambridge).

The single folio survives from what was originally a bifolium with the present outer edge originally the center fold and the three colored pipe runs in the middle continued across the fold to supply water to the *Piscina* (as they do also on *Drawing I*). The *Piscina* occupied the center of the lost page, possibly at large scale, and may even have been its principal subject (see this chapter and Chapter 8). The surviving folio depicts the water's journey from its source (upper left) to the main service terminals in the Priory's Green Court and strict enclosure, which are shown in diagrammatic form. The Water Tower is shown bottom center, and the pendulum-like feature below represents the fountain outside the west transepts on the south side of the Cathedral.

landscapes, and architecture illustrate the Psalms and the concluding canticles. And last, eight full-page narrative biblical scenes (comprising 160 subjects) once prefaced the Psalter, but these were cut out from the manuscript in the seventeenth century. They are now dispersed between the Morgan Library in New York and the Victoria and Albert Museum and British Library in London (Kauffmann 2003, 178).

Like every manuscript, the Eadwine Psalter was made as a copy from models or exempla. For the psalm drawings, the model was the Carolingian manuscript now known as the Utrecht Psalter (Utrecht, Universiteitsbibliothek, MS 32), then in the library at the Priory but written and illustrated more than 300 years earlier at the abbey of Hautevillers in the diocese of Reims. The Utrecht Psalter illustrated each psalm with a line drawing, and these formed the principal model for the Canterbury book.[5] However, the presence of other models was necessary to provide for the additional texts and images, the commentary, collects, canticles, interlineations, initials, and full-page illustrations, none of which appear in the Utrecht Psalter.

Despite much that is known about the Eadwine Psalter, its purpose remains unclear. With only a small percentage of the material relevant to the liturgy, some other intention underlay the manuscript's production. Various suggestions have failed to win agreement. They include a celebratory, display, compilatory, or commemorative purpose (Gibson 1992b, 211–13). In support of the last, William Urry suggested a variation, a chronicle role for *Drawing I*, which he hypothesized was "a spectacle of [Prior Wibert's] construction program," specifically "a pictorial record ... to preserve the memory of his improvements to the existing layout" (Urry 1986, 50). All such purposes fall outside the traditional work of monastic scriptoria. It may be this character that accounts for the manuscript's first recorded location. Normally a psalter of this size and splendor would be kept with the Priory's most precious books. Yet an inventory of its books made around 1320 by Prior Eastry lists the Eadwine Psalter among the "libri armariolo Claustri" (the books kept in the press in the Cloister) (James 1903, xxvii, 51). Further adding to the uncertainty, Margaret Gibson observed that the book was most likely outdated by the time it was finished (Gibson 1992b, 213). It bears no trace of the new ways of studying the Psalter based on detailed patristic analysis associated with Peter Lombard and much in evidence by the 1160s in Benedictine foundations, including Canterbury. On the question of patronage, Gibson suggests Prior Wibert as the most plausible benefactor. He had the means to commission such a manuscript and the bibliophile interests as well to push forward an undertaking of this complexity and ambition. Both inferences are based on the inventory of his own books made at his death in 1167 (James 1903, 143–45).

THE THIRTY-SEVENTH GATHERING

The final or thirty-seventh gathering of the manuscript fits in with the same puzzling character. The gathering is composed of one bifolium and a single folio (fig. 11). The bifolium (fols. 284v and 285r) provides the support for the drawing of the Precinct and its buildings referred to as *Drawing I*. The single folio (fol. 286v) provides the support for the drawing of the buildings just served by the water system referred to as *Drawing II*. Since the outer edge of the folio carries the dirt line of a center fold and in the middle three pipes are cut off, Pickwoad inferred the existence of a facing page which was probably removed from the manuscript in the early 1600s (Pickwoad 1992, 5). Further, since *Drawing I* shows three pipes feeding the fishpond (*Piscina*), the only such feature so supplied, the missing folio must have depicted the *Piscina* in the center of the image.

Many puzzles surround the thirty-seventh gathering. Was it an inserted addition to the manuscript? Or was it bound in as a blank gathering with the images painted later? Who made the images? What were they intended to convey, and how did they relate to the rest of the Psalter?

ROTATION OF THE BIFOLIUM

As it appears today bound into the Eadwine Psalter, *Drawing I* is almost certainly upside down (fig. 11). The Cathedral and buildings of the strict enclosure presently appear on folio 284 verso and the Green Court on folio 285 recto. Pickwoad has argued persuasively that its present orientation reverses the twelfth-century original and results from a rotation probably carried out when the manuscript was rebound in the early 1600s (Pickwoad 1992, 5–6). Seen thus, a twelfth-century viewer would have "read" the image from left to right, replicating the way a monk or visitor would have experienced the spaces.[6] Entering from the Green Court Gatehouse (originally on the verso at the left), he would have proceeded into the quasi-public Green Court, then entered

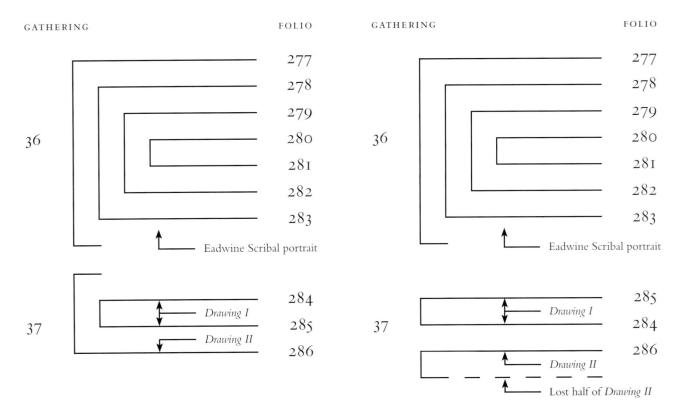

11 Collation plan of the last three images in the Eadwine Psalter. On the left is the present arrangement. On the right is the original arrangement (after Pickwoad 1992, 4–9).

the gated area of the strict enclosure, namely the Great Cloister and the Infirmary Cloister, and terminated at the Cathedral (originally drawn on the outer side of the opposite recto). Corresponding with this experience of spaces viewed from inside the Priory, it should be noted that the Cathedral was depicted as seen from the north: that is, from inside the monastery, a view unfamiliar to many in the present.

The present orientation of the bifolium reproduces the post-suppression experience of the Precinct. With the monks expelled and the Green Court and its buildings empty, the Cathedral became the sole goal of the visitor. It was arguably this circumstance that determined the binder's decision to rotate the bifolium and to show the Cathedral as the first structure encountered. The result is jarring whatever the explanation. The rotation of the bifolium means that the water source (now on the right folio) runs "backwards" towards its source at Horsefold. Throughout this chapter and in other chapters where reference is made to it, *Drawing I* is described with the corrected rotation suggested by Pickwoad.

CENTER FOLD AND LINE BREAKS

The argument about how and when *Drawing I* was made has much to do with the center fold of the bifolium and the artist's connection of lines across it. Dividing the Precinct into two distinct parts, with the Green Court on one folio and the strict enclosure and the Cathedral on the other, inevitably meant that some buildings, pipe runs, and the outer wall straddled the verso and recto of the two folios. The erratic linkage between buildings or pipes or walls of all the lines that cross the center fold (see fig. 8A) indicates that *Drawing I* was made *after* the thirty-seventh gathering was sewn and bound with the manuscript (Pickwoad 1992, 6).

On the other hand, it could be argued that that the artist anticipated the center fold and left a space between the folios, which he then joined up after the gatherings were bound. The process can be followed in a number of areas of the drawing where connecting lines have a different width than those on the adjoining folios (see fig. 5). Not all lines were completely joined up. For instance, the intersection of pipes just below the Bath

House (*Balneatorium*) suggests the artist's anticipation of this need and illustrates the unexplained neglect to complete them after the gathering was bound with the rest of the manuscript.

DATE OF THE PSALTER AND THE THIRTY-SEVENTH GATHERING

The Gibson, Heslop, and Pfaff monograph of 1992 argued persuasively for a date between 1155 and 1160 for the text rather than the late 1140s which had hitherto been accepted (Gibson 1992b, 209). Opinion remains divided, however, about the dating of the last gathering with the images of the Precinct.

Drawing I and *Drawing II* cannot have been started before Archbishop Theobald's gift of the water source at Horsefold, a thousand yards north from the city's walls and the Priory. Historians date his gift between 1155 and 1157 (Saltman 1956, 273–74, charter 46; Urry 1986, 54, n. 1; Woodman 1992, 169) based on an analysis of the witness list to the charter. The *terminus ante quem* is established by the artist's depiction of the Cathedral before the extensive changes that followed the fire of 1174 and the subsequent extension and rebuilding of the eastern parts, notably the Trinity Chapel and Corona.

To the information of the water gift can be added the evidence of the buildings shown on *Drawing I*. The artist draws the northwest part of the Precinct, a development made possible as a result of land purchases mentioned in *Rental A* (A.1, A.2, A.9; see Chapter 6). The first of these, A.1, was most likely completed in the period when Wibert was sub-prior (1148–52/54) and consisted of seven small holdings lying behind the Bakehouse (*Pistrinum*) between the Priory's surrounding walls and the city's Roman walls. The second (A.2), made around 1157, comprised additional holdings to the west of the Bakehouse and includes the land on which the *Aula Nova* was constructed. The third (A.9), also made around 1157, specified "the land next to the north gate of the city" (Urry 1967, 221). As Woodman noted, the building lots referred to in the three Rental Rolls are identified as razed, thereby implying that they were rebuilt or in the course of rebuilding (Woodman 1992, 174–75). Over these razed properties Wibert constructed the *Aula Nova*, the Almonry Chapel, and most likely the Bakehouse and Green Court Gatehouse. All these buildings are included on *Drawing I*, which therefore cannot be dated before 1157, as Urry was the first to work out.

Another clue to the date comes from buildings which do not appear in *Drawing I* but which are known to have been constructed by Prior Wibert. There is no sign of the Almonry outside the Green Court Gatehouse, although the artist does depict the *capella extra portas* which served it. Work on the Almonry was under way in 1161 when its "new wall" is referred to in a charter (Urry 1967, 221). The omission of the Almonry may not be central if the artist showed only the buildings within the Precinct. Yet the Almonry was one of Wibert's most cherished projects, and it should be noted that *Drawing I* included the *capella extra portas*. Equally omitted are the raised towers on the west side of the east transepts, the north range of the Cellarer's Court and its gatehouse, and the heightened story of the Treasury. All are acknowledged as among the last works carried out by the prior on the basis of their distinctive style. These omissions suggest a *terminus ante quem* of 1161 for *Drawing I*.

Further clues to the date of *Drawing I* come from the Cellarer's Court where the buildings around the entry underwent rapid alteration. These offer a rare if neglected chance to correlate archaeological, stylistic, and documentary references. On *Drawing I* the Guesthouse was entered through a gate rather than the Pentice Gatehouse. Surviving evidence shows that the Pentice Gatehouse was built in a separate campaign around 1160 (see Chapter 5). Since it does not appear in *Drawing I* but the Guesthouse does, the omission of the Pentice Gatehouse strengthens the case for dating the manuscript image before ca. 1160.[7] *Drawing I* also omits the additional buildings on the Gatehouse's eastern side (extending to the Larder Gate, see figs. 37B and 40) raised at the same time.

Documentary evidence adds support of a ca. 1157–59 date for the Guesthouse. A reference to staffing specifies: "Senescallus aulae hospitum, Janitor portae aulae, garcio ejus" (Urry 1967, 161, n. 14).[8] Among the names of the men who occupied the office of seneschal is Bartholomew, who assumed office in 1158. The appointment of staff suggests a completed building. A different milestone for the completion of the first phase of the renewal (including the Guesthouse) was marked by issuance of the Priory's Second Seal (see fig. 16) dated between 1155 and 1158 (Heslop 1982, 97). Although there is no record of what prompted the new design, an institutional event, like the completion of a major campaign of work, was often associated with such a commission. The same applies to the papal confirmation gained from the English pope Adrian IV in 1158 authenticating an internal administrative reorganization in which revenue was divided between three obedientiaries: the cellarer, chamberlain, and sacrist (Holtzmann 1930, vol. 2, 228–30). Cross-referencing the documentary with the archaeological evidence and both with *Drawing I* suggests a date around 1158 for the completion of this part of the renewal. This date coincides with the one proposed for the manuscript's texts and illuminations in the Eadwine Psalter monograph of 1992. Among other things, it would mean that *Drawing I* (along with the two other images) was completed and bound together with the rest of the manuscript at the same time.

TITULI

Two categories of *tituli* may be identified: labels written above or within individual buildings, and explanatory labels (Willis 1868, 197). Identifying labels consist of single words: *Refectorium, Necessarium*, and so forth.[9] Such economy contrasts with "The Plan of St. Gall" where each room's purpose is explained by sentences that even on occasion specify such details as the placement of furniture. On *Drawing I* the labels seem obvious to the point of being redundant, particularly if monks were the intended audience. Who would not have known the location of the Chapter House or the Infirmary? However, redundancy also marks the Eadwine Psalter's texts where every psalm was provided with a *titulus*. And in other Benedictine houses, cloister capitals with subjects of transparent clearness carry single-word, identifying *tituli*. Perhaps word and image should be seen as mutually referential.[10]

The few explanatory labels on *Drawing I* provide fuller information, although some again state the obvious. In the Cellarer's Court, we are told in an inscription above the gate with its two closed leaves: "Gate between the Guest Hall and Kitchen" (both flanking buildings are labeled in any case). Similarly, in the northern part of the Precinct, a *titulus* above the gate next to the *Aula Nova* reads: "Postern near the North Hall." More informative are the *tituli* which refer to the water system. Thus, we are told in the Great Cloister in front of the Parlor: "Small cistern before the door of the Locutory: the rainwater delivered into the gutters which are fixed round the Cloister is turned into this cistern, and conducted in a drainpipe under the passage which leads to the Infirmary Hall. This pipe, when it comes opposite the crypt door, is turned to the right, and continues its course outside the passage" (see fig. 26). Similarly, the *titulus* above the standpipe in the Infirmary Cloister

(quoted below) tells of its function in the event of drought or a breakdown in the water system.

A different category of information comes from three *tituli* placed on the east side of the Great Kitchen. Moving from north to south, we are told first of "the chamber where fish are washed" (*Camera ubi piscis lavatur*) (fig. 8A). A lower building with two windows fronts the narrow courtyard between the Great Kitchen and the Refectory with an explanatory *titulus*: "Window at which the portions are served out" (*Fenestra ubi fercula administrantur*), and then of the southernmost one: "Window through which the platters [or trenchers] are thrown out to be washed" (*Fenestra per quam ejiciuntur scutelle ad lavandum*). The down-to-earth specificity of what were relatively minor features of domestic organization at the Priory has nothing to do with either the water system or other suggested purposes for the image. Adding to the uncertainty of the labels' purpose is the obvious fact that they did not provide information discrete to Canterbury alone; other Benedictine foundations must have had similar practices.

DIVISIONING OF THE BUILDINGS
BETWEEN FOLIOS

The physical limits of the Convent alone are the subject of *Drawing I*. Nothing is shown of the Archbishop's Palace (which lay west of the precinct wall) or of the Almonry (in the northwest corner of the Precinct), both immediately adjacent.[11] The artist separates the Green Court with its eight buildings from the strict enclosure with more than twenty buildings. Clearly, functional divisions took precedence over pictorial needs.

For the folio featuring the Green Court, the artist uses the area outside the precinct wall to show at the outer edge a circular water tower and a second tower (partly trimmed). He then shows three fields through which the water travels and labels them as containing grain, vines, and apples.[12] At the end of each field he draws a settling tank to clean and purify the water. The pipes are shown on a steep diagonal which represented the water's descent of nearly 40 feet from source to monastery. Where the water reaches the city walls, the artist includes the small aqueduct which carried the water over the surrounding ditch, and where it meets the Priory's precinct wall, he includes the twin arched and crenellated superstructure.

Only a relatively small number of buildings are included on this folio. By contrast, the facing page includes a dense concentration of buildings. Their number and compression caused the artist many difficulties. The two cloisters dominate the center – the Great Cloister and the Infirmary Cloister. To the east the artist shows the Treasury, Infirmary Hall and its related buildings, and the prior's new residence with the separate bath and cistern (the latter three structures water damaged). The outer part of the page from top to bottom is taken up by the massive Cathedral with Anselm's large eastern extension (doubling the length of Lanfranc's earlier church). Towards the edge of the page, beyond the Cathedral, is a compressed space which formed the south side of the Precinct. In this the artist shows at the east the wall and gate closing the monks' "hortus" and the lay cemetery to the west. Between the eastern and western transepts he includes the large fountain without an aedicular covering and an adjacent older well, like the arrangement in the Infirmary Cloister on the opposite side of the Cathedral. To the south lay the large, free-standing campanile. It contained the massive bell, another of the prior's undertakings, which required thirty-two men to ring it (see Chapter 8).

SETTING OUT, PROJECTION, AND GRAPHIC CONVENTIONS

Overall, the artist presents the Precinct as a regular, rectangular space with neatly defined borders. In fact, a glance at a modern survey shows just the reverse: it is spread out and irregular. The buildings featured on the original right page of the bifolium are shown as if viewed from the north and those on the left folio from the south. The difference explains the image's distinctive folded out appearance. Buildings, courts, and cloisters are thus seen from inside the monastery. The insistent interiority conveys an effect of enclosure, of the interior viewed the way it was known by its users (fig. 13A). This is the opposite of a bird's-eye view such as that of the Cistercian abbey of Ter Duinen painted by Peter Porbus in 1580 (fig. 13B) where the intent was to show prospects and settings as seen from above and from outside.

How the artist composed his image can be reconstructed from *Drawing I*. Rotating the bifolium so that it was oriented vertically, he first drew the Cathedral at the top. The buildings below the church were then "dropped down" parallel to it. Lightly ruled vertical and horizontal lines served at the base lines for the buildings

to rest on. A number of these remain visible and can be noted at the west end of the *Necessarium* (fig. 12). As Willis observed, the lines were drawn when the bifolium was flat, in other words before the manuscript was bound (Willis 1868, 176–81). The artist often includes the front of a building set on the same base line as its side, for instance the Infirmary Hall or the Guesthouse, a feature which Woodman aptly characterized by observing that if each building was cut around and arranged on a true plan we would have a pop-up model of the monastery (Woodman 1992, 171). In the case of the Great Cloister, the Infirmary Cloister, and the Cellarer's Court, the artist used an exploded projection showing each of the four sides frontally. These features explain the resulting literalness of the image and its ordered aggregation of parts.

This process involved the artist in compositional pitfalls, and they provide clues to his working method. When he came to draw the Infirmary Cloister and the Water Tower, he needed to "fit" both under the Cathedral using the "drop down" procedure suggested above (fig. 14A). However, he exaggerated the width and height

12 Eadwine Psalter, *Drawing I*, detail showing west end of the *Necessarium*, Trinity College, Cambridge (courtesy the Master and Fellows, Trinity College, Cambridge).

The detail shows the artist has drawn setting-out overlapping lines at the west end of *Necessarium* to guide the positioning of the building.

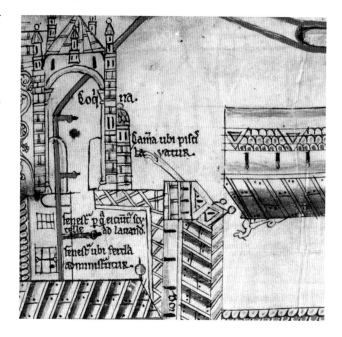

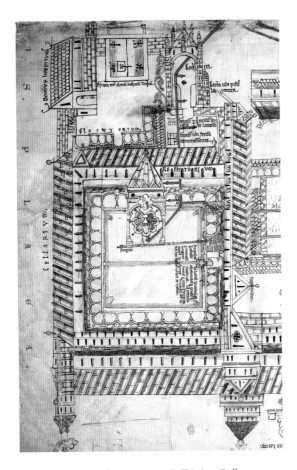

13A Eadwine Psalter, *Drawing I*, Trinity College, Cambridge (courtesy the Master and Fellows, Trinity College, Cambridge).

A detail of the Great Cloister showing the folded-out projection employed by the artist to convey his conception of what the image represented (rather than how it looked).

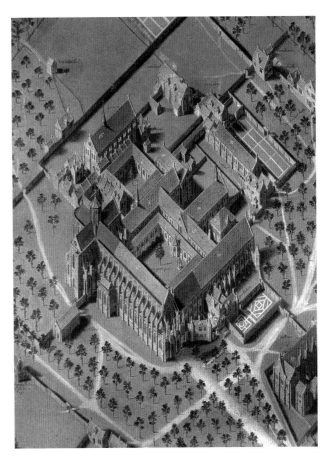

13B Pieter Porbus, *Abbey of Ter Duinen*, 1580, painting, Bruges, Musée Grunthuuse (courtesy Musée Grunthuuse).

The artist presents the abbey from a bird's-eye view with a consistent projection and single vanishing point. The painting clarifies the different intentions behind the projection used in the Eadwine Psalter's precinct drawing 400 years earlier (see fig. 3)

of the Water Tower with the result that its gabled roof projected "up" into the Cathedral, thereby enclosing the door into the crypt. Aware of the visual contradiction, the artist inscribed in the roof of the Water Tower the words *hostium cripte* (the door to the crypt).

A combination of projections built up the image.[13] The mix has long been recognized. As early as 1774 William Gostling, the cathedral archivist and antiquarian, observed in his *Walk in and about the City of Canterbury* that "the drawing is neither a plan, an upright, or a prospect" (147). Only a few parts of the monastery are shown from above, those immediately adjacent to the north side of the Cathedral such as the east alley and the buildings fronting it, and further east the Infirmary Cloister and the Treasury (labeled *Vestiarium*). Each is

simply noted as a façade, and they are stacked one behind the other as they might have been seen, possibly from a viewing location such as the northwest tower of Lanfranc's church.

The artist's distinctive graphic conventions included a penchant for depicting certain features at exaggerated scale. He expands the slender Water Tower in the Infirmary Cloister so that it is as wide as the massive north transept in front of which it stands (fig. 14B). Similarly, two of the three other fountain houses (at the entry to the Refectory and to the Infirmary Hall) are shown much larger than the buildings they front. Exaggeration may have been the consequence of the artist acting under instructions, although it is more likely that it reflected his pride in these features, which, in turn,

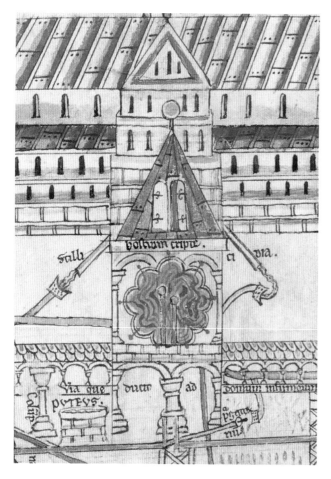

14A Eadwine Psalter, *Drawing I*, detail showing the Water Tower in the Infirmary Cloister with the northeast transept behind, Trinity College, Cambridge (courtesy the Master and Fellows, Trinity College, Cambridge).

14B Canterbury Cathedral Water Tower and northeast transept (photograph author).

The artist increases the scale of the Water Tower in relation to the transept. Many of the details of the Water Tower are accurately observed, even down to the interior arcading which still survives (cf. fig. 136).

tempted him not merely to show them large but to show them off. Another convention emerges in the artist's concern with the relationships of buildings and their adjacencies more than their scale or detail. Thus, he accurately shows the *Domus Hospitum* as lying outside the western boundary wall of the monastery between the east range and the entry to the Cellarer's Court, but shrinks the building from nine bays to three (as he did again with the *Aula Nova*). Such abbreviations occur more than once; the Dormitory is reduced from six aisles to two, and the Great Cloister's arcades from the twenty-four calculated by Tim Tatton-Brown (2006, 102) to the nine rendered by the artist.

The artist's adept graphic "editing" emerges when he faced the congestion in the Cellarer's Court or the Infirmary Cloister. For the former, lacking space to draw the Guesthouse with its east- and south-facing galleried walks extending across both sides of the building, he apparently transposed the arcades to the uncluttered wall on the opposite side of the court and then labeled them *Locutorium* to help the viewer grasp his transposition (see Chapter 5). Similar rearrangements mark the southeast corner of the Infirmary Cloister.

The image's projections are far from unified. Thus, the drawing is not a plan or a bird's-eye view, or a representation of the waterworks, or a literal rendering of buildings and spaces. Yet the image is rich in information and eloquent in its representations, and it is these features that form the basis for a number of scholarly questions such as its sources and context. Part representation, part map, part ideal, part inventory, part chronicle, the artist provides us with much more information than would have been possible had he shown us their appearance only. A term is lacking to describe these varied intentions. A working characterization may be borrowed from the work of Pierre Lavedan, who developed the notion of "l'idéogramme monastère," meaning a combination of ideas and images depicted as ideographs.[14]

THE WATER SYSTEM

Before Prior Wibert's installation of the piped, pressure-fed water system, the community had drawn its water from wells inside the Precinct.[15] Two such wells most likely left from the earlier system are shown on *Drawing I*, one on the south side of the Cathedral opposite the southeast transept in the area marked the cemetery of the laity, and the other in the Infirmary Cloister (Tatton-Brown 1980, 19–20). For the latter, the artist supplied a *titulus* which identifies the well (*Puteus*) and then next to it makes the observation: "standpipe into which, when the waters of the source fail, water raised from the well may be poured, and it will be distributed to all the offices." This improbable explanation (to prime the system would have taken many gallons more than could have been contained in the capital of the standpipe) nonetheless points to a need which existed during repair or drought in dry seasons.

The water system has never been investigated archaeologically. A field survey undertaken in 1983 by Tim Tatton-Brown identified some of the ponds in Old Park that fed the 1150s system (Tatton-Brown 1983, 45–51). Most of what is known about the new system comes from *Drawing I* and *Drawing II*. Documents record subsequent remodelings by Prior Chillenden (1391–1411) and, a century later, by Prior Thomas Goldstone II (1495–1517). After the suppression, a further overhaul and part renewal is recorded, and more extensive changes were made in the late 1600s. They are noted on maps of the Precinct such as the Hill plan of the 1680s (see fig. 5; see also Woodman 1992, 168–69). Parts of the pipe remain outside the Precinct, and some fragments are preserved in the cathedral archives (Urry 1986, 55).

Water in quantity was critical to every monastic community. The Priory was unusually large with about 120 monks and the same number of servants, plus staff, grooms and horses, and visitors. Water served many purposes: drinking, washing, laundry, cooking, plant cultivation, baths, stabling and smithing, and disposal of waste. Unlike rural monasteries where the identification of plentiful streams was a preliminary to foundation, older urban monasteries competed for water. Competition was most pressing when a community expanded. Thus, Archbishop Theobald's gift to the Priory of additional water from the Horsefold springs was hugely valuable. Further, the water's source outside the city had the additional advantage of being located on ground nearly 40 feet higher than the Priory, providing a gravity drop sufficient to ensure adequate water pressure for the piped system. Modern engineering estimates suggest a flow of fresh, filtered, pipe-fed water at the rate of approximately 10,000 liters an hour. From the source to the Priory the water had to pass over a number of properties. Each required negotiation and payment, as illustrated by an agreement between the Priory's monks and William, son of Drogo, to pay him one penny each year "for our aqueduct which passes through his land" (Urry 1967, 378, no. 30).

Designing, constructing, and controlling such a system has been rightly hailed as a major engineering achievement. At every stage it called for a high degree of technological sophistication. *Drawing I* includes a large number of components such as spigots, collection basins, conduits, filtration tanks, inspection covers, cisterns, scouring pipes, lavers, fountains, and standpipes. The claim has been made that the artist also shows us different qualities of the water according to its purity by the use of different colors: green for fresh water, orange-red for water after it had passed through the Great Cloister, brown for rainwater run-off, strong red for water fouled by sewage (Woodman 1992, 172).

Willis's assertion that the water system was the subject of *Drawing I* has been extended by some scholars who see the image in terms of a practical purpose such as a guide for routine maintenance or repair. Arguing against this, it can be observed that the piping and other hydraulic details constitute only an approximate plan of the Priory's system.[16] On occasion the artist shows piping running alongside or in front of buildings, rather than underneath them, as at the *Necessarium*. Although the prior's *obit* mentions the new system supplying water "through all the offices" (meaning buildings) in the Precinct, a number of such buildings are not hooked up to the system, such as the Servants' Hall and Common Hall (at the north end of the *Aula Nova*), the *Necessarium*, or the Guesthouse, even though it is known that

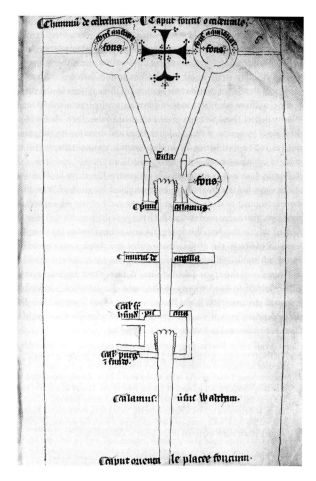

15 Waltham Abbey, water system, ca. 1200 (courtesy Jean Givens).

Compared to the Eadwine Psalter, the representation of the water system at Waltham Abbey uses formulaic symbols and lacks the observed detail of the Canterbury system.

water was supplied to the last (Grewe 1991a, 235). All three buildings were only a few feet from the water pipe and sewer, making connection a matter of relative ease. Despite such omissions, the water system's representation is remarkable for the site-specific details, as can be seen if it is compared with a drawing of a water system at Waltham Abbey dating to the 1220s (fig. 15).

Comparison with the ca. 820 "Plan of St. Gall," a Carolingian foundation a little smaller than the Priory, brings out further distinctive features. St. Gall's numerous *tituli* and precise details far outstrip those on the Eadwine Psalter. On the other hand, St. Gall omits pipe runs and infrastructure. *Drawing I* is the reverse of St. Gall. It shows the exteriors of buildings (rather than their plans), "opens" walls for the observer to see supply

pipes or specific water features, combines below-ground details with above-ground features, visualizes the monastery from the inside, and represents space and relationships. All these define a different intention from the Carolingian artist's plan.

COMPARABLE WATER SYSTEMS

Many monastic and secular institutions in the second half of the twelfth century replaced wells with water systems.[17] Searching for comparisons with Canterbury is frustrating because of the lack of archaeologically verified material. At Lichfield, for instance, documents record construction of a water system by Bishop Walter Durdent (1149–59) (Gould 1976, 75–79). The reference is tantalizing because Durdent had been prior at Canterbury Cathedral from 1143 to 1149 before moving to Lichfield. He was in office when Wibert was elected sub-prior. Details of the Lichfield system are lacking, and thus it is not possible to say if it was comparable or if it preceded or followed the one at the Priory.

At about the same date as Prior Wibert's system, the monks of neighboring St. Augustine's Abbey installed a conduit, although again few details are known (Bennett 1986, 98–99). Elsewhere in southern England, a pressurized water system has been proposed for Bishop Henry of Blois's palace court at Wolvesey in the early 1130s, citing Roman sources (Barlow et al. 1976, 284). It is mentioned in the late twelfth century by Gerald of Wales, who noted admiringly the bishop's sumptuous palaces, aqueducts, and hydraulic schemes (*Giraldi Cambrensis Opera*, VII, 45–49).[18] At the Cistercians' first foundation at Waverley in Surrey, documents record a water system by 1179 (Brakspear 1905, 89–90). The same is known at Benedictine abbeys at Battle, Lewes, Much Wenlock, and St. Nicholas Exeter in the third and fourth quarters of the twelfth century (Kahn 1991, 98 and n. 13). More specific information comes from Bury St. Edmunds during Walter de Banham's term as sacrist (ca. 1200). He is said to have "enclosed in lead the water supply from its head and spring for a distance of two miles and brought it to the cloister through ways hidden in the ground" (Gransden 2007, 90–92).

In the north of England archaeology provides a fairly clear chronology to follow the change from wells to channeled systems deriving from streams or springs. At Cistercian abbeys, these are known at Kirkstall Abbey in West Yorkshire in the 1160s and at Sawley Abbey in Lancashire between 1150 and 1180.[19]

Distinguishing between channeled and pressurized systems based on the documents is difficult. The existence of pipes is a guide but is not decisive. With the exception of Winchester, none of the water systems mentioned above can be proved to be earlier than the Priory's. More relevant, no system is known with anything like the same detail, making it impossible to compare technical aspects or the range of service. What can be shown is that the system represented on *Drawing I* and installed in the late 1150s was highly sophisticated and was drawn in considerable detail. It was directly credited to Prior Wibert, and precedes the buildings rather than being retrofitted to them.

No agreement has been reached on where the model for the Priory's pressurized system came from. In the Roman period Canterbury provided its citizens with two public baths whose remains emerged from archaeology following bomb damage in World War II. One was located opposite St. Margaret's Church, the other behind Woolworth's in St. George's Street. Whether parts of these survived in the 1150s to provide ideas for the Priory's hydraulics is doubtful. Roman baths included multiple facilities such as reading rooms, art displays, hot and cold baths, and bear no relation to the Priory's Bath House, thus essentially eliminating them as sources.

Water systems outside England would probably have been known to Prior Wibert. Cluny employed a subterranean conduit in the mid-eleventh century. St.-Bertin at St.-Omer had a similar system installed by ca. 1125 known to Archbishop Theobald and his curia from their exile from Canterbury (1148–52). Another source was Italy where Rome under Pope Calixtus II (1119–24) restored water to the city, including the Lateran Palace (Magnusson 2001, 6 and n. 10). At the Lateran a bath house is recorded (Ward-Perkins 1984, 146), and Cardinal Boso, the biographer of Adrian IV (1154–59), mentions the pope's construction of a new cistern, presumably to supply it (Bolton and Duggan 2003, 230–31). Visits to Rome from Canterbury were frequent during the 1140s and 1150s; Archbishop Theobald, John of Salisbury, and Becket are known to have undertaken the journey more than once. An Italian source is suggested by Prior Wibert's idiosyncratic interest in fountains at the Priory, where five were installed. The atriums of the large basilican churches in Rome such as Old St. Peter's, St. Paul's Outside the Walls, or the Lateran displayed pressure-fed piped fountains, as too did their cloisters. A further possibility derives from the influence of manuscript sources such as Vitruvius' *De Architectura*, book VIII.

ARCHITECTURE IN THE EADWINE PSALTER

Among the drawings and miniatures in the Eadwine Psalter are a substantial number with buildings. Some parallels with the Precinct's buildings and the Eadwine Psalter are worth mentioning and raise the question of interaction between the masons' yard and the adjacent scriptorium. Psalm 1 shows the psalmist seated under an elaborate aedicule. The twelfth-century artist's model, the Carolingian Utrecht Psalter (ca. 800), showed the psalmist seated within a classical circular tempietto (fig. 17A). Although Eadwine adhered to the composition (fig. 17B), he altered the classical tempietto to an aedicule. His adoption of a form similar to those used in the fountain houses (fig. 17C) suggests such an exchange of ideas. The laver in the Great Cloister as built included an array of gables above the aedicule, an effect which parallels the image used in the manuscript for Psalm 1.

A similar stimulus may explain the employment of heads in the towers of the Cathedral illustrated in the Second Seal of Christ Church, a detail which also derived from the Utrecht Psalter, as Heslop has noted (1982, 97) (fig. 16). Such transmissions among the Priory's workshops can be seen in the context of the multidisciplinary skills of scholars, scribes, miniature painters, and metalsmiths who produced the Eadwine Psalter.

16   Second Seal of Christ Church, Canterbury, ca. 1158 (courtesy Warburg Institute).

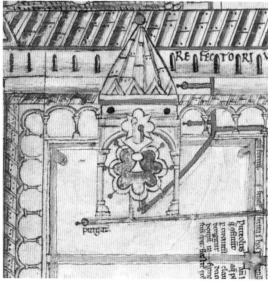

(Above left) 17A   Utrecht Psalter, Psalm 1, detail showing psalmist, MS Script. eccl. 484, fol. 1v, University Library, Utrecht (courtesy University Library).

(Above right) 17B   Eadwine Psalter, fol. 5v, Psalm 1, detail showing psalmist as Christ, Trinity College, Cambridge (courtesy the Master and Fellows, Trinity College, Cambridge).

(Left) 17C   Eadwine Psalter, *Drawing I*, Great Cloister, Fountain House, Trinity College, Cambridge (courtesy the Master and Fellows, Trinity College, Cambridge).

In contrast to the "insider" view employed for *Drawing I*, an emphatically "outsider" view dominated *Drawing II* (see fig. 10). The few buildings shown are reduced to icons more than images. Although the artist omits labels, some buildings can nonetheless be identified because they have features recognizable in *Drawing I* where the buildings are labeled. The subject of the drawing is the passage of water from outside the monastery to the buildings within the Precinct, and to emphasize it the Precinct's boundaries are eliminated and the pipework, sewers, and mechanisms simplified to snaking twin lines.

Pickwoad's codicological analysis in 1992 showed that the single surviving folio was originally the left half of a bifolium. The facing folio would have featured the fishpond (*Piscina*) fed by three pipes. That the draftsman devoted a large part of a folio to the fishpond has attracted little comment in the literature. The *Piscina* was also given detailed treatment in *Drawing I* where the containing walls are shown as scalloped and the central island is graced by sculpture. *Drawing II*'s rendering of the fishpond would have been larger and perhaps more detailed, and its prominence requires us to rethink this element in the life of the Priory and its unusual central placement in the Precinct (see Chapter 8).

The surviving half of the drawing shows the water system outlined in brown ink with green used for fresh water and orange-red for previously used water (if this distinction carried over from *Drawing I*). The composition begins in the upper left of the page with a structure drawn as three concentric circles. This depicts the holding tank rather than the spring house at Horsefold, as Woodman recognized. (A small length of pipe from the holding tank to the extreme corner of the folio connected to the spring house, which was assumed lost when the manuscript was later trimmed.) From the holding tank the pipe traverses the three-quarter-mile journey from Horsefold to the Priory, descending diagonally downwards at a sharp angle and passing through three fields, each with a settling tank to cleanse and filter the water. A further settling tank is shown outside the high curving walls of the Priory of St. Gregory, a favorite foundation of Archbishop Theobald, which owned the fields and was presumably connected to the water system. From there the pipe traveled onward to the Cathedral, whose precinct is signified by closed doors.

The water's passage inside the Priory occupies the bottom half of the folio. The artist shows nine structures which the water enters, and they are set at intervals along the single meandering pipeline without regard to their adjacency to one another or their spatial separation. First shown is an unidentified tower, then a large building with a tall hall and lower aisles, either the Infirmary or the *Balneatorium* with the prior's cistern and *cupa* (bath) represented by the adjacent circles behind it. The pipe next supplies the Water Tower with its eight-lobed laver and spigots; it then drops down like a pendulum to feed the circular laver to the south of the Cathedral before moving to the outer edge of the folio to supply the *Piscina*. Returning to the Water Tower, the pipe continues to the left to supply the laver of the Great Cloister. With little space now left at the bottom of the page, the artist changes the pipe's direction with a sharp, upturned diagonal to represent the water connections to the laver in front of the Refectory, which is distinguished by its roof gables like those shown on *Drawing I*. The pipe then enters the Great Kitchen, which is presumably the aedicule. Now back in the middle of the page, the pipe branches to service the Green Court *Aula Nova* with its fountain, and the Bakehouse, Brewhouse, and Granary with their three faucets. One further structure is shown near the center of the page, a square building with a wall-mounted water outlet. This must be the *Necessarium*. No attempt is made to show the Great Cloister or the Infirmary Cloister.

Although lacking the accomplishment and detail of the preceding bifolium, *Drawing II* was prized enough to be included in the manuscript. The artist omits the buildings which the water system did not serve. He focuses instead on a unilinear depiction of the water's journey from source to final destination in the now missing *Piscina*.

Recognition of a different intent for *Drawing II* is essential before proceeding to its interpretation. Several possibilities have been offered by different authors. Woodman judged *Drawing II* as unfinished or an earlier version superseded by the more detailed *Drawing I* (Woodman 1992, 170–71). Other possibilities include a conceptual or project drawing, an idea that could explain the abbreviated images which constituted a shorthand, or even a mystical or meditational rendering of the water system. Account has to be taken of why *Drawing II* was retained when *Drawing I* showed far more of the system and contained much information about how it operated.

Another approach considers the now missing page with the *Piscina*. Clearly it was a feature of considerable pride to the prior. It was singled out for mention in the *obit* written in 1167 (see Appendix A), and placed not as might be expected in a discrete, distant area of the Priory but within a stone's throw of the Cathedral's sanctuary. Could it be that the *Piscina* was intended as the main subject of the bifolium with the surviving folio serving as a prelude? The elaborate form given to the fishpond and its sculptural adornment is unique, and, likewise, its placement. They suggest an element of eccentricity on Prior Wibert's part. It is worth noting that within a century the fishpond had fallen out of use and been removed outside the Precinct, the reason, perhaps, for removing the image from the Psalter (see Chapter 8). A further explanation might link the drawing to an important individual whose authorship justified its retention. Possibilities include the master responsible for the system, the prior himself, or Archbishop Theobald, who donated the source of the water.

SCRIBAL PORTRAIT

Preceding *Drawing I* and *Drawing II* in the manuscript is the *Scribal Portrait of Eadwine* (fol. 283v) (fig. 18). Because it is separated from the manuscript by a blank folio and is thought to be a later addition, the *Scribal Portrait* is considered with the architectural drawings as the Psalter's concluding images. The foremost scholar working on the portrait, Sandy Heslop, has suggested that it was painted a decade and a half after the manuscript was completed (Heslop 1992, 178–92).

Eadwine is shown almost in profile, seated on a throne-like chair whose base is formed of three registers of round-headed arcades, a composition resembling a transept end. He faces left towards the texts on which he labored, bent down in focused concentration over an ornate writing desk and gripping the attributes of his profession, the quill pen and pen-knife or pen-sharpener. The desk is shrouded with a cloth in which the book was to be wrapped, a direct reference to its precious nature. Eadwine wears a thin, multifold habit which the artist organizes in a dynamic abstract pattern of swirls and eddies stretched across his torso, the plain areas painted with delicate arabesques. A trefoil arch surmounts the scribe with the spandrels filled with domed and basilica buildings. Enclosing the figure is an elaborate frame whose inner border contains the following inscription:

> **Scribe:** The prince of scribes am I; neither my praises nor my fame shall ever die. Cry out, O my letter, what kind of man I am. [**Scriptor:** s[c]riptorum

princeps ego, nec obitura deinceps laus mea nec fama. qu[-]is sim mea littera clama]

> **Letter:** That you, O Eadwine, whom the painted figure traces, are in reputation immortal, your writing proclaims – you, whose genius the beauty of the book declares, which, O God, take to yourself with the man himself as an acceptable gift. [**Littera:** te tua s[c]riptura quem signat picta figura. predicat eadwinum fama per secula vivum. ingenium cuis libri decus ind[-]icat huius. quem tibi seque datum munus dues accipe gratum] (Zarnecki 1981, 93).

The inscription takes the form of an animated dialog between the (writing) Scribe and the (written) Letter which was rendered articulate through its creation on the folio. The shift between the self-eulogizing first part and the petition-like second part has drawn different interpretations. To George Zarnecki, who was the first to question the traditional dating of the image as a "living" portrait, the second part indicated a posthumous portrait, possibly a commissioned memorial image. In contrast, Reginald Dodwell viewed Eadwine's last words in the inscription as a prayerful petition made while he was alive, thereby making the portrait a "living" image (Dodwell 1993, 355–57). He also drew attention to the tradition of showing scribes in large-scale images in contemporary manuscripts in northeast France (206, 355). The same petition-character has been noted by others and connected to the reference to Eadwine in the Psalter added after the collect for Psalm 150, when the scribe asks God "to allow your servant Eadwine to serve you faithfully, and will deign to confer on me good perseverance and a happy end. And may this Psalter 'that I have sung in your sight' be perfected for the health and eternal salvation of my soul."[20] More recently it has been argued that the portrait is a memorial image and connected via the surrounding inscription to grave slab inscriptions.[21]

(Facing page) 18   Eadwine Psalter, *Scribal Portrait of Eadwine*, fol. 283v, Trinity College, Cambridge (courtesy Trinity College Library).

The portrait of Eadwine, the main scribe of the team of ten or so monks who wrote the trilingual Psalter and produced the many drawings, paintings, and illuminated initials included in it. These make the manuscript the most lavish produced at the Cathedral Priory or anywhere else in England in the twelfth century. The inscription around the border begins at the top and refers to Eadwine as "s[c]riptorum princeps" (prince of scribes).

All that is known about Eadwine is contained in the inscription. His name does not appear with those of other monks known to have been at the Priory during these years. Nonetheless, he shows himself dressed as a monk. The assumption is that Eadwine headed the team of scribes, estimated as about ten to twelve men, which produced the Psalter's texts, based on the image and the inscription (Heslop 1992, 60–61).

Scholars have long noted the relationship of the portrait image to author portraits. These are usually placed at the beginning of the text and in the case of the Psalms would normally show King David. The Eadwine image adopts the author portrait type. However, its location at the end of the manuscript may be seen as a reference to scribal skills, as the inscription attests, rather than to authorship. As such, it mirrors other portraits in the Romanesque period such as the self-portrait of Master Hugo in Oxford.[22] For the distinctive figure style, Zarnecki compared the scribe to the prefatory figures in the Copenhagen Psalter of ca. 1170 (fig. 19). This comparison supported his association of the painting with the sculpted relief heads (see figs. 31A and B) discovered between 1968 and 1972, which he argued came from the screen in the Cathedral constructed in 1180 (Zarnecki 1981, 96). Heslop endorsed Zarnecki's dating and interpretation, placing the image within a tradition of monastic author portraits and supporting a retrospective intention (Heslop 1992, 59–61, 184–85). However, Jeffrey West's recent reassessment of the sculpture (see Chapter 4) links it to the Fountain House in the Great Cloister constructed by Prior Wibert from ca. 1160 (West 2012).

An alternative way of interpreting the *Scribal Portrait* is to see it in the tradition of the representation of Hebrew scholar scribes. These employed the same author portrait type. One famous example is the Ezra from the Codex Amiatinus (Florence, Biblioteca Laurenziana, Cod. Amiatino 1), an early eighth-century pandect Bible produced at Bede's monastery at Wearmouth-Jarrow. Ezra had the reputation as "the most learned scribe of the law of God" (1 Ezra 7:1–6), and it is his image which introduced the Bible text. Katherine Baker (2008) associates the image with Cassiodorus' *Institutiones*, a text known to Bede, who reported that it contained illustrations of the Temple and the Tabernacle. Cassiodorus thought of himself as a "second Ezra," and his commentary on the Psalms served as a widely known model for monks and monastic communities (fig. 20). Earlier, Dodwell had drawn attention to a late eleventh-century large-scale drawing of Jerome made at Christ Church

and added as an additional folio to an Anglo-Saxon manuscript (Dodwell 1954, 27). The analogy is compelling. The Eadwine Psalter displayed all three of Jerome's versions of the Psalm texts and synthesized different versions of other Old Testament books to create the Latin Vulgate Bible. To Eadwine, Jerome would have been the prototypical exemplar. In this context, the *Scribal Portrait* is neither a commemorative nor a self-assertive portrait of an individual, but an image in a lineal relationship to earlier scribal exemplars. As well as lauding Eadwine's scribal skills, the image makes explicit reference to biblical tradition.

INTERPRETATION

As seen above, there are strong reasons for discounting Willis's assumptions about *Drawing I* (principally that it was a "waterworks drawing" and was unrelated to the Eadwine Psalter's texts). Much more is known today about the Psalter than was available to Willis 150 years ago. Although basic questions remain unanswered, such as its purpose and why it was made, some matters are clearer. Analysis of the drawing and its relation to verifiable archaeology makes a date of around 1158 for its creation highly likely. As such, *Drawing I* is contemporary with the text rather than being later. Furthermore, a huge expansion of scholarly work on mid-twelfth-century manuscripts and their historical context in the last fifty years helps place the Eadwine Psalter within a broader artistic tradition.

Today, the most plausible published interpretation for the precinct drawing remains Urry's 1986 suggestion that it was intended to chronicle Prior Wibert's renewal (see above). Such an intention complements the picture of him as a confident and cultured personality, historically aware, and proud of his achievements as patron. On the other hand, Wibert's life was passed as a monk, and as such he was committed to Benedictine monasticism and to the practice of its theological precepts. Could it be that the Psalter's images and the text should be seen in the framework of monastic life and thought rather than as self-memorialization? And if so, does this offer an alternative interpretation?

The artist's adoption of distinctive formal strategies in *Drawing I* included the emphasis on interiority, the rearranging of components of buildings to create an ideal of organization, and the combining of the seen and unseen (in the above-ground and below-ground infrastructure of the water system).[23] The composite

19 Copenhagen Psalter, *The Magi before Herod*,
MS Thott 143 2°, fol. 10r, Royal Library, Copenhagen
(courtesy Royal Library).

20 Cassiodorus, *Institutiones*, representation of the monastery
with the fishpond at the bottom, ca. 800, Patr. 61 (J.IV.15),
Vivarium, Bamberg, Staatsbibliothek (courtesy Stattsbibliothek).

character allowed the image to carry several layers of
meaning, among others as chronicle, inventory, metaphor, memorial, and vision. The image's means of carrying several layers of meaning corresponds to the
general view of the period that reality was multivalent.

Recent scholarship, notably the pioneering work of
Mary Carruthers, has thrown light on the twelfth century's interest in visual and mental schema (Carruthers
1998, 222–24, 246–54; Carruthers 2008, 202–17). Monastic thought specifically encouraged the creation of *picturae*, a process involving meditation and imaginings
(Carruthers 2010, 103). Such a process can be recognized
in the tradition of architectural representation which is
found in several types of twelfth-century texts, notably
exegetical works and psalters from Channel School
scriptoria. Among the latter are included full-page
images of the city of Jerusalem which combine recognizable features such as pools, streams, and identifying
tituli with idealized representation designed to show the
city as a sacred site. Such images raise the possibility of
a context for the Canterbury drawing.

Establishing a parallel between the Priory image and
the city image of Jerusalem involves a theological analogy.
A clue to this process can be found in St. Augustine's
De civitate Dei (XV. 2), in which he argued that Jerusalem exhibited two aspects: "under the one it displays its
own presence; the other it serves by its presence to point
towards the heavenly city." Augustine's ideas influenced
the writings of Archbishop Anselm around 1100, as they
did fifty years later those of St. Bernard, who claimed
Clairvaux to be Jerusalem (Bredero 1996, 267–75).

Can the Augustinian concept be discerned in the
Eadwine Psalter image? The Precinct is shown as both a
material construct and a metaphor. It is recognizably the
Priory, but also an abstract ideal. The image shows us
nothing of the city of Canterbury or of the adjacent
Archbishop's Palace. Lifting out or abstracting the Precinct from its surroundings is further emphasized by the
artist's regularization of the Priory's boundaries and the
exclusion of urban context exemplified by the sealed
gates. Likewise, the interior is shown as a neatened ideal,
ordered, well-watered, spacious. Seen from Augustinian

43

tradition, the image resembles Anselm's likening in his *De Moribus* of Christendom to a city with God as its king.[24] The "city" allusion appears again on the Priory's principal gatehouse, where the entry arch is flanked by the Priory's carved symbols like those on city gates (see fig. 70). In this interpretation the decision to include the Precinct's hydraulic system can be seen as a site-specific (but far from literal) reference and as a symbol of spiritual anointing and cleansing which it made possible.

Similarly, the *Scribal Portrait* connects to an old tradition of pairing full-page author portrait with a full-page architectural image. Best known is the Codex Amiatinus with Ezra and the Tabernacle's sacred furniture (Chazelle 2006). It was familiar within monastic circles also through Cassiodorus' *Institutiones* where author and monastery are represented (fig. 20).[25] Channel School Psalters also pair author or scribal portraits of King David with biblical diagrams of Jerusalem. Examples of the latter include plan-views in Brussels, Bibliothèque royale, MS 9823 (fig. 22), and the Psalter in The Hague, Koninklijke Bibliotheek, MS 76 F 13.[26] Both images show "cut-out" buildings similar to those in *Drawing I*, and they include streams, settling pools, and *tituli*. The Eadwine Psalter's *Scribal Portrait* and precinct drawing should be seen as part of this representational tradition. Modern authors such as Marcia Kupfer have argued for their integration with the manuscript, seeing them as "self-representations of the monastic community" (Kupfer 1994, 1171).

Further affirming this tradition of representation were Richard of St.-Victor's mid-twelfth-century visualizations of the Temple in Jerusalem (Cahn 1994, 53–68). As a meditative mode Richard urged a combination of the "view from above" with an inventorying *picturae* and created large-scale plan-views of Jerusalem. Facilitating the process was the conquest of Jerusalem in the Crusades (First Crusade 1099, Second Crusade 1146), which brought these sites into the custody of the reform monastic movements, where they became both objects of antiquarian scrutiny as well as stimuli to association.

The representation of Eadwine as the scribal archetype and the Precinct as the *civitas Dei* form a linked unit. In the manuscript, exemplary scholarly monks of the past (notably Jerome, whose texts form its core) are seen as models to a living biblical tradition (Eadwine). In the architecture, the Priory is depicted as an ideal, with analogies to Jerusalem, a concept epitomized in the Cathedral's dedication as Christ Church. Transpositions involving Canterbury/Jerusalem, the Priory/the Temple occurred elsewhere. The Norman Staircase

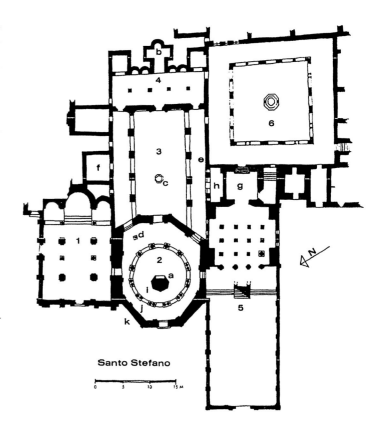

Santo Stefano

21   S. Stefano, Bologna, plan (Ousterhout 1981, 312, courtesy Robert Ousterhout).

The numbers indicate (1) church of SS. Vitale and Agricola; (2) church of S. Sepolcro; (3) Court of Pilate; (4) church of S. Trinità, formerly S. Croce; (5) church of S. Crocefisso, formerly S. Giovanni Battista; (6) cloister. The letters indicate (a) tomb aedicule; (b) former location of Calvary; (c) Cantino of Pilate; (d) copy of Column of Flagellation; (e) site of Denial of Peter; (f) Prison of Christ; (g) former location of House of Pilate; (h) former location of the Scala Santa (i) copy of the Pool of Siloam; (j) copy of site of Annunciation to the Virgin; (k) former location of Renaissance chapel of S. Giuliana, copy of site of Christ's appearance to the Magdalene.

leading to the Prior's Court alluded to the *porticum columnarum* of Solomon's Judgment Hall (see Chapter 6); the Second Seal of the Priory visualized Christ himself standing in the principal public entry to the Cathedral dedicated to him (see fig. 16); the columns surrounding the principal altar in Anselm's crypt recalled those of King Solomon; David the Psalmist and Christ the Lord are freely interchanged in Psalm 1 of the Eadwine Psalter (see fig. 17B); the Treasury paralleled the monks' building for sacred vessel and vesting storage with that of the Temple priests.

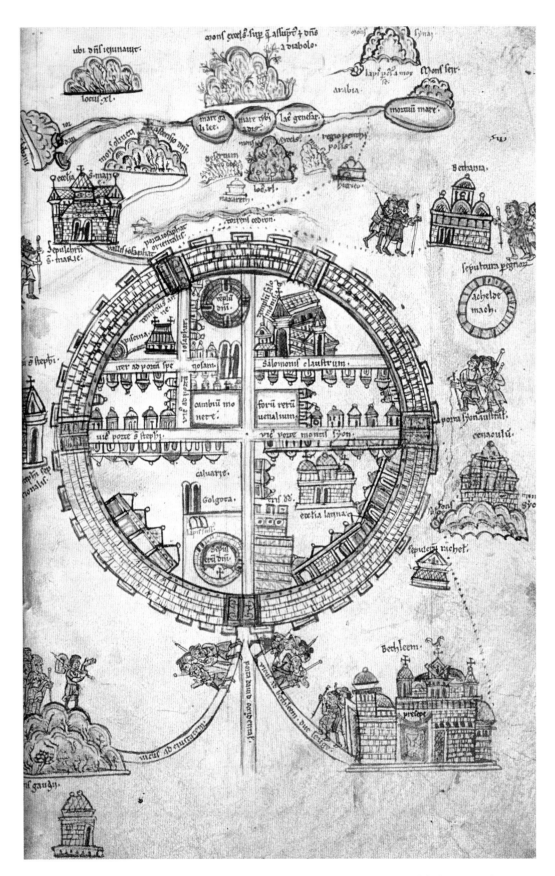

22   Jerusalem, plan of the city, MS 9823, Brussels, Bibliothèque royale (courtesy Bibliothèque royale).

The Priory was not alone in these allegorizing modes and elisions of identity. The heavenly Jerusalem and the earthly Jerusalem were synonymous, as already mentioned, and Bernard of Clairvaux went further to claim "celestia exempla sunt terrestrium" (Bredero 1996, 267–75). Ousterhout has detailed similar elisions in Italy and explained how sacred topography was viewed as being transportable, capable of re-creation through a combination of ritual and architecture, with examples in Florence, Pisa, Borgo San Sepolcro, and Bologna (Ousterhout 1998, 394). For the last, the Olivetan monastery of S. Stefano (fig. 21), the shrine of the city's patron, S. Petronio, constituted with the "seven" churches related to it and raised between ca. 1140 and 1160 a Nuova Gerusalemme replicating the *loca sancta* in Jerusalem (Ousterhout 1981, 311–21). Copies of the Mount of Olives, the Pool of Siloam, the church of the Ascension, and so forth made up the itinerary. Bologna was much in the awareness of Canterbury in these years. Two distinguished law magisters from Bologna – Master Vacarius and Master Lombard of Piacenza – formed part of Archbishop Theobald's curia in the 1140s and 1150s, and Becket had been sent to Bologna in the early 1150s for a year of study in its famous law school, returning in 1154 to take up his appointment as ecclesiastical advisor to Henry II (see Chapter 2) at the moment when Prior Wibert started work on the renewal and the Priory's scriptorium was at work on the Eadwine Psalter.

In presenting in succession at the end of the Eadwine Psalter the *Scribal Portrait*, *Drawing I*, and *Drawing II*, the artist would have seen them as pendants to the scholarly texts that preceded them. Considered as such, they suggest a further analogy. The Second Seal of the Priory was contemporary with the Eadwine Psalter and the renewal of the Priory. Rather than feature a ruler or ecclesiastical figure or sainted founder, the new seal adopted Anselm's Romanesque cathedral as the authenticating device of the Priory's charters and documents (Heslop 1982, 94–96). It was Christ Church and it was the Lord himself who stands at its portal. In a similar manner, the Priory's celebrated symbol of scholarly learning, the Eadwine Psalter, was provided with an authenticating "seal" in the form of the *Scribal Portrait*, *Drawing I*, and *Drawing II*.

The Precinct with the Cathedral and the Convent as rendered in *Drawing I* is conceived, then, as a temporal locus and a symbolic locus. Such a dualism was a standard mental paradigm for monks whose lives were focused on the celestial or New Jerusalem. This was not just a vague idea but a spiritual goal. On a daily basis the monks read and sang about the New Jerusalem and saw their lives as leading towards its walls. If the labors of the scribe Eadwine in the Psalter constituted "a prayer sung in [the Lord's] sight," the artist's view of the Priory in *Drawing I* should be seen as its graphic parallel.

4

THE GREAT CLOISTER

The Great Cloister encompassed much of the daily life of every Benedictine monastery. It took the form of an enclosed square surrounded by the community's most important buildings – church, chapter house, dormitory, refectory, guesthouse – with a light-filled garden (or garth) at its center. Covered galleries or walks linked the buildings along their fronts and provided a garland of arcaded daylight. The columns carrying the arcades stood on a waist-high stylobate (or plinth) which served as a low boundary framing the garden and as a bench for contemplation (McNeill 2006a, 11). Uses varied depending on the time of day. In the mornings the walks functioned for study and reading (the *lectio divina*) and the instruction of novices. Later in the day they provided the setting for rites, such as *collation*, the nightly refreshment and spiritual reading before the community retired to bed, or *lavings* of guests, or liturgical processions, as well as more mundane activities, such as drying laundry (with lines strung from the columns), shaving and tonsuring, bookbinding and preparing parchment. These activities gave the cloister a changing character spaced throughout the highly regulated monastic day, one switching between tasked movement and contemplative stillness, ordained routine and practical chores. With every day of every year passed within its confines, the cloister epitomized containment and stasis, values

that explain the etymology of the word "cloister" (*claustrum* in Latin), meaning something enclosed as well as the means of enclosing it such as a lock or bolt.[1]

Given the central role of the cloister in monastic life, ambitious abbots (or priors at cathedral monasteries) were drawn to its renovation and rebuilding. At Canterbury the process began with Archbishop Lanfranc's replacement of the Saxon cloister in the 1070s, thereby bringing it in line with Benedictine practice in Europe. Eighty years later, Prior Wibert supplied new arcades, renewed the six doorways of the prominent east range, constructed the Fountain House at the entrance to the Refectory, and renovated the west range (Guesthouse). In the late 1220s John of Sittingbourne remodeled the cloister doorway into the Cathedral and provided it with sculpture, and rebuilt the Refectory. Around 1304 Eastry extended the Chapter House and three years later constructed study carrels in the south walk. Starting in the early 1400s Chillenden replaced much of Wibert's work, leaving only two of his doorways in the east range. In the mid-1470s Selling renewed Chillenden's work with a new south walk (Sparks 2007, 14–23).

Interpreting these changes is not easy. For Willis, the patchwork of renewals in the north and east ranges prompted the wry observation that they "resembled a museum of medieval architecture against which examples of styles have been placed for the edification of students" (Willis 1868, 40). Some architectural historians today view the changes as marks of monastic decline, or as manifestations of institutional establishment and pride. More sympathetic readings see renewal as the guiding intention; changes in monastic culture prompted building changes. In some instances the motivations are recoverable. For Wibert, technological innovation geared to health and hygiene justified the new piped water system and the buildings dependent on it. For Eastry, education and university training required upgrading areas within the Great Cloister for "new studies" (or carrels) in the south range. For Chillenden, the urge for greater light, spaciousness, and the aesthetic delight in tracery divisions connected to the new Perpendicular style generated his extensive rebuildings. And for Sellyng, protection from the weather for users of the carrels prompted the glazing of the open arcading of the south range (Willis 1868, 45).

LANFRANC'S CLOISTER

Little is known about the Great Cloister in the Saxon period. Three years before Lanfranc's appointment as archbishop in 1070, fire devastated the Cathedral and the monastic buildings, sparing only the Refectory and Dormitory. The blaze was witnessed and described in the *Chronicle* of Eadmer, a monk and later secretary to Archbishop Anselm (Rule 1884, 12–13). His observation that the claustral buildings were connected by a wooden cloister indicates an unusual choice of building material and hints at an atypical form. To replace the lost buildings Lanfranc provided "in all haste the houses essential to the monks. For those which had been used for many years were found too small for the increased numbers of the convent. He therefore pulled down to the ground all that he found of the burnt monastery, whether of buildings or the wasted remains of buildings, and having dug out their foundations from under the earth, he constructed in their stead others, which excelled them greatly both in beauty and magnitude. He built cloisters, cellarers' offices, refectories, dormitories, with all the other necessary offices."[2] Eadmer's account also informs us of Lanfranc's intention to enlarge the community to 150 monks. Whether the number was reached is doubtful, but it was for this that Lanfranc's monastery was designed.

The overall scale of Lanfranc's cloister is recoverable thanks to Willis's recognition that the lower masonry courses on the north and east sides of the present cloister

date from his rebuild. Supporting this identification is the use of the term "quadros lapides" to describe the distinctive Norman manner of cutting the imported Caen stone ashlars for the Cathedral (Gem 1987, 91), Lanfranc's cloister measured just over 100 feet to a side, slightly longer on the north–south orientation (108 feet) than on the east–west (104 feet).

Of Lanfranc's work only the Dormitory remains, with some areas in use as the archives building (post–World War II) and some as ruins. The surviving parts reveal a surprisingly large and broad building measuring 148 feet north–south and 78 feet east–west. It was also distinctly atypical in shape for a dormitory, being set out in six aisles, three either side of a substantial spine wall. The undercroft was groin vaulted (surviving parts in the southwest corner) with the vaults received on two rows of columns (on each side of the spine wall) for a total of seventy-two vault compartments (Urry 1986, 52). No parallel is known with other dormitories from the 1080s such as Winchester, Ely, Westminster, Bury, Norwich, or Rochester. Decoration was severe and mostly limited to plain cushion capitals. At ground level, the space provided for a day room, locutory (or parlor), and warming room (in the southern bays), although none of these has been identified. The convent's beds occupied the upper story. Of the exterior a few details survive on the west side, notably a row of arcades with cushion capitals (fig. 23), their bases hidden below the lean-to roof covering the vaults of the galleried walk below; these provided unexpectedly rich decorative effects. Remarkably, the Dormitory's windows were glazed; the *Constitutions* specify the need to keep them repaired: "vitreas dormitorii facit, et reficit cum opus est" (Knowles and Brooke 2002, 127). More usually dormitories were closed with wooden shutters, a practice continued into the mid-twelfth century, as can still be seen at Cistercian Fountains Abbey in Yorkshire.

Further information about the cloister buildings comes from documents. Lanfranc's *Constitutions*, written as the community's *Customary*, detailed liturgical observance throughout the monastic year. It mentions buildings without providing information about their form, scale, or adjacency. In the Great Cloister Lanfranc mentions the chapter house, parlor, dark entry, refectory, dormitory, and guesthouse suggesting parallels to surviving continental examples. As just seen, the Dormitory was highly unusual, and the same could be said of its connection to the monks' choir via the night stair. Accessed through a doorway at the Dormitory's south end, adjacent to the Chapter House, a passage crossed

23   Canterbury Cathedral Priory, Great Cloister, east range (courtesy Stuart Harrison).

The remains of Lanfranc's Dormitory upper-story windows lie to the left of the Chapter House. Separating the two stories, the blind arcading below the windows survives with the arch heads visible above the cloister roof.

the west bay of the Chapter House and led thence into the gallery of the north transept of the Cathedral and down the night stair into the monks' choir. Willis interpreted the connecting passage as "of sloping ascent . . . [to rise] over the Cloister roof, and consequently landing the monks on the pavement of the upper chapel of the north transept, dedicated to St Blaise, which was on a higher level" (Willis 1868, 17–18). These features are represented in *Drawing I* by the triangular gable lit by three windows that links the Chapter House to the Cathedral.

The west range of the Great Cloister served as the Priory's guesthouse, although no part of it today can be identified with Lanfranc. The *Constitutions* fill out some of the range's uses. These included the daily rite of the *mandatum hospitum*, the washing of the feet and hands of visitors (not to be confused with the weekly *mandatum fratrum*, the washing of the feet of the community). The rite is described in the *Customs of Farfa*, which were based on the *Customs of Cluny* written under Abbot Odilo (1030–48).[3] The rite was performed by the community, which assembled in the Chapter House and

24 Canterbury Cathedral Priory, Great Cloister, east range, day stair to monks' Dormitory (photograph author).

25 Canterbury Cathedral Priory, Great Cloister, east range, day stair to monks' Dormitory, detail of jamb column (courtesy Stuart Harrison).

then processed to the cloister walk "next to the cellar" (*juxta promptuarium*). Warmed water and three towels for drying are prescribed. The practice is known at Norwich's Hostry of ca. 1100 (Gilchrist 2005, 134–42), at Bury and Ely, as well as at St.-Denis in 1137.

Of the furnishings for the guesthouse, Lanfranc's *Constitutions* detailed more extensive appointments than might be imagined. The archbishop specified the provision of "beds, chairs, tables, towels, cloths, tankards, plates, spoons, basins, and such like – firewood also" (Knowles and Brooke 2002, 129).[4] The same text specified that the guesthouse serve as a "parlor" (*locutorio*) where guests could talk with a monk if they so requested, and also mentioned it as the space where fugitive monks who sought readmission to the community awaited their call to appear before the Chapter (Knowles and Brooke 2002, 153–55).

Separating the Dormitory and the Chapter House, a much used passageway led from the Great Cloister to the Infirmary Cloister (Willis 1868, 24–25). The northern wall contains recesses for decorated piers (featuring torsade, diaper, and fluted decoration), presumably to

carry transverse arches; those on the facing southern wall are undecorated. At the suppression these piers were walled up. They came to light only in 1954 during repairs following the bombing in World War II. Unexplained is why the piers differ from side to side and from those used in the undercroft. There is also no agreement on the date of the decorated piers: whether they date from Lanfranc or from Anselm. Further muddling matters, halfway down the passageway is an inserted cross arch (corresponding to the spine wall) which is clearly the work of Prior Wibert. This carries decoration similar to the doorway in the Pentice Gatehouse (see fig. 41), and also the day stair (see below).

WIBERT'S GREAT CLOISTER

Before the twenty-first century, the little that was known of Wibert's Great Cloister came from its representation on *Drawing I* and the survival of two *in situ* doorways in the east range: the day stair doorway to the Dormitory at the north end (figs. 24 and 25), and the entry to

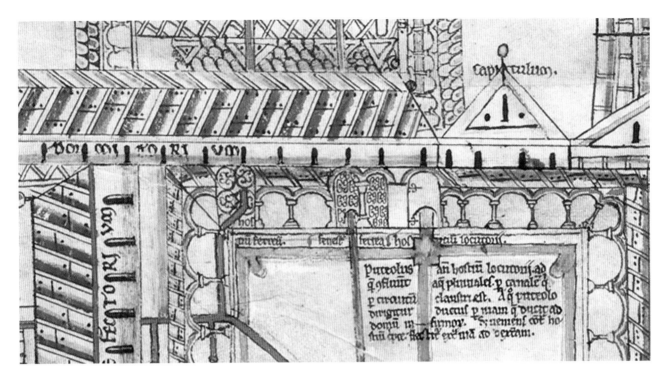

26   Eadwine Psalter, *Drawing I*, Great Cloister, east range, Trinity College, Cambridge (courtesy the Master and Fellows, Trinity College, Cambridge).

the former slype at the south end.[5] Everything else had been destroyed when Chillenden undertook his major remodeling in the late 1300s. The prospect of details emerging at a distance of 700 years was so remote as to be unthinkable.

Recent discoveries, however, have transformed the entire picture of Wibert's Great Cloister. It is now possible to know the extent of his renovation and much of its appearance, down to the color scheme employed, and even to recover something of its intended meaning. The discoveries began appearing in scholarly papers and lectures shortly after the millennium. Utilizing the new discipline based on the study of loose stonework, much of which had come to light during major repair work which started in 1939, resumed in the mid-1960s, and concluded in 1977, Tim Tatton-Brown was able to reconstruct Wibert's arcading, and Jeffrey West to reveal the form and sculptural program of the Great Laver at the entrance to the Refectory. To this published material can be added related finds such as the surviving parts of floors of the walks and the likelihood that the six doorways in the prominent east range were also Wibert's work.[6] Enough is now known to make the argument that the Great Cloister was intended to serve as the glittering showpiece of the Priory.

The material used for the recovery of this work was far from promising. It consisted of smashed columns, bases, arcades, spandrels, and sculpture re-employed by Prior Chillenden's masons in the late 1390s as masonry fill for the vaults, upper walls, and buttresses of his new cloister. The significance of this material and its potential for the reconstruction of Wibert's lost work emerged gradually. Central to its recognition was Tatton-Brown's appointment as director of the Canterbury Archaeological Trust in the early 1970s. Linking the recovered material with unprovenanced fragments stored in the Cathedral's *lapidarium* at Broad Oak Farm (at Sturry two miles to the north) as well as loose stonework immured in other parts of the Precinct such as the dean's garden and the wall of the Prior's Gatehouse, he saw the potential for reconstructing Wibert's cloister.[7]

Linking the four cloister walks to the central garden were twenty-four or twenty-five openings spaced at about 4-foot-wide bays per walk (fig. 26).[8] Given the scale of *Drawing I*, the artist showed each walk variously with seven to nine openings. Paired marble columns in the form of spirals, chevrons, and other incised designs, some with shaft rings (probably for the corners), stood on twinned marble spur bases with trefoiled leaf spurs at the angles (fig. 27). Capitals showed early foliate

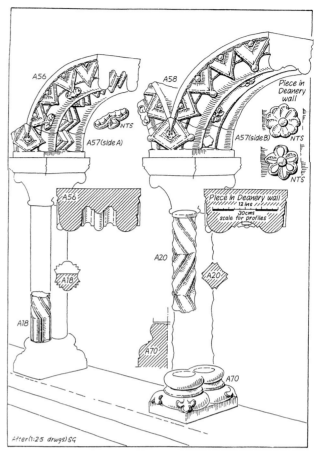

(Above) 27   Canterbury Cathedral Priory, Great Cloister, reconstruction drawing by Jill Atherton (Tatton-Brown 2006, 100, fig. 8).

(Right) 28   Canterbury Cathedral Priory, Great Cloister, reconstruction drawing by Jill Atherton (Tatton-Brown 2006, 101, fig. 9).

(Below right) 29   Canterbury Cathedral Priory, Great Cloister, arcade fragment, *lapidarium*, Sturry (courtesy Stuart Harrison).

designs along with beaded scallop. Arcades mixed chevron and incised designs with ball terminals on the extrados and carved fleurets on the twin molded intrados (fig. 28).

The Great Cloister's effects came from the rapidly repeating rhythm of low-rising, small-opening arcading extending the length of the walk. Enriched with carved detailing of high quality, and enhanced by semi-precious materials such as Purbeck and Tournai marble (fig. 29) for columns, bases, capitals, and archivolts, the arcades glittered with a light-reflecting gloss finish achieved through the high polishing of the stone.[9] The resulting ambiance was dense, busy, and glinting, giving an effect of shimmering fullness and richness.

The second important contribution to the understanding of Wibert's Great Cloister came from the work of Jeffrey West.[10] Beginning with a series of public lectures in 1997, he has argued persuasively that the sculptural reliefs discovered between 1964 and 1973 during the restoration of the west range originated from the Great Laver constructed in front of the Refectory.[11] Since the laver appears in *Drawing I* (fig. 30), the sculptures (figs. 31A and B) date from the 1150s. Furthermore,

West plausibly connects them with the cloister at St.-Denis outside Paris, the royal abbey of France, which underwent an extensive renewal in the 1140s and 1150s and included a fountain house with sculpture.

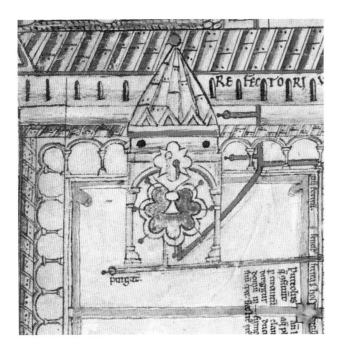

(Left) 30 Eadwine Psalter, *Drawing I*, Great Cloister, detail showing north range with Fountain House at entrance to the Refectory, Trinity College, Cambridge (courtesy the Master and Fellows, Trinity College, Cambridge).

(Below) 31 Canterbury Cathedral Priory, Great Cloister, Fountain House, sculptures, Cathedral crypt (courtesy Conway Library, Courtauld Institute of Art, London).

(Below left: A) Quattrefoil – king pointing upward.

(Below right: B) Roundel – prophet (?).

Like the rest of Wibert's cloister, the Great Laver was demolished by Prior Chillenden in the early 1400s. The stonework was smashed and reused as masonry fill. Replaced by Chillenden with a much more modest structure without sculptural imagery, it disappeared a century and a half later, the victim of post-suppression changes. Starting in the late 1960s a number of Prior Wibert's sculptural reliefs came to light during the repair of the fifteenth-century arcade buttresses where they had been used as masonry fill. At the time of their discovery, Frank Woodman suggested that they came from the Great Laver with their find-site located just a few

feet away (Stratford 1977, 212–16; Woodman 1981, 83–84). Subsequently, George Zarnecki proposed a different purpose, arguing that the sculptures came from the 1180 choir screen mentioned by Gervase in his account (ca. 1190) of the rebuilding of the Cathedral's east end and Trinity Chapel (Zarnecki 1976, 83–92). Kahn endorsed Zarnecki's opinion in her book on Canterbury's twelfth-century sculpture (Kahn 1991, 145–71). At the time of publication reviewers expressed reservations about the location and date of the reliefs, but no new suggestions were advanced until West's research.[12]

West's study of the entire collection of retrieved stonework – the carved reliefs and the architectural ornament – linked it to the Great Laver. Nothing is known archaeologically of the building's plan. The sole visual evidence comes from *Drawing I*, which shows the structure at exaggerated scale positioned roughly in the middle of the north range walk (rather than at its west end) and projecting into the cloister garth. The artist shows it

(Above) 32   Canterbury Cathedral Priory, Dean and Chapter, *Lapidarium,* Sturry, stringcourse or register separator (photograph author).

(Right) 33   Canterbury Cathedral Priory, Dean and Chapter, *Lapidarium,* Sturry, lower torso of king (courtesy Stuart Harrison).

topped by small gables at the base of the tall conical roof, a detail repeated on *Drawing II,* which suggests a complex timber-frame roof over an octagonal building.[13] The double-decker laver consisted of a large octofoil laver with spigots below and a smaller quatrefoil laver above with angular projections separating the semicircles.

The recovered stone assemblage falls into three distinct groups: five quatrefoils with bust-length figures (fig. 31A), nine roundels with heads (fig. 31B), and figurative and architectural fragments (West 2012).[14] West discerned that the quatrefoil blocks retain on their lower side edges the remains of shallow curves (their fronts are straight-faced). These curves correspond to the archivolt blocks reconstructed for the cloister arcades and indicate an original function as spandrel fillers. Whether the same spandrel context existed for the roundels is unclear; none retains the original lower side edges. For the architectural fragments one sizable piece of decorative stringcourse has two faces set at a 135-degree angle (fig. 32). These angles confirm an octagonal form for the Fountain House as suggested by *Drawing I.*[15]

How the quatrefoils and roundels related to the fountain has not been settled. The sculptures' contrast between the crowned and veiled bust-sized quatrefoil figures and the demonic roundels suggests a program featuring contrasting types. However, there is no way of knowing what proportion of the laver reliefs are represented by the ones retrieved. There are too many reliefs for a laver

base like the one at Much Wenlock Priory (Godfrey 1949, 91–97; Zarnecki 1984, 200–2; Coppack 1999, 37–43). A number of the reliefs carry a molding at their base indicating their function as a rim or register-definer. In addition, among the recovered sculpture at Broad Oaks is the seated figure of a king (now in three pieces; fig. 33) measuring ca. 26 inches in height, which was attached at the back to a column or screen and whose scale indicates a corner or interval placement.[16] The most likely arrangement is for a two-tiered laver with the water flowing continuously from the upper into the lower basin, the upper part with the quatrefoils in spandrels, the lower part with the roundels, the two tied together by single figures such as the king. Two-tiered fountains survive in small number from the later twelfth century, with several surviving octagonal examples in Cistercian foundations such as Maulbronn (in Württemberg-Baden), although none retains the same arcade format suggested for Canterbury.[17]

For the subject of the laver, the quatrefoils include two figures with crowns, plausibly Old Testament kings such as David and Solomon, one veiled female figure, and two pointing figures, most likely prophets. By contrast, the roundels include human, animal, and monster heads but lack attributes to indicate their identity. A sharp stylistic difference distinguishes the quatrefoils from the roundels. The former have carved natural-falling drapery, heads with carefully modeled features and calm expressions, and a defined spatial ambiance within their compositional formats. The roundel heads are more abstract; they fill their compositional space without any suggestion of depth, and the faces strike extravagant, even grotesque, expressions. Easy as it would be to classify the quatrefoils as Gothic and the roundels as Romanesque and to see them as the work of two distinct periods, it is as valid to see the quatrefoils as reflecting a more composed – even a more classical – style and the roundels as reflecting a freer style, each suited to their different subjects.

A plausible typological program would consist of mounting zones of representation with pre-law at the base (the roundels), subjects under the law above (the quatrefoils), and the era of the new law (the linking single figures). Similar arrangements juxtaposing New and Old Testament types had been established at Canterbury by Anselm ca. 1100 (Heslop 2011, 107–24). They mark compositions from the mid-twelfth century such as the Stavelot portable altar (ca. 1150) in Brussels, the Malmesbury Ciborium (ca. 1155) in the Morgan Library, New York, and Suger's Great Cross (1147).[18] Such a typological program would complement the extravagant materials lavished on the arcades with their mnemonic allusions to the Temple in Jerusalem (see below).

Sculpture programs for twelfth-century fountains await study. At Much Wenlock an octagonal laver base is divided on each side by three arches supported on twinned shafts. The diameter is 28 feet. West calculates a somewhat larger structure for the Canterbury Great Laver, 32 feet in diameter, based on Tatton-Brown's estimate of the bay lengths (and therefore nearly 11 feet larger than the Water Tower; see fig. 134). The second example comes from St.-Denis where the cloister was constructed in the period 1150–65, complete with a lavabo in the southeast corner (Pressouyre 1986, 230), of which a small quantity of stonework survives (Johnson and Wyss 1992, 355–81). Based on this material West reasons a relationship between these two prominent Benedictine foundations for their fountain house designs (West 2012).

How many of the four Cloister ranges were rebuilt or remodeled by Wibert as part of his renewal is undecided. West cautions against attributing all four ranges to Wibert and reserves judgment about claims for his complete remake of the Great Cloister. On the other hand, the limited archaeological evidence supports a tentative case for attributing three of the ranges to him (the north, west, and east).[19] The remaining range may also be his, if *Drawing I* (which shows no difference between the arcading for all four ranges) is to be trusted.

The extent of Wibert's renewal also needs to take account of his remodeling of the doorways of the east range. *Drawing I* shows four doorways, and two others are also known (see fig. 26). Those shown by the artist are the *in situ* day stair to the monks' Dormitory, the dark entry doorway (depicted without door leaves), the *Locutorium* or Parlor (so indicated by the *titulus*), and the day room doorway to the undercroft. Two further doorways may be assumed: the entry to the Chapter House and the slype (of which fragmentary parts survive). By far the most complete is the day stair doorway. It survived because it was walled over, like the piers of the dark entry (Willis 1868, 26, n. 1), almost certainly after the suppression. Rediscovered in 1813, the doorway revealed the semicircular head carved with three sumptuous orders (outward-facing chevron on the intrados, a multi-roll middle order consisting of triple rolls with the center decorated with drilled pellets, and a crowning crenellated motif) (see fig. 24). Scalloped capitals are supported on richly detailed angle shafts with registers of interlinked circles with drilled pellet ornament. These motifs resemble those on the wellhead (cf. fig. 110B). Kahn has drawn attention to similar ornament in St. Augustine's Abbey and in east Kent churches, such as Minster-in-Thanet, St. Margaret's-at-Cliffe, and Sandwich. She links them to the Cathedral, and also to Norman work at La Trinité in Caen from the same period (Kahn 1991, 123–27).

The claims for Wibert's renovation of the west range are slight but worth mentioning. As seen above, this served the Priory's visitors from Lanfranc until Wibert's renewal. Only the cloister wall is retained today, where it acts as a screen wall to separate the Archbishop's Palace from the Great Cloister. At either end medieval doorways survive: at the south, three Perpendicular doorways (Chillenden renovations), and at the north a single doorway which is Romanesque towards the Archbishop's Palace and Perpendicular towards the Cloister.[20] The wall itself is packed with broken fragments from Wibert's arcades and fountain house.[21] The depth of the medieval range can be established from the bay next to the Cathedral. Scars remain from the lobby that connected the range to the church. They show a width measurement of 21 feet. This indicates a narrow building, but one close to other west ranges begun before 1160.[22]

On the cloister side, medieval evidence apart from the doorways is obscured by twentieth-century replastering and use of the wall for twentieth-century memorials. On the palace side, Willis's elevation drawing and plan

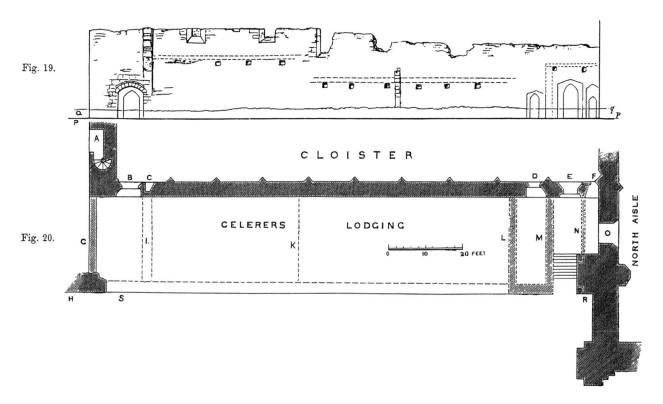

Fig. 19.

CLOISTER

Fig. 20.

CELERERS   LODGING

NORTH AISLE

34   Canterbury Cathedral Priory, Great Cloister, west range, elevation and plan (Willis 1868, facing p. 115, figs. 19 and 20).

(made in the late 1840s before subsequent consolidations) preserves valuable information now obscured (Willis 1868, 115–19) (fig. 34). Willis discerned evidence of two halls at ground level, a taller one with holes for the floor joists. This was probably the Common Hall and the Servants' Hall and could well have been retained from earlier building, either by Wibert or Lanfranc. Where the halls joined at ground level, Willis shows a doorway. Above lay the Dormitory, of which Willis recognized the lower parts of two window jambs.

The west range has similarities with the Hostry at Norwich recently studied by Gilchrist (2005, 134–42) (fig. 35) and with St. Mary's Guildhall, Lincoln, of the mid-1150s (fig. 36). Remodeling of the Canterbury range can be assumed under Wibert at the same time as he expanded the guest quarters to the Guesthouse (for gentry visitors) and the *Aula Nova* (for the Common Hall and the Servants' Hall). Under Chillenden the upper story was used for the novices' school (Sparks 2007, 237), and documentary records indicate the range's use as temporary accommodation for the Priory's secular professionals such as working lawyers and master masons when they needed housing for visits (Sparks 2007, 15, 45). Both the west range and north range with the

Refectory were the responsibility of the cellarer. The flint rubble used for the west range, in contrast to the ashlar for the other ranges, indicates a lesser value placed on the fabric.

Together the new discoveries and the surviving fragments allow for a reasonably complete reconstruction of Wibert's Great Cloister as well as insights into the intended effect. Woodman was the first to discern the Great Cloister's dazzling quality resulting from the use of different colored marbles for the arcades and blue and brown marble for the floors, and to note the distinctive reflective glitter achieved through painstaking polishing (Woodman 1981, 83). His hypothesis that the Great Cloister represented the major work of Wibert's rule is plausible. Compared with the prior's other buildings such as the Water Tower, Treasury, and *Aula Nova* built from Caen stone, the Great Cloister stood out clearly as the burnished hub of the Priory. Yet arguing such claims requires balancing them against Wibert's other major achievements, such as the development of the Green Court (see Chapter 6) or his installation of the water system (Chapter 3).

The Great Cloister offers a unique and detailed insight into Wibert's tastes. One is face to face with his color

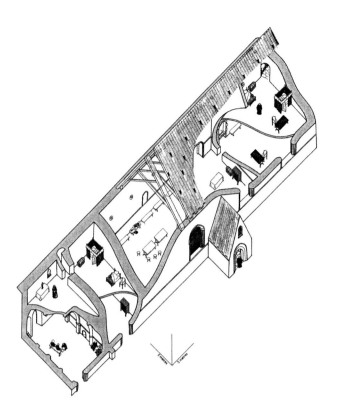

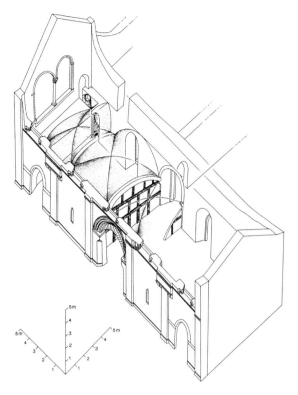

35 Norwich Cathedral, Great Cloister, west range, Hostry, reconstruction drawing (Gilchrist 2005, p. 137, fig. 49).

36 St Mary's Guildhall, Lincoln, isometric section, ca. 1157 (Stocker 1991, 30).

preferences, delight in lavish carving and high polish, penchant for small-scale repetition of units, and insistence on meticulous detailing. His enthusiasm for conspicuous effects and rich expenditures needs to be placed in a wider context. At Cluny, a century earlier, Odilo's cloister (before 1049) was "admirably decorated with marble columns from the furthest parts of that province" (Conant 1968, 65). Wibert's use of expensive marbles was followed by large-scale Purbeck marble piers in the rotunda of the Temple Church in London ca. 1160 (Wilson 2010, 34–35), in the piers cut for the intended Lady Chapel at Durham Cathedral ca. 1170 (later transferred to the Galilee Chapel at the west end), and, after the 1174 fire at Canterbury, in the piers, capitals, and stringcourses of the choir and Trinity Chapel of the Cathedral.[23]

Modern perceptions of monasticism tuned to notions of frugality and simplicity are confounded by the glitter and costly materials displayed at the center of the Priory. But the question is less our response and more that of the monks for whom the work was carried out eight hundred years ago. For them the issue of cost most likely receded before the invocation of models and their intended promptings to consider higher matters. For monks and visitors signification outweighed expense. St. Augustine's concept of the faithful as a *civitas Dei* – a physical and a metaphorical entity – invoked by Archbishop Anselm, rotated around the ideal epitomized by Solomon's Temple in Jerusalem. Its sanctuary, surrounding buildings, and courts constituted the archetype for all patrons and builders. Biblical accounts described them as made with "costly stones, cut according to measure, sawed with saws, back and front, from the foundation to the coping, and from outside to the great court" (1 Kings 7:10; cf. Ezekiel 40–44, and 2 Chronicles 3–7). Interest at Canterbury in Solomon's Temple is manifested in Anselm's use of torsade (or Solomonic) columns for the bays reserved for the main altar in the crypt (ca. 1100) (Fernie, 1989, 18–29) and in Wibert's structures such as the aedicular fountain houses, Norman Staircase, and Treasury, which recall the same Jerusalem model. As mentioned in the preceding chapter, the Temple became the subject of explicit scholarly and exegetical analysis as the result of Victorine scholarship in Paris at mid-century, as well as first-hand experience following from the Crusader occupation of the *loca sancta* in Jerusalem (Cahn 1976a, 247–54; Cahn 1994, 53–68; Schröder 2000, vol. 1, 137ff.).

To see the columns, capitals, moldings, and sculptures of Wibert's Great Cloister as a genre of expensive interior decoration notable as markers of period style and exemplars of masons' skills misses the intention underlying their creation in the 1150s. Designed to underpin meditation, these components functioned collectively as an architecture of representation. For the 250 years in which they served this purpose, they provided changing generations of monks with connection-making links rich in association to biblical models, compass points on their mnemonic 'journeys' within the locked confines of the cloister enclosure.

5

AN ARCHITECTURE
OF HOSPITALITY FOR
DISTINGUISHED GUESTS

The expansion of Benedictine cathedral communities after the Norman Conquest posed difficulties for foundations settled in former Roman cities such as Winchester, York, Lincoln, and Canterbury. Located on the cities' margins and hemmed in by formidable defensive wall systems, they had little land for expansion and for the development of traditional monastic layouts. The best the communities could hope for was some reorganization of the buildings which formed their inner courts consisting of the entry gate, guesthouse, stables, forge, bakehouse, granary, brewhouse, and storage buildings. An outer court was beyond their expectations no matter how necessary such buildings as barns, watermills, woolhouses, workshops, tanneries, and dovecotes or such features as orchards, fishponds, vineyards, and meadows were deemed for the realization of the ideal of self-sufficiency inscribed in the *Rule* of St. Benedict (ca. 540).[1] These functions had to be outsourced to farms or manors, an inconvenience involving constant transport and difficulties of management (Coppack 2006, 109–31).

Canterbury dramatically illustrates the situation and suggests the innovative architectural and administrative solutions the Priory devised to handle these restrictions. Two ancient Benedictine foundations – the Priory and St. Augustine's – lay virtually next door to each other. The Priory, set within the confines of the old Roman city, constructed only buildings associated with an inner court, and this with much ingenuity and expense.[2] St. Augustine's, by contrast, located a mere 300 yards to the east, lay outside the city's walls and enjoyed the freedom to develop both an inner and an outer court, the latter extending into the countryside and providing the monks with the industrial and economic components crucial for the development of a full monastic economy (Tatton-Brown 1991b).

Further complicating precinct development in the case of the Priory was the Archbishop's Palace, which lay immediately adjacent on its western side. To overcome the tight confines of their precinct, the monks divided their inner court into two parts: the Cellarer's

Court to the north of the Great Cloister, the subject of this chapter, and the Green Court far larger and further north, the subject of Chapter 6. Each court was separately walled and gated, served distinct purposes, and was staffed differently.[3] The names given to the parts are admittedly imprecise. On *Drawing I*, the Cellarer's Court is not named as such, and the Green Court is simply referred to as "the court." For once Willis does little to help; he heads his chapter on the former "The Hospitate and Private Buildings of the Celerer" (Willis 1868, 119–42).

When the Benedictine reform began at Monte Cassino in the 540s, St. Benedict assigned the cellarer the responsibility for provisioning the monastery recommending that the individual assigned this responsibility be "sober and no great eater" (McCann 1952, 84). Originally his duties were relatively circumscribed, but over time they developed into a sprawling, complex monastic office. Thus, at the Priory by the mid-twelfth century the cellarer's domain extended from the Refectory and Guesthouse (and their galleried walks) out into his court with the Cellar and Great Kitchen, and then out again into the Green Court to include the Common Hall and Servants' Hall, the Bakehouse, the Brewhouse (through his subordinate, the bartoner), the Granary (through his subordinate, the granger), and, finally, further to the east, the prior's *Nova Camera* with guest accommodation and the Infirmary Hall with its own kitchen and specialized needs (see Chapter 7). The running of these buildings with their staff, provisions, and fabric responsibilities saddled the cellarer with heavy administrative duties, including personnel management, budgeting, and the handling of endowment income. Inevitably, these involved disputes and, in turn, judicial procedures to resolve them. To deal with these the Priory provided the cellarer with his own law court, which convened in the door of the Brewhouse in the Green Court (Urry 1967, 23ff.). The considerable demands placed on this office holder required social status as well as administrative and judicial skills. The kind of men who held the office is best grasped through the names and social rank of the cellarers listed in the twelve Cellarer's Rolls which cover the years 1392–1474 (Sparks 2007, 24).

The decision to physically divide the functions and buildings between the Cellarer's Court and the Green Court complicated the placement of the Guesthouse. Archbishop Lanfranc had assigned the west range of the Great Cloister to this purpose (see Chapter 4). Other monasteries followed this model, as may still be seen at Norwich or in France at St.-Denis where Abbot Suger's renewal retained the west range as the *Domus Hospitum* in the late 1130s (Grant 1998, 243). The location of the Guesthouse in the Great Cloister nonetheless caused problems. At Canterbury these focused on access, a condition compounded by the increase in visitors in the peaceful conditions that followed the end of King Stephen's reign and the proximity of the different social classes to one another.[4] To solve such problems Prior Wibert took the drastic decision to remove the Guesthouse from the Great Cloister altogether. Finding a new location in the existing Cellarer's Court was impossible; available space was nonexistent. The only way to break out of its tight footprint was to persuade the archbishop to cede to the Priory a site from his own adjacent palace grounds. Even though the amount of land was modest, about 3,000 square feet, Prior Wibert's skill in persuading Theobald to assign it to the Priory must rank among his major achievements. That successor archbishops regarded Theobald's gift with less than enthusiasm (seeing the Guesthouse as an intrusion into the Palace) may be sensed in the aftermath of the suppression, when the land and the building reverted back to them, the hall at the same time changing its purpose from hospitality to law (to serve as the Court Hall for the archbishop's Liberty – see Chapter 6).

Today, the entire area of the Cellarer's Court and the Guesthouse (fig. 37B) is occupied by the garden of the archdeacon of Canterbury, also known as No. 29 The Precincts. Strictly private, the area is consequently little known.[5] Equally, as the most heavily wrecked part of the Priory, it is hard to piece together. Ruined structures border it on all sides: those of the Refectory on the south, the Dormitory on the east, the north range and Great Kitchen on the north, and the Guesthouse on the west. Despite these conditions, the Cellarer's Court is an area of exceptional if overlooked interest and reveals much about how the community organized its response to distinguished visitors. Scattered throughout what is now the archdeacon's house is a wide range of mid-twelfth-century material. Particularly notable is the entry passage, which remains essentially intact. Outside, the Guesthouse hall and Parlor emerge improbably from the archdeacon's flower borders and rockery and rank as the best appointed and most interesting of any known from the period.

Drawing I shows the Cellarer's Court (fig. 37A) as an open space bordered by buildings – the Great Kitchen (*Coquinam*), the Parlor (*Locutorium*), the Guesthouse (*Domus Hospitum*) – and the high wall and gate. The artist presents the area as approximately square, with the buildings neatly folded outward to give the impression of generous separation and openness. The degree to which the artist's depiction was an ideal can be grasped by comparing *Drawing I* (fig. 37A) with the 1989 survey of the same space by the Canterbury Archaeological Trust (fig. 37B). Far from regular, the area was, in fact, pinched at its northern end and formed a narrow trapezoid as it extended to the Refectory, and then opened to the south in a tight space between the Great Kitchen and the Refectory. The former sits nearer to the center of the north range, rather than forming the east boundary. What the artist represents as ordered and spacious was, therefore, compressed and tightly bounded by two-story buildings. On the other hand, *Drawing I* presents us with a number of verifiable details. It shows accurately the new Guesthouse extending into the Archbishop's Palace grounds, the paired windows in the upper story, the Great Kitchen as a multi-chimneyed and vaulted building, and the awkward open area between the Guesthouse and the west range of the Great Cloister as plant (or herb) filled.

Impossible to recognize today is *Drawing I*'s depiction of the Cellarer's Court's northern boundary. The artist shows an ashlar wall opened more or less in the middle by a huge gateway with twin leaves surmounted by a pediment. A *titulus* underneath tells us: "Porta inter Domus Hospitum et Coquinam." The gate carries no implication of a gatehouse. As drawn it resembles other gate openings cut through wall enclosures on *Drawing I*, such as the presently named Memorial Gateway on the south side of the Cathedral which separated the monks' from the lay persons' cemetery (see fig. 146). Of the twin gate leaves, the western one is provided with the serviceable feature of a small paneled opening that could be slid back for oral communication. This served presumably for guests who, in St. Benedict's words in the *Rule*, "arrive at irregular hours" demanding entry.

Just as puzzling is *Drawing I*'s depiction of the *Locutorium* or Parlor at the southern end of the Cellarer's Court. No trace of this feature has been found (Willis 1868, 35–39, 135–36, 197). The artist depicts an L-shaped *porticus*, the longer side backed against the Refectory, the shorter side turned perpendicular to it and seemingly

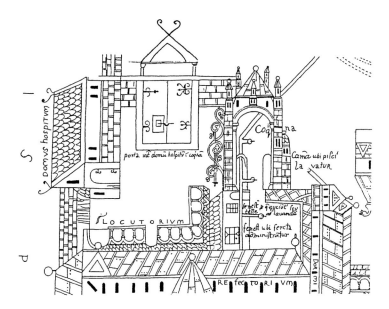

37A   *Drawing I*, Willis's tracing, detail showing the Cellarer's Court, Trinity College, Cambridge (Willis, 1868, pl. 1).

aligned with the west side of the Great Kitchen. The *porticus* is shown with a center opening flanked on either side by three arches resting on a stylobate on which the word "locutorium" has been written; the openings are about half the width of those in the Great Cloister. At the west, the porch has a high-rising single arch, suggesting a separate feature since the tiled roof is omitted

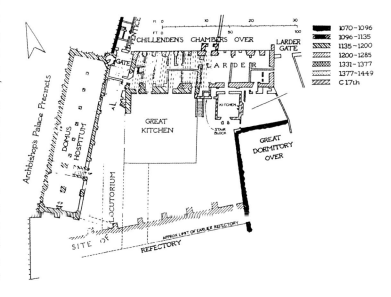

37B   Canterbury Archaeological Trust, Cellarer's Court, plan (courtesy Canterbury Archaeological Trust).

above it and on the west side. The shorter arm of the porch has four arched openings resting on a stylobate. Modern surveys of the Cellarer's Court treat the *Locutorium* with some uncertainty. The 1987 Canterbury Archaeological Trust's survey shows a dotted-in, free-standing structure positioned between the southern end of the Guesthouse and the Great Kitchen.

The Cellarer's Court as shown on *Drawing I* raises once more the image's complexity. As seen in Chapter 3, the artist represents the Priory in terms consistent with a view of Christ Church as an idealized *civitas Dei*. While far from a literal blueprint, it represents the buildings as recognizable entities. The image requires "reading" as well as looking. It "tells" us more and shows us more than a single-point perspective rendering. At the end of this chapter it will be necessary to return to *Drawing I*'s depiction of the Cellarer's Court to suggest a way of reconciling what it represents and what was physically there.

A brief sketch of its users and their relation to the Priory helps in understanding the physical remains of the Cellarer's Court as well as the Guesthouse. Wished for or not, an unbroken stream of visitors was a fact of life at the Priory. With thirteen saints buried in the Cathedral, Canterbury was famous as an important site of pilgrimage in southern England long before Becket. Adding to the pilgrims were numerous church officials who came with business to the adjacent Archbishop's Palace, the administrative center of the Primate of All England, and further visitors from those who used the main road from London to the Channel ports.[6] Accommodation represented just the start of monastic hospitality. For those who arrived on horseback, high quality stables were essential along with a forge. Then came the need for food, escorts within the Precinct, and medical attention. Candles (or candle ends for those lower down the social scale) had to be produced to allow visitors to see their way inside and outside once daylight faded. Visitors naturally expected access to the church and cloister, and demanded tours of the Precinct (the tours graded according to social rank). Given these factors, it is no surprise to find the monastery's documents listing at regular intervals the complaints of the prior and chapter about their oppression by visitors.

Admission of guests and their appropriate placement in accommodation depended on their social status. The responsibility of determining who went where fell on the keeper of the Green Court Gatehouse, a lay appointment and one within the gift of the archbishop. No document survives to inform us about how the keeper

made such decisions, but the *Customaries* of other large Benedictine houses such as Bury St. Edmunds and Ely provide reliable guidance (Kerr 2007, 56–57). At least four distinct categories of guest can be identified, and they were each accommodated in separate areas. Top rank visitors such as royalty or aristocracy resided as guests of the prior in the "Nova Camera Prioris" (on *Drawing I*) just north of the Infirmary Hall or in the Archbishop's Palace. Such visitors traveled with riding households. A minimum of thirteen horses was required to qualify for this top category of residence (Butler 1949, 39). At the other end of the social scale, the servants, grooms, and cooks who accompanied the top social rank of visitor lodged in a separate Servants' Hall in the *Aula Nova* in the Green Court. Higher socially than servants were pilgrims or visitors, messengers, mariners, chaplains, and clerks who arrived on foot; they were accommodated in the Common Hall. Even among these three groups, determination of location cannot always have been easy, nor either the arguments about which monastic official within the institution was responsible to pay for their upkeep and at what rate. At Vézelay in the 1160s it was this issue that became the touchstone for the communal movement.[7] In England, a flavor of these distinctions comes from the historian and chronicler Gerald of Wales, who complained bitterly around 1200 of the accommodation offered to him at the Cistercian abbey of Strata Florida in Wales, where he was "harbored in the public hall among the common guests and the noise of the people."[8] In addition to these distinct classes, it is worth noting provision for the indigent outside the Green Court Gatehouse in the Almonry in the Mint Yard (with limited lodging) and for visiting clergy (either in the Dormitory or the city).[9]

This leaves until last the social class accommodated in the Priory's Guesthouse, which included vassals, knights, squires, royal agents, or gentry of rank. It was for them that the building discussed in this chapter was designed. This class of visitor arrived with a riding household of fewer than thirteen horses. The single structure provided by Archbishop Lanfranc ca. 1070 in the west range of the Great Cloister was clearly deemed inadequate to meet the needs of this group in the mid-1150s. Prior Wibert set about the problem of hospitality with characteristic boldness and dispatch.

Guesthouse visitors underwent a two-part scrutiny on their arrival at the Priory. Dismounted at the Green Court Gatehouse and their identity established by the gatekeeper, they would then have been conducted along the covered pentice (a 240-foot open-sided, roofed structure set against the Priory's west precinct wall which provided all-weather protection), at the end of which they encountered a second substantial gatehouse, the Pentice Gatehouse. The visitor now came under the responsibility of a new official, the keeper of the Pentice Gatehouse. It was his responsibility to refer them to the principal monastic official in charge of the Guesthouse, the seneschal (see below), who assigned accommodation, meals, firewood, candles, and arranged for tours of the Precinct and Cathedral. If a guest so wished, the seneschal would contact the guestmaster to arrange for meetings with the monks or procure an invitation to dine in the monastic Refectory at the prior's table. Invitations on major feast days were much sought, and a description of one such meal survives. On Trinity Sunday 1179, and thus a high feast day, Gerald of Wales, the archbishop's legate in Wales, joined the prior's table in the Refectory. In a parody of ordered refectory routine, he recorded how "...all of [the monks] gesticulating with fingers, hands, and arms and whistling one to another in lieu of speaking all extravaganting in a manner more free and frivolous than was seemly" (Butler 1937, 71). He also dwelled disapprovingly on the appearance of sixteen separate dishes (known as "pittances") in addition to the two basic dishes of cooked food prescribed by St. Benedict (known as "generals") (Butler 1949, 42; Harvey 1993, 11).

PENTICE GATEHOUSE

Documents refer to the Pentice Gatehouse by different names. In 1382 a donation by Prior Chillenden mentions the structure as the "porta interior juxta Aulam Hospitum" (Somner 1640, 111–12). At the suppression in 1540 it is referred to as "The Pentise Gate" (Willis 1868, 125), a derivation from the wooden pentice one still sees, a Chillenden replacement built in 1393 (figs. 38 and 39). None of this appears on *Drawing I* (see fig. 8A). The artist shows a gate in the center of an enclosing wall. Explaining the gate's disappearance is its replacement by the gatehouse ca. 1158 soon after *Drawing I* was made (fig. 40). This idea is supported by extensive modifications still visible in the physical fabric. The reasons may be inferred from the changes. The construction of a gatehouse indicates the need for greater security. At the same time, the addition of accommodation leading to the construction of the northern range extending from the Pentice Gatehouse to the Larder Gate indicates increased visitor demand. Just as important, the archi-

tecture of the Pentice Gatehouse reflected the prestige of its visitors and their expectations for hospitality. To make the high class visitors feel more suitably accommodated, the new gatehouse provided clearer accents of authority in line with those being adopted elsewhere for secular residences. An embellished entry surmounted by an imposing upper story lit by a large glazed window adorned with sculpted capitals balanced security with unmistakable signs of status.

Today the Pentice Gatehouse is substantially concealed by a drastic refronting undertaken by Prior Chillenden in the early 1400s. The changed appearance resulted from a timber-framed addition constructed 6 feet in front of the twelfth-century building. Willis likened the effect to "a picturesque grange of studwork" (Willis 1868, 138). Chillenden's refronting deliberately altered the building's identity. He wanted a residence redolent of manorial domesticity. What he had inherited from Prior Wibert carried all the wrong inflections. With its ashlar structure, wide entry arch and flanking stair turret, tall upper story lit by a single, large, square-headed window, and, most likely, a crenellated parapet, the Pentice Gatehouse referenced the old Angevin power elite rather than addressing the new gentry class of Chillenden's era.

Despite Chillenden's changes, the residence still retains some memory of the original building's overall disposition. From the front, the three-story block (on the west) with its own pitched roof marks the position of the Gatehouse and is set perpendicular to the two-story range. In contrast to the reworked exterior, the interior retains an unsuspected wealth of mid-twelfth-century work. On the ground floor the most notable features are the vaulted entry passage and a finely detailed lateral doorway (fig. 41). In the floors above, embedded in the walls and in the roof, are parts of the grand chamber over the Gatehouse entry passage.

The phasing changes were elucidated by Willis more than 160 years ago. His pages on the Inner or Pentice Gatehouse and on the Cellarer's Court and the Great Kitchen constitute a *tour de force* of accurate observation and lucid interpretation (Willis 1868, 122–36). The Gatehouse's entry arch against which the gates themselves were hung has left no trace – the arch was removed in Chillenden's refronting – but Willis calculated its position by observing the truncated southern bay of the pentice (fig. 42). The disruption in the spacing of the pentice's principal joists and roof trusses where it meets the residence signified the position of the entry arch. Willis's deduction is confirmed in the interior in the

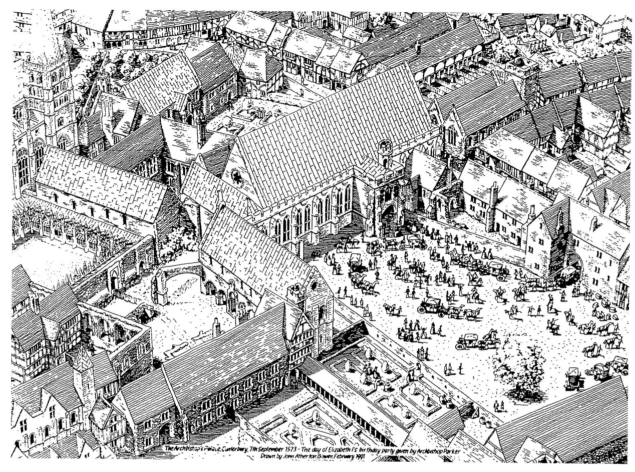

38 Canterbury Cathedral Priory, Cellarer's Court after the suppression. Reconstruction drawing from the north by Jill Atherton (courtesy Canterbury Archaeological Trust).

The bird's-eye view of the Cellarer's Court in 1573 shows the surviving pentice in the lower right leading to the Pentice Gatehouse with the east range extending to the Larder Gate. In the center is the Guesthouse with the Great Cloister and west range and northwest tower of the Cathedral at the top left. In the lower left the Dormitory is shown unroofed following the ejection of the monks and with domestic residences raised inside. In the left corner are the western bays of the *Necessarium* similiarly remodeled as domestic residences. The buildings in the right half are part of the Archbishop's Palace.

present closet storage space next to the archdeacon's kitchen (Willis 1868, 126, 136–42).

The archway leading to the entry passage is barrel vaulted and extended southwards with the adjacent bays being groin vaulted. The passageway served for the reception of visitors (the cellarer's supplies for the Great Kitchen entered through the Larder Gate on the east side of the Cellarer's Court). Chillenden's donation of 1382 also mentions a "custodiae portae interioris" (Somner 1640, 112). His chamber can only have been on the east side of the entry passage, and it thus formed part of the northern range built at the same time. The entry's two southern bays are articulated by a blind

arcade with uniform bay widths on the passageway's west wall (fig. 43), but the vaulting of these bays is skewed to the southeast with the transverse arch of the groin vault adjusted to accommodate the wide inner doorway that led to the flanking residence on the east (although the rise in ground level in the passage now requires three steps down to enter it). The severies of the vault overlap the molding of the arch and are provided with a corbeled support inserted into the wall (fig. 44). Connecting the passage to the northern residential range and to the Great Kitchen is a handsome arched doorway. Although the arch springs awkwardly on the south, the elaborately decorated moldings with outward-facing chevron and a

39   Canterbury Cathedral Priory, Cellarer's Court, digital reconstruction model, view from the south (courtesy Stuart Harrison).

The model shows at the bottom the monks' Refectory with the connecting passageway to the Great Kitchen in the center of the image. Above and to the left is the Guesthouse with the *Locutorium* on the east and south side of the Guesthouse. The Pentice Gatehouse appears at the top with the east range on the east side.

40   Canterbury Cathedral Priory, digital reconstruction of Pentice Gatehouse (courtesy Stuart Harrison).

41   Canterbury Cathedral Priory, Cellarer's Court, Pentice Gatehouse, doorway to east range (courtesy Stuart Harrison).

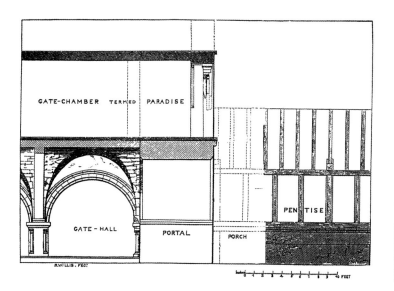

42 Canterbury Cathedral Priory, Cellarer's Court, Pentice Gatehouse, section (Willis 1868, 129, fig. 24).

43 Canterbury Cathedral Priory, Cellarer's Court, Pentice Gatehouse, passage looking south (courtesy Stuart Harrison).

44 Canterbury Cathedral Priory, Cellarer's Court, Pentice Gatehouse, entry hall, drawing of corbeled support for inserted groin vault (Willis 1868, 128, fig. 23).

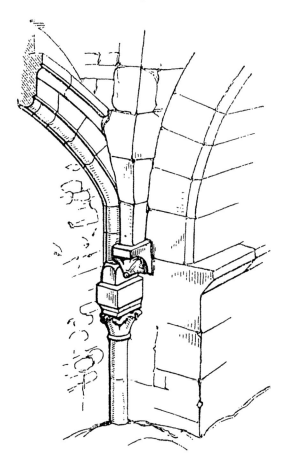

sculpted head in the keystone required no adjustment. A Greek key motif enriched by drilled pellets serves as a hood molding, a motif resembling that on the west side of Prior Wibert's Treasury (see fig. 126). In the next bay south, as Willis's plan shows, an angle of the original twelfth-century Great Kitchen butts into the southernmost bay of the entry passageway.

Above the entry passage a handsome, tall upper chamber rose through two stories of the present residence. The chamber was lit by a large square-headed window opening, the lintel supported by robust foliate capitals (fig. 45) with curled tips and beaded stems.[10] A relieving arch surmounts the window in Willis's illustration. Further accommodation formed the north wing of the range. Linkage at the second story to the upper-story room indicates a unified program of work for the Gatehouse and northern range.

THE CELLARER'S COURT AND THE KITCHEN COURT

Once inside the Cellarer's Court (now the archdeacon's garden) the visitor would have confronted the Great Kitchen at close quarters. With its multiple chimneys in the form of turrets, the Great Kitchen was impressive in scale and function. It featured prominently on *Drawing I*. However, it further narrowed the courtyard, and the space was restricted by the galleried porch labeled

45 Canterbury Cathedral Priory, Pentice Gatehouse, capital of center window (courtesy Stuart Harrison).

46 Abbey of Fontevrault, Great Kitchen (photograph by A. F. Kersting, courtesy Conway Library, The Courtauld Institute of Art, London).

Locutorium (discussed at the end of the chapter) that extended along the entire east-facing and south-facing flanks of the two-story Guesthouse (see below). On the Great Kitchen's eastern side lay a small courtyard entered from the Larder Gate, which served for the transport of its supplies and fuel. On the southern side another courtyard was divided by a corridor which connected it with the Refectory.

The Great Kitchen served the monks' Refectory, the Guesthouse, the Common Hall, and the Servants' Hall. Originally free-standing (as it is shown on *Drawing I*), the sole surviving fragment is the building's northwest angle which was absorbed into the new gatehouse entry hall (with the base partly buried in the garden). The Great Kitchen is drawn as a tall and compact space with chimneyed angles (each to serve a fireplace). What little is known about the interior comes from *Drawing I* where the artist removes the south-facing wall, thereby allowing us to glimpse the interior. The space was covered with a central vault and topped with a pyramidal roof sheeted with lead. The artist also draws two open arches, possibly windows or fireplaces. Water was supplied from a pipe coming from the Fountain House in the Great Cloister; the artist shows two faucets. In its twelfth century version, the kitchen would have resembled the standing kitchens at Glastonbury and the abbey of Fontevrault in Normandy (fig. 46).

Wibert's twelfth-century kitchen was replaced and enlarged by Prior Hathbrand (1338–70). The resulting

kitchen was square, 47 feet to a side, a larger version of the kitchen still extant at Durham Cathedral of 1367–74 (which measured 36 feet to a side).[11] The building lasted to the suppression, but with the community gone, the Dean and Chapter decreed its demolition five years later in 1546 (Sparks 2007, 110). The surviving northwest corner (protruding into the south end of the gatehouse passage) shows a diaphragm arch for a flue and indicates corner chimneys, perhaps the sole surviving detail from Prior Wibert's kitchen (fig. 47).

On the east side of the Great Kitchen *Drawing I* shows an extension to the building and carries the *titulus* "chamber where fish are washed" (see Chapter 3; also Willis 1868, 35–37). On the opposite or west wall, with a favored southwest prospect, the artist draws a vine in vigorous growth. South of the kitchen, in line with its western side, a smaller lower building fronted a second narrow courtyard. It linked the Great Kitchen to the Refectory, doubling as a serving station and a pantry or scullery, the latter function affirmed by the provision of piped water and a faucet. The building is shown with two windows, the northern one labeled "window at

47 Canterbury Cathedral Priory, Pentice Gatehouse, south elevation, drawing (Willis 1868, facing p. 139, fig. 30).

Made during the clearance undertaken in the late 1840s, the drawing shows the Pentice Gatehouse from the south, and the remaining wall of the Guesthouse. Willis also included the revealed twelfth-century ground level in the lower left corner and, on the right, the surviving angle of the Great Kitchen.

which the portions are served out," and the southern one "window through which the platters [or trenchers] are thrown out to be washed." Presumably what is being shown are two window hatches in the covered passage extending from the Great Kitchen to the Refectory. Through them food and plates were passed and soiled dishes returned. The *tituli* provide us a rare glimpse into twelfth-century kitchen organization.

CELLAR AND CELLARER'S BUILDINGS

The location of the Cellar probably lay at the north end of the west range of the Great Cloister. *Drawing I* suggests a two-story arrangement, and the artist shows both a gable end and immediately above it the wide arch attached to the west end of the *Locutorium*. Willis interpreted this western bay as containing the butteries, pantry, and passage to the cellarage beneath the Refectory and, above, the cellarer's lodging reached by a turret stair (Willis 1868, 35); he was uncertain whether the

Refectory had a low vaulted substructure or was more equally divided into two stories. In any case, a two-story form was used at other cathedral priories like Durham, Worcester, and Carlisle. After the suppression at Canterbury, the Dean and Chapter modified the Refectory, turning it into a residence for the seventh prebendary and at the same time specifying that it include "the long seller under ye frater" (Willis 1868, 35, n. 1). For reasons unrecorded, the residence was found unsatisfactory and in 1546 the building was unroofed. The walls remained a century later, when a garden is recorded in the space (Sparks 2007, 23).

THE GUESTHOUSE

The Guesthouse (*Domus Hospitum* on *Drawing I*) forms the western side of the courtyard (Willis 1868, 126, 133–36). It is shown as a compact, two-story rectangular building covered by a tiled roof and entered from the east. The upper story was lit by paired windows placed at either end. At the south a lower structure extends towards the Great Cloister and terminates a short distance from the Refectory. Between the two buildings a small open space is filled with plants or herbs against the boundary wall.

As built, the Guesthouse enjoyed exceptional appointments. It was fully vaulted, beautifully detailed, lit by glass windows, adorned with monumental sculpture at its main entry door, warmed by generous fireplaces, and supplied with running water. Such luxuries met the expectations of gentry for hospitality in the mid-1150s. The building was divided into two parts (fig. 48). To the north of the main entrance lay the seven-bay long hall which served as day room and dining area with dormitory above. To the south of the main entrance was a lower, centrally planned, fully rib-vaulted building which served as the formal parlor or meeting area of the guests with a room above provided with a fireplace.

Some sense of the Guesthouse's importance in the medieval period comes from the list of officers charged with its running and maintenance (under the overall authority of the guestmaster and, in turn, under the cellarer). This included: "Senescallus aulae hospitum, Janitor portae aulae, garcio ejus" (Urry 1967, 161).[12] The names of some men who occupied the important office of seneschal are recorded, beginning with Bartholomew in 1158. To align his name with the completed building is justified by fabric evidence which indicates a date in the late 1150s.

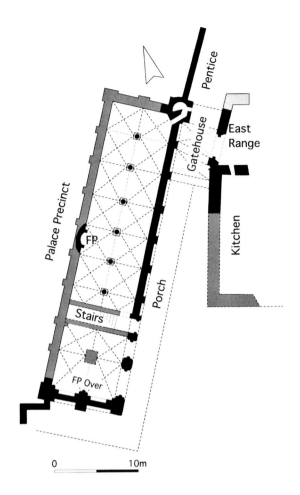

Palace Precinct

Pentice

Gatehouse

East Range

Kitchen

FP

Porch

Stairs

FP Over

0   10m

48   Canterbury Cathedral Priory, Guesthouse, plan
(courtesy Stuart Harrison).

At the suppression, the Dean and Chapter returned the Guesthouse to the archbishop, on whose land Prior Wibert had raised the building 400 years earlier. Specified as the Court Hall, it was reserved for the legal business of the archbishop's Liberties (Sparks 2007, 237). A hundred years later Somner could write that the hall was "perfect still" (Somner 1640, 110). By 1650, however, like other palace buildings under the Commonwealth, the former Guesthouse part was dismantled. As such it remained into the late 1840s, when Willis drew the exterior complete with an accumulation of about 2 to 3 feet of debris (fig. 47). In 1878 the Dean and Chapter acquired a tenancy of the site and created a garden within the shell of the Guesthouse. A clearance of the northern part of the garden was undertaken in 1951–52 and exposed the column bases of the mid-twelfth-century hall, where they remain unprotected and weathering away into the present.

Today, much of the Guesthouse's east wall stands up to the first stringcourse (fig. 49). The building was fronted by a galleried walk (fig. 52) covered by a lean-to roof, with the corbels to support the wall plate or rail visible in de Cort's 1807 drawing (fig. 51). The wall was articulated by blind arcades like those noted on the interior of the Pentice Gatehouse entry passage, and continued outside for five bays. The arcades carry a single order of moldings (a plain rounded angle) and are surmounted by a hood molding; they rest on pilasters with angle shafts and bear handsome foliate and water-leaf capitals (fig. 50). Four of the bays have the same dimensions as those in the interior passageway; the fifth bay is narrower to allow for the entry door (fig. 53). Beyond the entry are two further bays now infilled but originally open. They were likewise fronted by the same porch, which was returned around the south end of the building for a further two bays (at the building's south-east corner an attached shaft with a capital remains to indicate this). Architectural detailing – capitals, responds, and arch moldings – can be matched with that from other Wibert buildings such as the Treasury.

The Guesthouse's south gable wall survives, although heavily rebuilt. In the early sixteenth century the end of the building caused structural concerns and led to the construction of a massive, 26-foot-long flying buttress composed of molded bricks (visible in fig. 38). Willis realized that the upper line of the buttress "nearly corresponds to the floor of the Celerer's Hall and also to the level of the old floor of the Refectory...both having been raised upon subvaults" (Willis 1868, 135). The buttress would have met the northern wall of the now disappeared Refectory more or less diagonally between its corner buttresses.

The Guesthouse's entry doorway was elaborately decorated with two tympanums placed one over the other (fig. 54). Sculptural enrichment is unusual for a guesthouse and no other example is known in England. Equally distinctive is the piggyback composition. The upper tympanum is pushed through the stringcourse dividing the two stories, a difficult design requirement to incorporate with the fronting porch. The lower tympanum is supported by a segmental lintel with dogtooth decoration, and the entry door is flanked by coursed shafts with elegant foliate capitals (fig. 55). The upper tympanum is surmounted by a segmental arch and supported by columns with foliate capitals.

On the interior, traces of a small room survive just inside the entry along with a stairway to the upper floor, the latter built on two semicircular vaults. This

49 Canterbury Cathedral Priory, Guesthouse, remaining east elevation (photograph author).

The inner wall of the covered porch that extended from the Pentice Gatehouse passageway along the length of the Guesthouse.

50 Canterbury Cathedral Priory, Guesthouse, east-facing porch, capital from north bay (photograph author).

51 Canterbury Cathedral Priory, Guesthouse, drawing by Henri de Cort, ca. 1807 (courtesy Canterbury Cathedral Archives–Printdrawer /2/0/3).

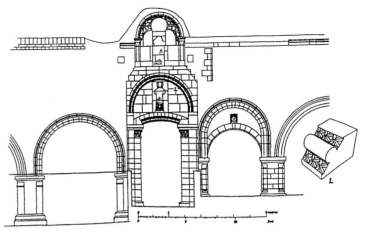

(Left) 52 Canterbury Cathedral Priory, Guesthouse, porch, digital model (courtesy Stuart Harrison).

(Above) 53 Canterbury Cathedral Priory, Guesthouse, east elevation, drawing by Jill Atherton (courtesy Canterbury Archaeological Trust).

(Left) 54 Canterbury Cathedral Priory, Guesthouse, entry doorway (photograph author).

(Below) 55 Canterbury Cathedral Priory, Guesthouse, entry doorway capital (photograph author).

56 Canterbury Cathedral Priory, drawing of interior of Parlor by Jill Atherton (Courtesy Canterbury Archaeological Trust).

must be the remains of the space used by the "janitor portae aulae." The jamb of a small window lighting the stair remains to the north of the entry door (see fig. 54). To the south of the entry lay the parlor area, a centrally planned, fully vaulted space with a room above. Four rib-vaulted bays sprang from a central pier, the vaults rising from triple attached columnar responds on the north and south (fig. 56), and were received on the outer walls by three-columned responds (the evidence of the western wall has disappeared in later rebuildings). The southern end wall is composed of two arches, the eastern one wider and taller than the western. Since the gable wall is made up of old fragments and reused loose stonework, little is known about the upper story except for the chimney flue. The structure originally opened towards the porch on both the eastern and southern sides.

To the north of the entry on the ground floor lay the Guesthouse's hall (fig. 57).[13] A long axial two-story structure extending seven bays, measuring 120 feet in length and 22 feet in width, the hall was also fully vaulted like the Parlor. The space was divided into twin aisles by a central row of slender columns which rested on bases with elegant, finely scaled rolls and hollows and with angle spurs (fig. 58). Columns supported rib vaults, evidence for which survives in the form of vault springers in the northeast corner where the hall joins with the Pentice Gatehouse. The rebuilding of the present

57 Canterbury Cathedral Priory, Guesthouse Hall, looking north (photograph author).

58 Canterbury Cathedral Priory, Guesthouse, ground-story hall, detail of base (photograph author).

wall top has eliminated all trace of the responds, although Willis tells us that they were visible to him on the eastern wall in 1847 (Willis 1868, 125). In a comment added twenty-two years later, he also noted that the recent garden work had obliterated "the remains of projecting piers" (meaning the aisle respond shafts). No trace survives of dividing screens on the ground floor to elucidate the different uses of the Guesthouse.[14] A large fireplace constructed in the fifth bay against the western wall provided warmth; it is flanked by spurred bases to support columns and has a curved back with herringbone construction. In the northeast corner where hall and gatehouse share the wall, a door (now blocked) provided entry for food from the Great Kitchen, indicating use of the north bays for dining. In the angle on the south face of the spiral stair, another doorway gave access to the chamber above the gatehouse entry passage, probably a withdrawing room (Willis 1868, 141).

In the dormitory above the hall, the sole surviving details come from the windows that lit the interior. The bay coterminous with the entry passage contains a blocked double window which dates from the earliest building phase and was closed only with the later construction of the upper room over the entry passage. The twin-light, round-headed composition coincides with the window arrangements shown on *Drawing I*, where the artist draws one set at the south and another at the north end of the building. Further, in the bay adjacent to the Pentice Gatehouse, an angled window jamb dressed with cut stone retains a hole for a glazing bar.

Turning to the sculpture, both tympanums are heavily weathered, making identification of the subjects difficult. De Cort's drawing shows a few details more clearly (see fig. 51) but not enough to firm up the subjects.[15] In 1640 Somner described the tympanums: the upper one bore "the resemblance of the Holy Ghost in the Dove's form, descending on our Saviour," and the lower showed "the statue of an Archbishop (haply the Founder) in his pontificals" (Somner, 1640, 110). Neither can be recognized today. Kahn describes the upper tympanum as "a seated Christ," while Sparks sees Christ on the Cross with adoring angels either side holding candles, with the lower tympanum showing Becket (Kahn 1991, 180–81; Sparks and Tatton-Brown 1987, 37).

Clues to the identity of the figure in the lower tympanum come from dress and insignia. The sculptor shows the single figure with a nimbus, bearded, robed, mitered, holding a crozier, and blessing with his right hand. The case made for Becket has ramifications for the date as well as the subject. His canonization took place in 1174,

three years after his murder. A nimbed Becket would be possible only if the building post-dates that year, or if the sculpture was added after the building was completed. The earliest representations of Becket occur in the late 1170s (not counting the Guesthouse figure). Were Becket the subject there is no reason why he would be thought appropriate to greet visitors to the Guesthouse, and Somner's identification in 1640 of the figure as "the Founder" does not fit Becket. Whether this title could be stretched to include Anselm is debatable. He was the object of a lay cult at Christ Church in the 1150s and 1160s (Urry 1967, 165) and was raised to a *Beatus* (the early stage to canonization) in 1163. Two features do not fit: the half-length tunic and the stepped support on which the figure stands. Other possibilities may explain the representation, such as the Tree of Consanguinity (Shilling 1963, 31; also Cahn 1975a, 55–56). More likely the figure depicted Gregory the Great who dispatched Augustine to re-Christianize the English in 597.

Piggybacked tympanums are not known in England. The closest parallels come from double-storied porch portals in the Po Valley of northern Italy such as Modena (fig. 59) or Ferrara.[16] This area also favored large-scale, standing single figures above doorways as at S. Michele in Pavia.[17] Connections with this region can be explained by the water system and the buildings it served and also by the prior's court buildings (see Chapter 6). Similarly puzzling is the relationship between the two subjects. The sainted bishop under a celestial grouping suggests a theme of homage. This genre of linkage parallels the 1123 fresco in the Lateran Palace in Rome in the S. Nicolas Chapel, where the seated Virgin as queen surmounts the niched standing figure of the haloed, mitered pope with crozier paying homage to her (fig. 60).

The sculptures also address the date of the Guesthouse. Were they attached to the building shown in *Drawing I*? Or do the standing remains come from a later rebuilding? The second idea is espoused by Sparks and Tatton-Brown, who argue that the compact building shown on *Drawing I* corresponds to an earlier guesthouse and the present nine-bay-long building dates from the mid- to late 1170s.[18] Such a date conflicts with the remains. Positing a small early building is based on a literal reading of *Drawing I*. Arguing against this is the artist's use of truncation as a graphic device elsewhere, particularly for buildings set on a north–south axis, or those set perpendicular to the incised base lines which the artist used to organize his composition. Thus, the artist shows the *Aula Nova* with three bays instead of nine and Lanfranc's Dormitory with two aisles instead of six. Sparks and

73

59 Modena, Cathedral, west façade (photograph Scala)

60 S. Nicolas Chapel, Old Lateran Palace, Rome, 1123, fresco, after engraving of 1638 (courtesy Pontificia Commissione di Archeologia Sacra).

Tatton-Brown also justify their later date by pointing to the foliate capitals (see fig. 55) supporting the doorway's segmental lintel, which clearly imitate those of the Gothic choir and so must post-date 1174. This is undeniably the case. However, the entry door capitals are a retrofit undertaken when the doorway's lintel was changed in the mid-1170s. They differ from the capitals used throughout the Guesthouse, which are waterleaf and bunched foliate capitals from ca. 1160.

Taking the evidence of the Guesthouse together, there is no reason to doubt the prior's responsibility for its construction. The changes to the north side of the Cellarer's Court are secondary, most visibly the Pentice Gatehouse entry passage which entailed adjustments of the vaulting to make it "fit" the work of the first campaign (Willis 1868, 130). A second campaign of ca. 1160 saw the replacement of the gate shown on *Drawing I*

with the Pentice Gatehouse, the construction of the handsome upper chamber over the entry passage, and the addition to the Court of the two-story northern range. None of these appear on *Drawing I*. As seen, their omission helps to date *Drawing I* to ca. 1158–60. Documents broadly confirm this sequence. The Guesthouse is mentioned as the object of gifts in three documents in *Rental B* (1163–67; see Urry 1967, 227–33, nos. 23, 51, 84), all of which imply that the building was in use at the time of the gifts.

INTERPRETATION

Monastic hospitality was a central concept of the *Rule* of St. Benedict, and all monastic orders honored its history and found meaning in its practice. The idea originated in the Gospels. St. Matthew records Christ's words: "I was hungry and you gave me food, I was thirsty and you gave me something to drink, I was a stranger and you welcomed me" (24:35). How this noble idea was to be realized was left to subsequent centuries to work out.

From late antiquity forwards, guests to monasteries not only expected hospitality but expected it on a level consistent with their social status. In St. Benedict's *Rule* the community's responsibility for the reception and care of guests is clearly articulated. Chapter 53 begins: "Let all guests that come be received like Christ for he will say I was a stranger and you took me in" (McCann 1952, 118). Care of pilgrims and clergy is specifically mentioned, and St. Benedict urged particular attention for the poor "because in them is Christ more truly welcomed." As for the rich, he observed that their capacity to inspire fear is enough to secure them honor. Beyond these prescriptions St. Benedict supplied few detailed directions about hospitality, except to command that all guests be shown "fitting honor."

Three hundred years later, "The Plan of St. Gall" embodied St. Benedict's words. Seven areas were set aside for guests and their providers, with separate houses allocated for them at the west end of the church. Pilgrims and paupers were assigned buildings on the south side, and distinguished guests buildings on the north side (Horn and Born 1979, vol. II, 155–67). These houses were single-story, timber-frame constructions, and Horn linked them to a tradition of vernacular architecture distinctive of northern Europe. They were not separated into courts. Later centuries simplified the handling of guests and their location in the monastery. Separate areas emerged constituting an inner court to the west of the monastic church close to the entry gate (the St. Gall plan omitted both precinct wall and entry gate). The court arrangement had the advantage of providing a firmer separation of visitors from the community. At the abbey of Cluny in Burgundy, the guesthouse constructed by Peter the Venerable (1122–56) comprised an entry court of unmatched splendor with a palatial residence capable of accommodating forty-five men and thirty women (Conant 1968, 110, figs. 47–59).

At Canterbury Cathedral Priory an arrangement similar to Cluny was ruled out by the Archbishop's Palace, which occupied the area to the northwest of the Cathedral. Monasteries of similar size provide some context for Prior Wibert's planning of the Cellarer's Court. At Bury St. Edmunds (fig. 61), the *Gesta Sacristarum* (ca. 1300) credits Abbot Anselm (1121–48) with the construction of the inner court buildings, which were accessed from the Cellarer's Gatehouse, as at Canterbury.[19] Adjacent to the gate lay the cellarer's range, and between it and the Refectory stood the Kitchen as an independent structure. The monks' dormitory sealed the narrow courtyard to the east, and the cloister's west range contained the Great Hall over the cellarer's undercroft: in other words, the hall for guests of social rank (rather than the Common Hall for pilgrims, clerks, and chaplains, or the Servants' Hall for servants, cooks, and grooms). The same arrangement was anticipated a decade earlier at Norwich Cathedral (fig. 62) and at Ely (fig. 63). At Norwich, the west range of the Great Cloister contained the single-story Great Hall accessed through a projecting porch in the middle of the range, with double-story chambers at the north and south ends over an undercroft (Gilchrist 2005, 134–42) (see fig. 35). Ely repeated this arrangement in a five-bay structure with the Prior's Hall adjacent to the southwest angle of the Kitchen with the Queen's Hall and the guest halls forming a separate court to the south.[20] These adjacencies bear comparison with Canterbury. At Norwich and Ely the use of the west range for guest functions probably reflected Lanfranc's late eleventh-century arrangement at Canterbury. Both show two-story ranges with vaulted undercrofts serving as the hall and with the dormitory on the upper floor.

Although two-story halls were well established for guesthouses in the mid-twelfth century, with a small-scale contemporary example at St. Augustine's Canterbury and larger scale versions at Norwich and Ely, none furnish models for Canterbury's Priory. Similar social stratifications surface in the reform orders. At the Cistercian Fountains Abbey (Yorkshire) ca. 1160, two guesthouses were constructed for distinguished visitors, both located to the south of the adjacent Common Hall. The east was clearly the grander of the two and must have served for the top rank of visitor. It provided a heated, vaulted lower-story hall with toilets and a timber-roofed upper-story dormitory complete with a wheel window (Coppack 2006, 114–16). A huge aisled Common Hall of seven bays was revealed by geophysical survey, perhaps screened at the west end to serve as the Servants' Hall. At Cistercian Kirkstall Abbey excavation has revealed a variant type a few years later, a Common Hall flanked at either end with double storied accommodation blocks (Wrathmell 1987, 8–17). A similar structure is suggested at St. Albans, where the *Gesta Abbatum* records that Abbot Geoffrey (1119–46) constructed a "large and noble hall" with two roofs for guests. The forerunner of this

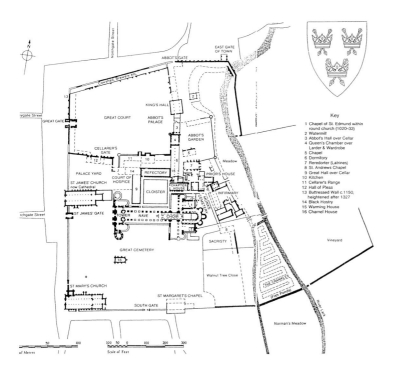

61 Bury St. Edmunds, plan (courtesy English Heritage).

The Palace Yard on the plan with access to the Guesthouse and the Hall of Pleas is the counterpart to the Cellarer's Court at Canterbury.

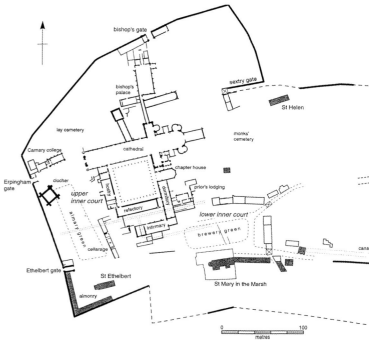

62 Norwich Cathedral, Cellarer's Court, plan (Gilchrist 2005, p. 42, fig. 7).

The Upper Inner Court on the plan with access to the Guesthouse is the counterpart to the Cellarer's Court at Canterbury.

type was Norwich's Hostry of ca. 1100, where it formed the west range of the cloister (Gilchrist 2005, 134–42).

At Canterbury the architecture, scale, and furnishings of the Pentice Gatehouse and Guesthouse set the Priory apart from other large Benedictine establishments. Furthermore, the Guesthouse included a number of distinctive features: a vaulted twin-aisled, ground-story hall, vaulted centralized Parlor, sculpted entry doorway, wraparound porch fronting the east and south elevations, and amenities such as heating, glazing, and running water. The most striking addition was undoubtedly the fully vaulted Parlor with its eastern and southern sides opened towards the fronting porch, although the novelty of this feature has not been recognized.

Turning to the purpose of the Parlor, earlier scholars have held divergent views. Willis called the building "a vestibule of considerable height" (Willis 1868, 134), and Sparks suggested it served as storage for carts used to transport the cellarer's stores (Sparks 2007, 26). Some clues come from its use under Archbishop Lanfranc. His *Constitutions* indicate that the guests' parlor in the west range served as the area where secular guests were

permitted contact with the monks. Such an encounter required the permission of the prior, who then instructed "the Guestmaster . . . to take the monk from the cloister to the guest house" (Knowles and Brooke 2002, 131).[21] All large monasteries provided two parlors within the cloister, the outer parlor for guests in the west range and the inner parlor in the east range for the community, the door to which is shown on *Drawing I* and identified in a *titulus*. By the mid-twelfth century other functions are mentioned for the outer parlor. They included liturgical and ceremonial roles, notably the *mandatum hospitum*.[22] Given particular prominence at the period, the rite exemplified service and humility and epitomized the Priory's response to strangers (*hospes*) modeled on Gospel precedents. As a principle of community life, the washing of visitors' feet was performed daily as opposed to the once-weekly *mandatum fratrum* for the community. Of the two rites the *Rule* of St. Benedict endowed the *mandatum hospitum* with the greater importance. Prior Wibert's incorporation of the rite into a new discrete space in the Parlor of the Guesthouse, however, constituted an important development. It should be seen

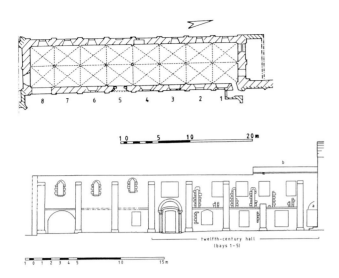

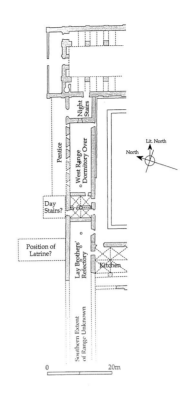

(Above) 63 Ely Cathedral, plan of Guesthouse (Holton-Krayenbuhl 1999, 128).

(Right) 64 Rievaulx Abbey, plan of west range (Fergusson and Harrison 1999, 52, fig. 18).

as part of the overall importance in the mid-twelfth century attached to ritual laving at the Priory. The Guesthouse was connected to the water system, as attested on documentary grounds (Grewe 1991a, 235), although a multipurpose use was likely.

Further ceremonial associated with the Parlor included the exchange of gifts between important visitors and the community. At Battle Abbey, mention is made of a visit by Bishop Hilary of Chichester shortly after his consecration in 1147. After preaching to the community in the Chapter House, Bishop Hilary proceeded to the Guesthouse, where the monks loaded him with gifts.[23] Further, the Guesthouse served as the setting for the formal welcome and greeting of guests, mention of which occurs in the Abingdon *De Obedientiariis* (Kerr 2007, 67), a ceremony doubtless centered in the Parlor. These would be persons of high social standing, although not the grandees lodged with the prior, who would have been introduced to the community in the Chapter House. Lanfranc's *Constitutions* as already mentioned specify the Parlor as the place where fugitive monks who wished to return to the community needed to wait before being summoned to the Chapter (Knowles and Brooke 2002, 153).

Several Benedictine houses retain the arrangement of outer parlors in west ranges. At Gloucester, ca. 1120, the outer parlor was located at the south end of the west

range; it was accessed down five steps from the cloister walk and reached from the outside by a doorway facing directly onto the inner court. The space was provided with a bench on the south side and covered by a barrel vault with transverse arches springing from carved capitals. At Norwich and Worcester the parlor was placed nearly identically but was larger with four bays and again barrel vaulted (Gilchrist 2005, 132–34). More convincing parallels for the adjacency of the two-story hall and the centralized vaulted structures at Canterbury come from the reform orders. At Rievaulx Abbey (North Yorkshire), a Cistercian foundation, the west range contained an early aisled hall (late 1130s) for the *conversii* along with an outer parlor adjacent to the church, an arrangement similar to Gloucester and Norwich. This was deemed inadequate around 1180, and a new multicell, rib-vaulted space was constructed in the middle of the range to serve as an upgraded space for the *conversii* to meet with relatives (fig. 64). Monastic architecture also provides examples in eastern ranges of the adjacency of a vaulted hall serving as day room and a vaulted central-plan structure serving as chapter house. Familiarity with these areas would have furnished Prior Wibert with the idea for the Priory's new parlor.

A further feature of the Guesthouse lay in its connection to the monks' Great Cloister. The existing doorway at the northern end of the west cloister walk may have served this purpose, although as an entry it was surprisingly modest. At St. Augustine's the doorway from the cloister into the west range (serving as the Guesthouse) was treated with some magnificence and received Purbeck marble shafts in the setbacks of the jambs.

Unexplained in the above is one of the most puzzling features of the Guesthouse: the porch running the length of the exterior and turned at right angles along the southern elevation.[24] To understand its purpose, it is necessary to return to another feature of the Cellarer's Court shown on *Drawing I*, the *Locutorium*. There it appears as an arcaded porch, north-facing, set against the back wall of the Refectory. If the hypothesis is accepted that the southern part of the Guesthouse served as the parlor (or *locutorium*), it is inconceivable that two such spaces were provided for the same purpose separated from one another by only a few feet and with the one depicted divorced from any related building. Furthermore, modern surveys show the Cellarer's Court as narrow and insufficient to accommodate a free-standing, two-sided *porticus*, facing inward into the courtyard and therefore interrupting the linkage of the Great Kitchen to the Refectory. For these reasons, doubt may be cast on *Drawing I*'s depiction of this feature. The doubt comes not from suspicion that the *Locutorium* was an invention of the artist, but because of our interpretation of it.

As seen, the fronting *porticus* extended along the side of the Pentice Gatehouse and was returned along the south end of the Guesthouse (see fig. 52). In depicting this feature the artist faced severe compositional problems. To show it in an "exploded" view (like the Great Cloister) would have meant that the *Locutorium* "collided" with the gate. The artist's solution, it may be suggested, was to displace the porch from the Guesthouse and place it on the opposite wall. In this reading, the main opening dividing the porch arcades corresponds to the Guesthouse's entry door (with its doubled tympanums projecting into the roof). The single arch added to the west end of the *porticus* related to the cellarer's buildings for the ebb and flow of supplies. The L-shape given to the *Locutorium* was a literal rendering of the wraparound porch which made a perpendicular turn around the end of the Guesthouse.

The disassembly of parts and their displacement from one side of the Cellarer's Court to the other calls into question the artist's overall intention for *Drawing I*. Were the *Locutorium* the sole example of this process of displacement, the argument would be speculative. However, as seen in Chapter 3, the artist employs the same process to mark other areas of the monastery. When faced with the need to show the confluence of architectural elements in the southeast corner of the Infirmary Cloister, or for the prior's gate, he rearranges the parts by disengaging them as the means to clarify them. Within the Cellarer's Court the *Locutorium* was not the sole example of the artist's use of this technique. To show the hatches on the east side of the Great Kitchen, he uses a similar process of rearrangement.

Consistent with this line of thinking outlined above, the artist lists for our inspection the parts of the *Domus Hospitum*. He shows the building double-storied with a lower southern feature, most likely the Parlor. Separately, he takes the wraparound porch and sets it against the north-facing wall of the Refectory, clarifying his license by labeling it *Locutorium*. He does the same in the south transept when faced with the crypt door appearing in the gable of the Water Tower. Again, it is necessary to remind ourselves that the intention of *Drawing I* was to present the parts rather than to show them as they looked, to render account of what was there more than to render appearance.

Seen together, the Guesthouse with its hall and parlor constituted one of the most striking buildings from Prior Wibert's program of reconstruction. Each relates to other buildings at the Priory. The Parlor shared with the Treasury (see Chapter 8) a similar square plan and employed four vault compartments which sprang from a central support. Changes to the Treasury in mid-campaign are reflected in the Parlor.[25] Similarities also link the Guesthouse to the *Aula Nova* (discussed in Chapter 6). Both joined separable functions into one building, were nine-bay structures, twin-story, twin-aisled, and fronted by an arcade. The architectural detailing of the Guesthouse is, however, clearly distinct from that of the *Aula Nova*, later in sequence, and bears comparison with the Norman Staircase and the Treasury. The use of more delicate forms, slimmer and more refined detailing, and more up-to-date vaulting can be understood not simply developmentally but as reflecting the different tastes and expectations of its users.

The Guesthouse and Parlor reveal with particular clearness the resourcefulness of Prior Wibert. They display his eye for models capable of adaptation to fulfill the architectural needs discrete to Canterbury. Grasping the way arrangements in monastic east ranges offered a model for the free-standing Guesthouse, and the way this could be elaborated and combined into a residence of elegance and distinction, may have had the effect less of meeting a need than of creating a demand. Was the popularity of the prior's Guesthouse the reason for the additional campaign of building undertaken almost at once and leading to the construction of the northern range extending from the Pentice Gate to the Larder Gate? Just as interesting was the addition of the Pentice Gatehouse. It affirmed an entry whose forms were intelligible to men of means with the room over the Gatehouse serving as a grand apartment.

6

THE GREEN COURT
AND THE PRIORY'S
JUDICIAL RESPONSIBILITY
AS A LIBERTY

The Green Court (fig. 66) remains Prior Wibert's most ambitious undertaking.[1] Even at a distance of 850 years it is possible to grasp the scale, range of services, and definition of the monastic and human environment which gave the area its identity. These qualities were captured by the artist of *Drawing I* (see fig. 3), who conveyed the spaciousness of the 3-acre open center with the surrounding buildings placed at ordered intervals around its periphery.[2] For the latter, the separations provided firebreaks for buildings prone to fire risk in the case of the Bakehouse, Brewhouse, and Bath House. Just as plausibly, their placement reflected the prior's concept of an ordered world of distinct responsibilities, a disposition referencing a regulated, rational, law-dominated world. To contemporaries the powerful effect of the Green Court was the consequence of conscious contrast. Everything about the ambiance reflected St. Augustine's

notion of the monastery as a *civitas Dei*. As such, the Green Court represented the antithesis of the urban counterpart, the *civitas terrena*, with its compressed residences, erratic streets, clamorous markets, and odoriferous open-drainage channels.

The development of the Green Court required the coordination of many elements of architecture: land acquisition, programming, planning, circulation, water supply, sewer and drainage infrastructure, design, and construction. A precise count of the new buildings attributable to Wibert lies in future archaeology, but it is likely they totaled eleven, or more if the Almonry and Chapel, a particular pride of his and lying immediately outside the Gatehouse, are included (fig. 67). Of these, the Green Court Gatehouse and the *Aula Nova*, the Bath House, and the Pentice Gatehouse (the entry to the Guesthouse – see Chapter 5) are sufficiently known to

65   Canterbury Cathedral Priory, Norman Staircase
(photograph author).

66   Canterbury Cathedral Priory, Green Court, view of buildings forming the north side (courtesy Stuart Harrison).

From left to right: the Green Court Gatehouse, *Aula Nova*, Bakehouse, Brewhouse, and Granary. On the right is the fourteenth-century Forrens Gate leading to the Stables. All these buildings have been remodeled for the King's School.

allow discussion. Of the other seven or eight buildings, the remains amenable to identification suggest origins with Wibert.

Much of this chapter focuses on the Green Court Gatehouse and the Bath House. Both are of exceptional interest for the monastic historian. The Gatehouse and the related buildings formed an entry complex, the earliest known in England whose forms were conditioned by one of the fundamental intellectual achievements of the mid-twelfth century and the entire Middle Ages: the revival of Roman-based law and the emergence of canon law. Similar interest surrounds the Bath House, which provides clues to the culture of health and hygiene important to Prior Wibert and enriches our understanding of monastic life and culture in the mid-twelfth century.

As seen today the Green Court carries forward the old monastic tradition of education in the guise of the King's School. From thirty scholars at the time of the suppression in 1540, the school has expanded over the past 450 years, and particularly in the last 150, to the present 800 students, nearly all of whom are housed within the domain of the medieval Precinct (fig. 68). But the school's realm is distinctly separate from that of the Cathedral. A visitor wandering into the Green

Court today has to contend with a sense of trespass, and confronts an emphatic disconnection of place and purpose. Reconstructing the mid-twelfth-century's inter-dependence of court to convent and of convent to cathedral requires analysis and background knowledge. Only with this effort is it possible to grasp the range of functions and architectural forms provided by the Green Court, and to see the achievement of the prior in realizing them.

Although secured within the walls of the Precinct, the Green Court served quasi-public or business needs in contrast to the strict enclosure of the monks. It was here that the Priory interacted with the world on its own terms, providing hospitality, legal process, stabling, food and beverage production, and the restorative qualities of the new water system. To dispense or to benefit from these services, a wide range of medieval society passed through the Priory's Gatehouse: pilgrims, guests of every social degree, clergy and religious, petitioners, plaintiffs, defendants, clerks, notaries, corrodians, commercial suppliers and tradesmen, grooms and horses, mariners, and cooks. Such visitors needed to deal with the Green Court's five nodes of entry and circulation and to interact there with the full hierarchy of monks, monastic officials, porters, gatekeepers, and servants. For

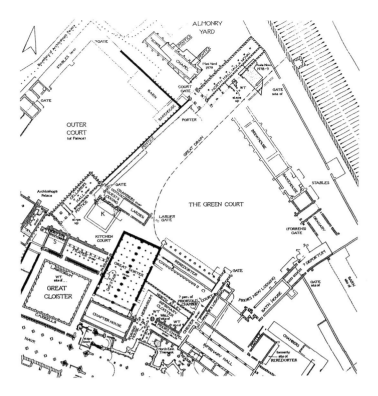

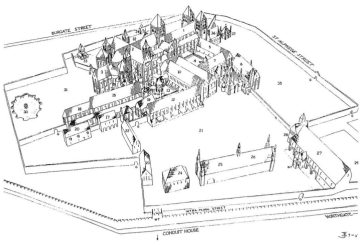

(Left) 67 Canterbury Cathedral Priory, Green Court, plan (courtesy Canterbury Archaeological Trust).

(Above) 68 Canterbury Cathedral Priory, Green Court, reconstruction drawing by Jill Atherton showing ca. 1160 condition (courtesy Canterbury Archaeological Trust).

the last, Knowles's estimate of the ratio of servants to monks of approximately 1 : 1 would mean about 120 to 130 of each (Knowles 1963, 439–41). To think of the servants as distributed throughout the Convent is misleading. They were clustered with the major monastic officeholders, such as the fifty-one servants of the sacrist noted at the end of the twelfth century (Urry 1967, 157–61) or the more than forty who served the prior (Smith 1943, 199).

The realization that the Priory's needs required additional land was long-standing. In the early 1100s Archbishop Anselm had purchased land to the east of the Cathedral for the community's burial ground and infirmary as part of his near doubling of the size of the church. Wibert's expansion was more ambitious and focused on the Precinct's northern, eastern, and southern boundaries. Important developments drove the process. The Priory's offering of hospitality required more separated areas, and to provide for them Wibert constructed the Guesthouse, the *Aula Nova* (with the Common Hall and the Servants' Hall), and the Bath House, all either accessed from or contained within the Green Court. For the administration of the new jurisprudence, discrete buildings were constructed as part of the entry complex to the Precinct. They included the Gatehouse, Tower, Court Hall, Prison, Norman Staircase, and Fountain House. For fresh running water

and the disposal of waste, Wibert installed the piped pressurized water system throughout the Precinct, an innovation marveled at by his contemporaries. And last and by no means least, the principal entry to the monastery called for a dignified and ennobled space, one which displayed as frame and backdrop the full length and magnificence of Lanfranc's and Anselm's huge Cathedral, a quality powerfully conveyed in *Drawing I.*

The Green Court renewal was not developed in a vacuum.[3] The layout drew on knowledge of the inner courts at other Benedictine cathedral monasteries in England. Known in all likelihood to Wibert at first hand, they included the Palace Green at Durham (ca. 1105), the Upper Inner Court at Norwich (ca. 1110) (see fig. 62), and the Great Court at Bury St. Edmunds (mid-1120s forward) (see fig. 61).[4] Bury St. Edmunds seems to have made particular impression on Wibert. A number of ideas for the Green Court and the Cellarer's Court reflect those of the Suffolk abbey.

The first sign of the prior's intention to develop the entry complex comes from land acquisitions. These included the purchase of a number of domestic properties on the Precinct's northern edge. Detailed in the Priory's Rental Rolls, the documentary entries, dry as they seem, speak to the straitened physical circumstances in which the Priory believed itself constrained and the means it saw to escape from them. The earliest,

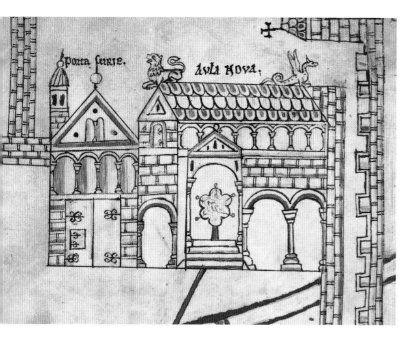

69 Eadwine Psalter, *Drawing I*, detail showing the entry complex, Trinity College, Cambridge (courtesy the Master and Fellows, Trinity College, Cambridge).

From left to right: Green Court Gatehouse, *Aula Nova*, and Norman Staircase.

Rental A (Rental 87 in the cathedral archives), compiled between 1153 and 1165, lists forty-four properties acquired in the city by the prior, most by purchase, including those subsequently absorbed into the Green Court (Urry 1959, 583; Urry 1967, 221–25). The process began when Wibert was sub-prior. Over time, domestic residences had come to fill the area to the north between the old Roman city walls and Lanfranc's priory boundary wall. Wibert bought out the owners, who were relocated a short distance to the northwest, razed their dwellings (lessening the risk of fire spreading from them to the priory buildings), and absorbed the land into the Precinct. The enlarged area accommodated the new entry complex, provided for the entry and exit of the piped water system and sewer infrastructure installed by Wibert, created space for the Priory's expanded need for stables to accommodate its own horses and those of its growing number of visitors (Urry 1967, 204–6), and provided land for the construction of the Mint Yard, Almonry, and Almonry Chapel immediately outside the Green Court Gatehouse to serve the city's poor. The process entailed the construction of a new lane – Queningate Lane – and a new precinct wall.[5]

THE ENTRY COMPLEX

The buildings forming the entry complex are usually discussed as unrelated. In the following pages I want to make the case that they need to be seen as united by function and planned together to serve the legal needs of the Priory. Seeing them thus is justified by their representation in the contemporary drawing in the Eadwine Psalter, where the artist shows the Priory's entry as a complex of several buildings without any separation between them or preference given to one building over another (fig. 69). Faced with the difficult challenge of compressing the buildings which made up the entry complex into the small area of the page available to him, the artist adopts several short cuts. The *Aula Nova* posed the biggest problem. A large building just under 160 feet in length, it stood on a north–south axis on the newly acquired land. To fit it within the limited space at his disposal, the artist shortens the building from nine to three bays and draws only its most important part, the prior's Court Hall. At the same time he rearranges some components, notably the ceremonial Norman Staircase to the Court Hall, which he places proudly in the center of the new buildings (rather than at the northern end).

At Canterbury the construction of the entry buildings was put in hand to meet the Priory's responsibilities for law and finance encoded in the august title of the "Liberty of Christ Church" (Smith 1943, 83–99). Monastic Liberties had come into being in the early eleventh century, but their powers were strengthened and expanded by the new king, Henry II. He saw them as a means of eroding the power of proliferating local lordships and as the first steps in the establishment of a more uniform system of legal administration (Bisson 2009, 269–78). Monastic Liberties acted in effect as indirect agents of the king. Liberties enjoyed judicial independence from shire and hundred courts, as also did their free tenants. To carry out the responsibilities of the Liberty, the prior was granted immunity from knight or military service (Smith 1943, 83).

A number of major monasteries were classed as Liberties. In the southeast of England they included Bury St. Edmunds, St. Albans, the Isle of Ely, Ramsey, Peterborough, Battle, Westminster, and within Canterbury the abbey of St. Augustine as well as the Priory (Cam 1944, 184–204). Free tenants living within the bounds of the Liberty were subject to the prior's justice and as plaintiffs or defendants were brought to Canterbury for trial and judgment (Smith 1943, 87). For the Priory, the largest Benedictine foundation in England in the 1150s, the importance of the Liberty lay in the extent of its lands, which were spread across eight counties in the south and east of England. They incorporated fifty-five manors, the ownership of between a third and a half of the domestic property in the city of Canterbury, control of the ports of Dover and Sandwich, and scattered properties in London, Southwark, Devonshire, and Ireland (Sparks 1995, 566–70). To convey a sense of the powers of the Liberty, it is useful to bear in mind that the prior's court had its own pillories, tumbrils, and gallows.[6]

The prior's decision to locate the buildings dealing with the legal administration of the Liberty at the furthest remove from the cloister on the outer margins of the Precinct at the Green Court Gatehouse was partly determined by practical reasons. In this position the risks of secular intrusion – represented by the world of plaintiffs, bailiffs, defendants, notary clerks, lawyers, relatives, and kinsfolk of those called before the prior's court – were reduced. More important, however, this location dovetailed with biblical precedent. The association of the gate with justice recalled ancient practice in Judaism, Christianity, and Islam. In the Hebrew scriptures, judicial business was conducted at the gate of the city. Numerous examples could be cited, but four allow for illustration. In Ruth 4:11, Boaz goes to the gate and sits with ten elders of the city to negotiate the purchase of land, a transaction witnessed by "all the people there at the gate"; in Amos 5:15 the Lord enjoins Israel "to establish justice in the Gate"; in Deuteronomy 21:19 parents take their recalcitrant son for judgment "to the elders at the gate of the town"; and in Zechariah 8:16 the prophet has the Lord commanding the people to "render in your gates judgments that are true." Such communal jurisdictions, in effect popular courts, were carried out by the city elders. For complex legal issues, judgments were delegated to the priests. In Jerusalem, a court of priests, the Levites, was established by King Josephat to act as a court of first instances for the inhabitants of the city (2 Chronicles 19:8–11) and as a court of appeal for cases referred from other towns. For the same purpose King Solomon later constructed several buildings at the Temple complex. They included the judgment hall, the Hall of Pillars, a structure 50 cubits long and 30 wide, fronted by a canopied porch with pillars (1 Kings 7:6).

An understanding of the Priory's entry buildings needs to start with the Green Court Gatehouse and then to turn to related buildings composing the overall complex.

Green Court Gatehouse

A visitor approaching the Priory from the city of Canterbury traversed a lane which led past the Mint Yard and Almonry and faced the Green Court Gatehouse, or Magna Porta to give its Latin name (fig. 70). Like all gatehouses, it secured entry to the Precinct.[7] Designed to impress and to convey a muscular presence, the façade was dominated by the wide, high entry arch, topped by two stories with crenellations at the roof line, and flanked by an imposing four- or five-story tower, of which only the lowest story survives (fig. 71).

The entry arch carried twin-roll archivolts with human and animal reliefs supported by imposing *en délit* colonettes (the bases obscured by the rise of the ground level). Tall-profiled blind arches on slender coursed-in colonettes flank the entry arch and are decorated with chevron. In the spandrels sunken roundels enclose crosses, symbols signifying the Priory's name and alluding to city gates.[8] The clustering of columns, arches, and light-catching moldings assembled an array of three-dimensional motifs to ennoble the outward-facing entry to the Priory, to anchor the imposing volume of the spanning arch, and to declare to all who passed through the Green Court Gatehouse a clear message of authority, power, and privileged responsibility (fig. 72).

The Gatehouse enclosed a 36-foot-long interior gate-hall or passage (fig. 73). This provided for the admission of inbound visitors on foot and horseback and allowed for the monitoring of outbound traffic. Doorways opened from the passage to lateral chambers. On the south side, the inner chamber contained the original porter's lodge, while the outer chamber afforded access to the pentice leading to the Guesthouse. Opposite, a single door led to spaces within the undercroft of the *Aula Nova*, probably those used as a prison for defendants required to appear in the courtroom overhead (see below). The office of porter in a large institution like the Priory was prestigious and valuable. A papal letter of ca. 1187 describes the Priory's two doorkeepers as *seruientes*, thereby indicating lay status. As a mark of their importance, appointment to the office was normally made by the archbishop and even on occasion during a vacancy by the king (Kerr 2007, 71, 79).

Establishing the original disposition of the Green Court Gatehouse is complicated by the extensive modifications undertaken by Prior Chillenden in 1393–94.[9] The Eadwine Psalter drawing shows a pair of heavy doors under a lintel, a second story with round-headed windows, and an attic story with twin round-headed

70   Canterbury Cathedral Priory, Green Court Gatehouse from the west (photograph author).

71   Canterbury Cathedral Priory, Green Court Gatehouse, west façade and remains of the adjacent Tower (photograph author).

72   Canterbury Cathedral Priory, digital reconstruction model showing the entry complex from the west (courtesy Stuart Harrison).

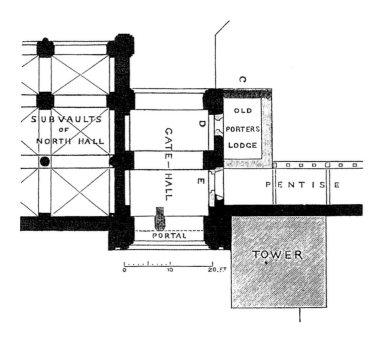

windows. In contrast, the present building shows that Chillenden reduced the height from three stories to two, lowered the roof pitch, reorganized the window composition to reflect Perpendicular tastes, and inserted Perpendicular doorways under the western arch, the smaller for pedestrians, the larger for wheeled vehicles (a modification repeated under the east-facing arch by George Austin in his restoration of 1843–84). Chillenden's new doorways required the removal of the mid-twelfth-century rebates against which the doors closed and, probably, the moldings attached to them. Their existence is hinted at by the chopped back impost and scarred intrados (fig. 74A) and can be compared to a contemporary gatehouse at Peterborough Cathedral (fig. 74B) where the main arch moldings remain intact. In their place, Chillenden's masons constructed a wall of untidy coursed masonry, a jarring contrast to the precise mid-twelfth-century ashlar construction, although it was doubtless plastered and painted with false jointing. Fortunately, Chillenden left the two extrados moldings of

73   Canterbury Cathedral Priory, Green Court Gatehouse, plan (Willis 1868, 144, fig. 31).

74A   Canterbury Cathedral Priory, Green Court Gatehouse, interior passageway, arch intrados (photograph author).

74B   Peterborough Cathedral, Gatehouse, interior passageway, arch intrados (photograph author).

the mid-twelfth century, which retain their relief carvings (see below).

A clue to the building's original use comes from the access to the space over the Gatehouse's entry passage. It could not be reached from the ground. Entry to the space came one story higher from the adjacent Court Hall (in the *Aula Nova*), a feature that indicates functions related to the Court Hall such as the storage of legal documents and the provision of working space for the notary clerks.

Chillenden's and later changes to the Gatehouse have had the effect of lessening its presence. Diminished in height, shorn of its adjacent tower, deprived of the drama of the imposing arched entrance, the Green Court Gatehouse lacks the powerful accents of the original. Their recovery is essential in order to grasp its intended message of authority and to make intelligible its references and associations. A first step is to survey the structures that formed the entry complex. Based on this the sources of the architecture can be sought. Second, the sculpture of the archivolts surrounding the twelfth-century entry arch will be examined. They complement the purposes of the building in which they are set and help in an understanding of its intended meaning.

Tower

The adjacent flanking Tower can be glimpsed in *Drawing I*. Since the artist's viewpoint was from inside the Priory, he shows the Gatehouse from the east with the Tower's upper stages tucked behind, rising above the roof. This viewpoint diminishes the Tower's intended purpose, which was related to its exterior placement. Once four or five stories high and constructed in flint with stone dressings, it was an imposing structure, as a glance at the plan and model confirms (see figs. 72 and 73).

Towers in general were a universally recognized feature of defense and, just as important, an accepted marker of power and authority. Both justified its use at the entry to the Priory. It was also a recognized symbol of Solomon based on the tower of the Temple in Jerusalem (1 Kings 6). Finally, the Tower's tolling bell signified the gathering of the court in the Court Hall of the prior in the *Aula Nova* (see below).

The Green Court Tower survived until the eighteenth century, when it was reduced to a single story. As such, essentially dismantled, it survived as a stump. Attempts to disguise it followed, including topping it with a gable (fig. 75). Later, efforts to make what remained appear continuous with surrounding structures, to melt the

75   Job Bulman, *Green Court Gatehouse*, ca. 1776, watercolor (Canterbury Cathedral Archives, Add. MS 45, no. 32).

The tower flanking the Gatehouse is disguised by a sloping roof.

Tower's identity into the surrounding townscape, have had the effect of concealing this important feature of the entry complex.

Prison

Every court in a Liberty required a prison or holding chamber for those awaiting trial. They are recorded at many sites including Westminster Abbey, St. Mary's York, the Archbishop's Palace at York Minster, and the Priory (Pugh 1970, 136–37). At Canterbury, the jail occupied the undercroft below the Court Hall, probably set back to correspond to the hall above, thereby leaving the arcade open. During the rule of Archbishop Hubert Walter (1193–1205), so many prisoners were held in "the gaol of the Prior near the gate of the *curia*" that some had to be accommodated in the stone chamber next to the Granary (*camera lapidea ante granarium*) (Smith, 1943, 96). To deal with the prisoners, the Priory created the office of jailor to assist the *custos curie*.

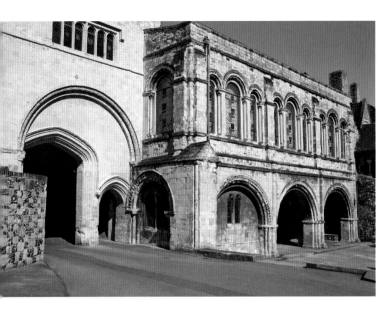

76 Canterbury Cathedral Priory, *Aula Nova*, south end, and east elevation (photograph author).

Aula Nova

The *Aula Nova* was by far the largest and most elaborate of Prior Wibert's entry buildings. Construction started soon after the completion of the Gatehouse; the south end of the *Aula Nova* butts awkwardly across its eastern arch (fig. 76), a miscalculation unimaginable were the building to have been constructed from south to north. With an exterior length of 154 feet and an interior with a broad, twin-aisled hall above an undercroft, the building measured 35 feet across, including a 9-foot-wide aisle for circulation on the eastern side (fig. 77). These dimensions compare with those of the Guesthouse in the Cellarer's Court (see Chapter 5) and the Infirmary Hall (see Chapter 7).

Drawing I (see fig. 69) shows the *Aula Nova* as a two-story building resting on an open arcade, three bays in length, facing inward to the Green Court, its gable end wall at right angles to the Gatehouse and lit by a single opening closed by wooden shutters. The artist gives prominence to the Court Hall's entry, the Norman Staircase, which is depicted in the center of the buildings lying to the north of the Gatehouse. At the top of the steps leading from the court, he draws a fountain and laver with five spigots. The Court Hall's upper story is lit with a continuous band of arcaded windows. Care is taken to depict materials; ashlar blocks are emphasized, as also are roof tiles. The artist exaggerates the finials on the

ridge terminals, showing a lion on the south, a dragon on the north. As with other parts of the drawing, some details are reasonably accurate, while others display the artist's loose concerns with scale and his penchant for rearranging parts. Thus, the *Aula Nova* as built was three times larger than as drawn and extended northwards from the Gatehouse for a total length of nine bays.

The undercroft of the *Aula Nova* needs some reconstruction. Evidence remaining in the King's School Memorial Chapel (created in 1935 to honor the many boys killed in the Great War) and in the Armory located in the adjacent Galpin's House (of the school) shows that the undercroft was groin vaulted with the supporting piers resting on square sub-bases with leaf spurs. The capitals were scalloped (one survives in the Memorial Chapel, a second in the Armory, and a third in bay two). The east-facing arcade on the ground level carries three orders of moldings, the outer a chamfered hood molding, the middle a forward-facing chevron, the inner a single roll set against a square-edged soffit (fig. 65). The arches rest on piers with indented corner angle shafts with molded bases and foliate capitals. On the front of each pier, single, coursed rounded shafts stand on molded bases and rise to a double stringcourse where they terminate with an odd bell-shaped top, an Austin addition.

Austin's 1853 upper story is noticeably stepped back (fig. 79), and pilasters separate the bays rather than the shafts used below. The Court Hall over the undercroft is harder to envision. The 36-foot width of the building was undivided and covered by a timber roof (figs. 77 and 78). On the east side a 9-foot-wide corridor provided circulation. It was groin vaulted and supported on the hall side on simple, squared piers resting on chamfered bases (as can be seen in the Memorial Chapel). The only surviving pier from the upper story carried a single chamfered order and is found at the top of the Norman Staircase on the outside (southeast corner) of Galpin's House (Willis 1868, 146, n. 2; fig. 80). It must relate to an unrecorded reconstruction of the upper story, one most likely connected to the 1239 redesign of the windows which replaced Wibert's round-headed windows (Willis 1868, 147; Hussey 1881, 6). A valuable eyewitness description before the demolition of the northern bays in the 1730s comes from the antiquarian William Gostling, who described the interior as "a very large and lofty room, much like some of our parish churches, having one third of its breadth parted by pillars and arches of stone (like a side aisle) which were continued for the length of the whole building, and are to be seen in what remains of it" (Gostling 1774,

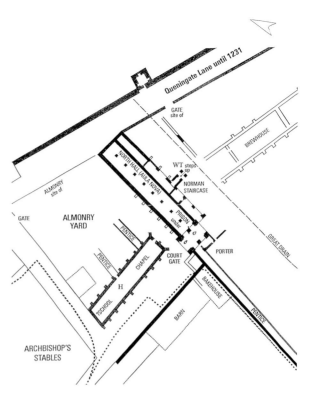

77 Canterbury Cathedral Priory, *Aula Nova*, digital reconstruction model of interior, section (courtesy Stuart Harrison).

78 Canterbury Cathedral Priory, *Aula Nova*, plan (courtesy Canterbury Archaeological Trust).

167). In consequence, the building would have been covered by an asymmetrical roof, the eastern slope with two pitches to cover the aisle as well as half the main Court Hall.

To follow the *Aula Nova*'s history in medieval and post-suppression times, the building's three distinct purposes need to be recalled. The southern three bays provided for the prior's court and included one additional bay for the ceremonial entry stair, the Norman Staircase. Bays five, six, and seven comprised the Common Hall for the pilgrims and visitors who arrived on foot, and bays eight and nine accommodated the Servants' Hall for cooks, grooms, and servants of the Priory's upper class of visitors. These functions changed relatively little throughout the Middle Ages. At the suppression, however, the Distribution Document of 1546 refers to both halls under the generic title "Hogg Hall," namely "high hall" (Somner 1640, 111). By 1730 they were deemed redundant. Demolition of bays seven, eight, and nine was put in hand and witnessed by Gostling from his house in Mint Yard adjacent to the *Aula Nova* (Gostling 1774, 170).[10] The adjoining bays – five and six – were left heavily ruined.

The prior's court continued to provide residual legal functions as the registrar's office into the early nineteenth century, as also did the jail in the undercroft (Sparks 2007, 176). In 1790 Thomas Rowlandson's lithograph of the Norman Staircase contained a caption which identified those shown sheltering within it or sprawled over the courtyard in front as French prisoners. Such functions safeguarded the medieval building. Change came in the 1820s when both the registry and prison were moved to a more central location within the city of Canterbury. Shortly after, the Dean and Chapter decided to remove the entire superstructure of the *Aula Nova*, leaving only the undercroft intact. Drawings and prints show it thus, as do early photographs from the 1840s (fig. 81).

Discussion of how to use what remained of the *Aula Nova* occupied the Dean and Chapter in the mid-1840s (Sparks 2007, 177–78). The King's School asked for the construction of a new house, Galpin's, to be located over its former northern bays. The work was given to George Austin, who was surveyor and architect to the Cathedral. In 1843 he had restored the Green Court Gatehouse with relative restraint, but the following

(Left) 79   Canterbury Cathedral Priory, *Aula Nova*, stepped-back upper story (photograph author).

(Above) 80   Canterbury Cathedral Priory, *Aula Nova* and Galpin's House, view from the north (detail), lithograph by W. A. Bone, 1865 (courtesy King's School Library).

(Below left) 81   Canterbury Cathedral Priory, *Aula Nova*, photograph by C. R. Jones, 1843, showing condition prior to the 1853 addition of the upper story (© Victoria and Albert Museum, 1937–3089).

(Below) 82   George Austin's design for the *Aula Nova* from the Austins' *Sketchbooks*, n.d., unpaginated (Canterbury Cathedral Archives and Library, © Dean and Chapter).

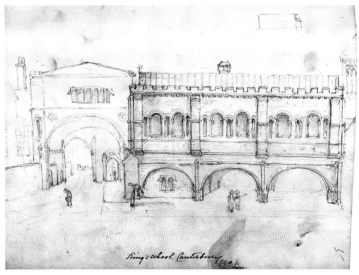

83   Canterbury Cathedral Priory, digital reconstruction model showing the entry complex from the east (courtesy Stuart Harrison).

year his cavalier rebuilding of the northwest tower of the Cathedral in a subdued Gothic style drew heavy antiquarian protests. For the *Aula Nova*, the Austins' *Sketchbooks* show the search for a satisfactory design for the new upper story.[11] George Austin opted for an elevation in a Romanesque style divided into clearly articulated bays. For the window composition of the upper floor, Austin spurned the early Gothic windows and sketched different variations (fig. 82). He favored the construction of a tower over the new north-facing gable (visible at the extreme right). Funding difficulties intervened. By the time the project was revived, George Austin had died (in 1848) and his position had been taken by his son, H. G. Austin. In 1852 the Dean and Chapter instructed him to develop a design "in a Romanesque style . . . [to fit] over the Norman arches" (Sparks 2007, 178). Passing over his father's ideas, H. G. Austin devised a design with triple openings, one large window flanked by smaller ones, the motif copied from the Treasury (see figs. 76 and 124). The new work was distinguished from the medieval by the unusual device of setting back the elevation (fig. 79).

The new house for the King's School, Galpin's, built over the former bays five, six, seven, eight, and nine, adopted a two-part design. For the bays adjacent to the prior's Court Hall, Austin produced a Romanesque design; for the rest of the building he opted for Gothic forms (fig. 80).[12] To provide entry to the former Court Hall, Austin designed a new north-facing gable wall

entered through a faux Romanesque doorway.[13] The doorway's detailing copied that on the western arch of the Norman Staircase.[14] For architectural detailing on the building's exterior, Austin based his design on the Treasury. The *Sketchbooks* show his grandson, Frederick, measuring and copying details of the Treasury in drawings dated August and September of 1853 (see fig. 128).

When the southernmost bay of the *Aula Nova*'s undercroft was turned into the school's Memorial Chapel after World War I, the adjacent bays two and three were formed into an open-sided undercroft continuous with the memorial courtyard lying immediately to the east. Above, in the reconstructed upper story, an undivided space serves as the music practice room for the school. A limited excavation undertaken by the Canterbury Archaeological Trust in 1978 at the north end of Galpin's revealed that the medieval northern bays were raised on a continuous wall and lacked the arcade of the southern bays.

Norman Staircase

Connected to the *Aula Nova* on the Court Hall's eastern side, the Norman Staircase survives largely intact (figs. 83–86 and see fig. 65). It is the most remarkable such structure in Romanesque England. Its elaborate decoration and use of semi-precious materials, the provision of an entry fountain, the canopy given to its parts, and, most important, its relation to the Court Hall with the

(Above) 84 Canterbury Cathedral Priory, *Aula Nova*, Norman Staircase with Galpin's House behind, seen from the south (photograph author).

(Right) 85 Canterbury Cathedral Priory, Norman Staircase (photograph author).

latter's intended associations and meanings reflect its ceremonial character. Although the Norman Staircase forms part of the *Aula Nova*, the robust and forceful architecture of that building was not deemed appropriate. Instead, an architecture notable for its delicacy, use of small-scale forms, and display of polished materials was chosen.

The Norman Staircase is formed of two parts, both reached by flights of steps.[15] From the courtyard, four steps (as in *Drawing I*) lead to a landing covered by an aedicule supported on stout columns with prominent abaci. Both look overscaled for the slender arches they carry. Scalloped capitals support arcades with an outer order of carved chevron, and an inner order with triple rolls separated by a small angle fillet. The aedicule's western columns are backed by ashlar, but then for no obvious reason the wall gives over to flint rubble

construction. The second stage consists of a covered staircase (fig. 85) whose sides are lit by five small arches with uniform-height arch heads but stepped up bases as the staircase ascends, supported on semi-precious shafts of Purbeck, Tournai, and onyx marble (Kahn 1991, 105). Some bases have delicate bands of chevron or drilled roundels on their scotias. Moldings display fulsome chevron with petaled flowers separating them (fig. 86A). Capitals are scalloped with beaded heads and sides (fig. 86B) and, at the top of the stair, waterleaf archivolts display three-petaled or split-palmette flowers. A surmounting hood molding is carved with a loose chevron.

In *Drawing I* the Norman Staircase is positioned in the center of the entry complex, the unusual prominence signifying the structure's novelty and importance. The artist also shows a fountain placed under the

86A Canterbury Cathedral Priory, Norman Staircase, interior arch (photograph author).

86B Canterbury Cathedral Priory, Norman Staircase, capitals and arcade of staircase, south side (photograph author).

aedicule on the landing platform. In 1978 during a repair and renovation of the roof over the Staircase, Tatton-Brown saw a channel worked in the superstructure of the aedicule, evidence for a cistern to ensure water pressure for the fountain, and in 1993–4 emergency repairs on the staircase's northern side revealed a drainage channel.[16] Even with this evidence the location of the fountain remains problematic. The landing platform measures only 3 feet by 3 feet. Even a small laver would have largely blocked entry, and *Drawing I* indicates a sizable one since five spigots are shown. Was the fountain placed possibly at the top of the Norman Staircase, or at ground level in the court, or located at the rear of the first platform?

The composition of the Staircase used two distinct forms: an aedicule (ciborium) and a staircase. The forms provide a clue to the prototype on which it was based. The same purpose of entry and court hall is described in the Bible for the judgment hall of King Solomon in the Temple complex. The building was entered through the *porticum columnarum* (1 Kings 7:6). The text describes the Hall of Pillars where Solomon pronounced judgment as fronted by "a porch . . . with pillars" with "a canopy in front of them" (v. 6). It was also adorned with "costly stones" (v. 9), and the carved ornament included split-palmette, three-petaled foliage, and lily work (v. 19). At Canterbury the sculptors' choice of these motifs has the quality of quotation (see below). It may also be added that the roof ridge shown on *Drawing*

I features a lion, an old symbol of justice connected, not least, with the throne used by Solomon.[17] Such biblical prototypes would have been ever present to the monks as they heard the texts in choir and studied them in their daily two-hour *lectio divina*. It is also possible that the stimulus depended on first-hand experience of the *loca sancta* in Jerusalem resulting from the Second Crusade in the late 1140s. At Canterbury at least one of the Dionisii (the guild of votaries of Anselm), Vivian of With, is mentioned as among those who had made the journey to the Holy Land. His name provides a means of connecting local knowledge with the far-distant *loca sancta* in Jerusalem (Urry 1959, 581).

Aula Nova Context

Court functions at Canterbury have a long history. Before the Norman Conquest ecclesiastical courts were connected to the Cathedral. Eadmer describes the Baptistery of Archbishop Cuthbert (741–59) as serving for "judicial trials of various sorts . . . intended to correct wrongdoing," but then adds that the trials were "normally held in the church" (Wharton 1691, vol. II, 186). Eadmer also mentions that the "Suthdoor" of the Cathedral, represented at large scale on the Priory's First Seal, was the site of ecclesiastical courts "from time immemorial" (Willis 1845, 11; Heslop 1982, 97) Unfortunately, nothing is known of Archbishop Lanfranc's arrangements. They presumably followed continental tradition;

before leaving Italy to take up the abbacy of Bec in 1037, Lanfranc enjoyed a distinguished career in the judiciary in Pavia during the years when the dramatic developments in the law were beginning in Italy. From the twelfth century forward, ecclesiastical cases continued in the Cathedral and were held under the northwest tower (Rady, Tatton-Brown, and Bowen 1991, 4).

In contrast to ecclesiastical courts, the Priory's legal proceedings in the mid-twelfth century required the use of three separate courts. The sacrist's court dealt with gifts and income to the Cathedral's altars, the repairs and fabric of the church (and thus of the masons' yard and the plumbers' yard, the glaziers' and the carpenters' shops), the provision of candles, vestments, and the administration of the cemeteries. It convened under the great campanile on the south side of the Cathedral (Smith 1943, 68–82) (see figs. 5, 6, 8 and 146). The cellarer's court adjudicated matters arising from the provisioning and accommodation for the community and visitors and for the building for them, as well as for the Infirmary. It met at the doorway of the Brewhouse on the north side of the Green Court (Urry 1967, 23ff.). The prior's court handled cases concerning the Liberty and met in the upper hall of the *Aula Nova*. It was by far the most important of the three courts and the only one to have its own building. At first it was presided over by the prior, but around 1200 he deputed this responsibility to a trained jurist, who was given the title of "Steward of the Liberty of Christ Church."[18] The court assembled for business every three weeks (Smith 1943, 90–92). Clerks and officials supplied help and record keeping. The status of the Court Hall in the thirteenth century may be glimpsed from a reference in 1238 or 1239 to "the great hall by the Gate." Another, during the archepiscopal vacancy of 1270–73, refers to it as the "aula juxta portam prioratus ecclesie Christi pro tribunali sedente" (Donahue and Adams 1981, 16, n. 5), and again in 1290 as "the great hall next to the Court Gate" when its repair was listed among the work carried out by Prior Eastry.

Similar courts for monastic or cathedral Liberties are recorded in other urban centers. In York, at St. Mary's Abbey, Richard I granted a legal jurisdiction comparable to that exercised by the archbishop at his palace by the minster. A timber-frame building housed the courtroom, which functioned as such until 1722 (Wilson and Burton 1988, 12). A royal mandate issued in 1301 gave to the justices of the court at St. Mary's the right to hold sessions for assizes relating to the abbey's Liberty "infra portam abacie predicte," adding "as had customarily been done in the past" (ibid.).

The buildings forming the entry complex to the Priory – Gatehouse, Tower, Court Hall, Prison, Norman Staircase, Fountain House – constitute the earliest known in England for the administration of law in a monastic Liberty. They mark the revival of Roman civil law and the emergence of canon law.[19] The revival of Roman civil law had begun in the 1070s in Lombardy with the rediscovery in Pisa of a copy of Justinian's *Digesta seu Pandectae*. Combined with his *Codex* and *Novellae*, the three volumes underpinned the discipline of jurisprudence within a few generations (Kuttner 1982, 299–323; Radding 1988, 92–93). The establishment of canon law in the mid-twelfth century formed a parallel discipline and was centered in the law school in Bologna in its earliest years.

Sources

An architecture for the administration of the law involved assimilating elements necessary for its operation and then subjecting them to a design process. Monastic Liberties in England as an architectural type await study. On the available evidence, however, a case can be argued that the Canterbury entry complex combined English elements for the hall and undercroft accented with features drawn from committal halls in France and episcopal halls in Italy. Such a process of adaptation suggests that monastic Liberties developed an architecture of the law separate from royal court halls and castle courtrooms where the king's justice was dispensed, such as Westminster Hall in the Palace of Whitehall or the Tower of London.[20] Canterbury's entry complex was copied at Peterborough within a few years. The gatehouse and parts of the prison survive, and the court hall is documented at the end of the twelfth century.[21] Much later examples survive at Lambeth Palace, in Morton's Tower, and at Hexham (Northumberland) in the Moot Hall of the archbishop of York, whose titles included "Lord of the Liberty and Regality of Hexham" (Ryder 1994, 194).[22] At Hexham the components assembled at Canterbury 200 years earlier are incorporated into the Moot Hall's entry complex – entry gate, tower, court hall, external stair, prison – albeit in a more compact design (fig. 87). Interestingly, the Moot Hall is some years earlier than Chillenden's changes and updating of the Green Court Gatehouse, and it shares some of the same features.

The Canterbury complex may be linked to similar complexes in France and Italy in the mid-twelfth century. Counts and bishops sympathetic to the communal movement's attempts to pry control of civil affairs from

87　Moot Hall, Hexham, east elevation (courtesy Stuart Harrison).

88　Saint-Antonin-Noble-Val, Tarn-et-Garonne, Committal Hall, drawn from rectified photograph (courtesy *Mémoires de la Société archéologique Midi de la France*, 1989, © M. Scelles).

imperial authority with the help of the new jurisprudence granted use of their residences for this purpose.[23] Depending on their political leanings, the popes aided or opposed the communal movement. Between 1154 and 1189 three successive popes – the English Nicholas Breakspear, Adrian IV (1154–59), Alexander III (1159–81), and Urban III (1181–89) – did much to establish the new legal processes. Adrian had studied Roman law at Arles, Alexander at Bologna where he went on to become a law magister, and Urban also at Bologna where he in turn became a law magister. The most influential was Alexander III. His support for the communal movement, notably the Lombard League cities formed to combat Frederick Barbarossa's repressive imperial policies, was acknowledged in 1168 by the naming of Alessandria after him.

Architecture in France and Italy in or near centers that were connected to the revival of jurisprudence follows these broad historical outlines. From France, in

the Midi, the *maison romane* at Saint-Antonin-Noble-Val (Tarn-et-Garonne) of ca. 1155 served the counts of Saint-Antonin for the administration of law and justice (fig. 88) (Pressouyre 1986, 256–68; Scelles 1989, 45–119). The court was located in the first-floor hall, generously lit by a band of windows raised over a vaulted undercroft, and provided with a flanking tower. Separating the windows are two piers which carry relief sculptures, one showing Justinian holding an open book on which was inscribed the *incipit* of the famous *Institutiones*, the other showing the fall of Adam and Eve. Pressouyre demonstrated that the image affirmed the influence of the *corpus iuris civilis*, probably derived from the school of law at Montpellier.

In Italy the evidence is more fragmentary. At Ferrara, Verona, Piacenza, and Modena documents from the early twelfth century record that justice was administered "sub portico," meaning the porch portal of great churches, or "protiro" or "intra ecclesiam."[24] These

96

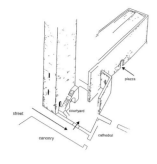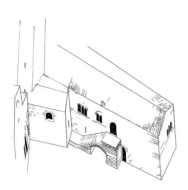

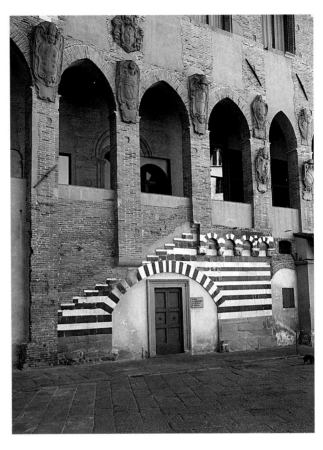

(Above) 89 Bishop's Palace, Pistoia, reconstruction drawings showing condition ca. 1100 (left) and after 1170 (right) (Miller 2000, pp. 150–51, figs. 49, 50).

(Right) 90 Palazzo dei Vescovi, Pistoia, ceremonial staircase, ca. 1170 (photograph author).

adhere to the centuries old tradition of administering justice at the gate (discussed above). They provide few clues, however, to the appearance in the second half of the twelfth century of a new type, the Palazzo Comunale. Located in the heart of the city (rather than at its margins), the development of the Palazzo Comunale was centered in Lombardy and the Po Valley. The emergence of the type is associated with the formation of the Lombard League after the Peace of Constance in 1183 (Miller 1995, 175). Closer in time to Canterbury, an early Palazzo Comunale is noted at Padua in 1166 on the site of the still-standing Palazzo della Ragione, late twelfth century (Miller 1995, 183, n. 3), and at Piacenza in 1171 where the commune's consuls had taken over the bishop's palace. In these examples a distinctive grouping of architectural components similar to Canterbury can be recognized. To these can be added the definition of the area carrying judicial protection known as the *broletto* (from *brolo*, Latin for a lord's hayfield), as Jürgen Paul and Maureen Miller have shown (Paul 1969, 18; Miller 2000, 168–69). In these examples influence can be tracked through typology even when there is slight influence discernible through style. What mattered was the citation of models, a well-documented process outlined by Richard Krautheimer (1969).

In the Italian cases, the conduct of law rapidly involved the creation of the ceremony of law. Elaborate entry staircases were part of this. Composed of luxurious materials, they began appearing in the second half of the twelfth century. An example in Tuscany from ca.

1170 survives at Pistoia, along with a two-story *aula* and adjacent tower embedded in a later building (fig. 89). The ceremonial staircase in black and white marble was carried up the flank of the *aula* and then turned at right angles on a generous platform or balcony to enter the bishop's hall (fig. 90) (Miller 2000, 150–54).[25] Various coverings have been proposed for the balcony, including an aedicule. Such ceremonial staircases were called *veroni* and served as the setting for proclamations, greetings, the publication of indulgences, and so forth. In general, the wide ornamented staircase defined rank, but, just as important, it opened to scrutiny those making judicial decisions, thereby extending visibility to the law's administration as well as to those petitioners seeking its help. Other examples before 1200 are provided by Padua (fig. 91) and Bergamo (fig. 92) where the staircase to the communal palace rises in two flights, like Canterbury. These staircases became one of the hallmarks of the new Italian buildings. Adding to their meaning was association with the Scala Santa at the papal palace at the Lateran, where tradition held that the steps had been traversed by Christ on his way to trial and judgment before Pilate (Donadono 2000, 28–30). It is within this context that a fountain for ritual cleansing is included,

(Left) 91 Palazzo del Ragione, Padua, east façade, ceremonial staircase, ca. 1190 (photograph author).

(Above) 92 Palazzo Comunale and entry staircase, Bergamo (photograph author).

(Below left) 93 Palazzo Comunale, Como, upper story added later (photograph Alinari).

(Below) 94 Duccio, *Maestà*, detail showing Pilate judging Christ, ca. 1308 (Siena, Museo del Duomo).

with examples at Bergamo and Viterbo from ca. 1260 where it sits within a loggia.[26]

By the early 1200s court halls in northern and central Italy such as Como (fig. 93) or Viterbo display many of the constituent parts noted for the entry complex at Canterbury. These were widely enough recognized to be employed in early trecento painting to illustrate the trial and judgment of Christ. In Duccio's *Maestà* (ca. 1308) the scene is set within a gatehouse courtyard (shown on the lower left) with an elaborate entry staircase leading up to a balcony and then into the first-floor court hall (fig. 94). To reveal the interior Duccio uses the device, familiar to the artist of *Drawing I*, of removing the outer wall to reveal the trial in process.

Other ceremonial symbols of justice appeared at the same time. Most prominent was the tower, with surviving examples at Como, Viterbo, Florence (the Bargello), Milan, Venice, Verona (S. Zeno), and elsewhere. Another was the canopy (a kind of fabric aedicule) and ring given by Pope Alexander III at the Peace of Venice in 1177 to Doge Sebastiano Ziani, who sealed the treaty with Frederick Barbarossa in front of the basilica of San Marco.[27]

Given the importance of Bologna and its close links with Canterbury (see Chapter 3), it would be satisfying to see the same influence manifest in architecture as in jurisprudence. However, the oldest buildings in the Piazza Maggiore date to the early years of the thirteenth century and form the north side, the *palatium vetus* (Palazzo della Biada), which served as the Romanesque communal hall on the site of the present Palazzo del Podestà. It consisted of a two-story structure with a vaulted undercroft supporting an upper hall with an external staircase; the Torre d'Arengo was attached.[28]

Archivolt Reliefs

Complementing the architectural development of the entry complex at Canterbury are the mid-twelfth-century relief carvings on the entry arch of the Green Court Gatehouse.[29] The outer archivolts intersperse human and animal motifs with densely decorated foliage, both enclosed in medallion-like frames (fig. 95A and B). On the north side five subjects are shown (reading from the bottom): a seated musician with a *vielle*, a dancing figure with raised arms (fig 96A), a harp-playing animal with an enormous tongue, a wild-man musician with bells (fig. 96B), and a knife juggler.[30] On the south, there are three subjects: a man and woman with arms over each other's shoulders holding what looks like a cord, a

dancing mermaid with raised arms, and a horn blower in a small boat.

The entry arch proper has supporting capitals from the same period. Their subjects include animals and coiled snakes, a grotesque head with flaming hair, hunters, an acrobatic group of animals, and winged dragons "cavorting among twining stems," in Newman's words (1969, 219). The last resemble those on the roof ridge of the adjacent *Aula Nova* in *Drawing I*. Similarities of style are noted for the capitals with those in Anselm's crypt of ca. 1100. Interest in Anselm's work at a space of fifty years may be linked to strenuous efforts to promote his canonization (partially successful in 1163) with the active support of an influential lay guild of votaries known as the Dionisii (Urry 1959, 582).

For the archivolt sculptures the identification of subjects remains difficult. Scholars suggest secular subjects connected with music and dance, an appropriate secular interest corresponding to the outward- or city-facing side of the Green Court Gatehouse. In my interpretation I suggest an alternative related to the established purpose of the Gatehouse and entry buildings which, as seen above, had to do with the judicial administration of the Liberty of Christ Church. The first illustrated manuscripts on canon law, notably Gratian's *Decretum* written around 1140 in Italy in the law school at Bologna, are contemporary with the entry complex buildings. Of the eight subjects, two can be related to illustrations in these early law books, and three more to episodes in King David's life that stress his humility and penitence.

The two archivolts with *Decreta* references are on the right or south side, and include the couple with their hands over each other's shoulders who stand under an arch supported by columns, of which one is a spiral (fig. 97A), and the horn blower standing in a boat (fig. 97B).[31] Both suggest knowledge of the full-page illustrations which appear in part two of the *Decretum*.[32] Gratian presented a range of legal matters using thirty-six cases or *Causae*, which cover such matters as property regulations, obligatory payment of tithes, disputes over taxes and contracts, and the jurisdiction of canonical courts over clerical crimes. *Causa* XXXV devoted to marriage and church proscriptions on partners within seven degrees of interrelationship (rather than the five proscribed by Roman law), employed the image of the Trees of Affinity and Consanguinity. The branches of the trees list the relatives by marriage forbidden to fulfill the role of second spouse upon the death of the first (L'Engle, Gibbs, and Clarke 2001, 87–96, 106). An early example now in Sidney Sussex College, Cambridge, MS 101,

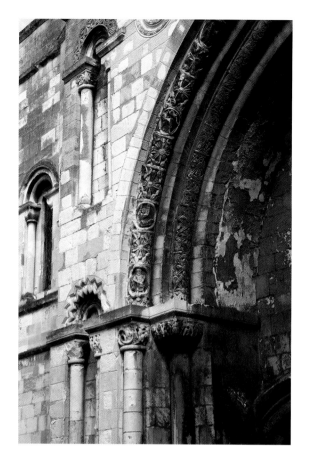

(Above left and right) 95 Canterbury Cathedral Priory, Green Court Gatehouse, entry arch: (A) north side archivolts; (B) south side archivolts (photographs author).

(Below left and right) 96 Canterbury Cathedral Priory, Green Court Gatehouse, entry arch, north side: (A) David, dancer; (B) wild man with bells (S. Onuphrius?) (photographs author).

97A   Canterbury Cathedral Priory, Green Court
Gatehouse, entry arch, south side: Man and Woman,
Tree of Affinity (photograph author).

97B   Canterbury Cathedral Priory, Green Court
Gatehouse, entry arch, south side: Horn blower in boat
(photograph author).

made around 1175, shows a Tree of Affinity (fig. 98) with
a man and woman with their right arms crossed over
each other's shoulders who hold cords leading to tablets
detailing the degrees of interrelationship. The scene is
set under the framing arch of a gatehouse, within the
central tower of which a horn blower, a standard image
of summoning, sounds his horn. The frame with its
crowning towers and crenellations and the arch overs-
panning the figures clearly allude to the gatehouse location where legal issues connected with marriage were
adjudicated. In the Canterbury sculptures the horn
blower is featured, although why he appears in a boat
is unexplained.

On the north side the archivolt subjects relate to the
psalmist. Shown at the springer of the arch is a seated,

(Right) 98   Gratian, *Decretum*, *Causa* XXXV, Tree of Affinity,
MS 101, fol. 210 (courtesy Cambridge, Sidney Sussex College).

99 Psalter, Psalm 1, MS 53, fol. 151r, Trinity College, Dublin (courtesy Trinity College Library). David as harpist (left) with supporting horn blower and bell ringer, and as dancer (right).

cloaked, instrument-holding musician who resembles King David.[33] This identity is strengthened by the upper figures: a leaping dancer with raised arms – a popular reference to David's humility affirmed when he danced before the Ark of the Covenant – and a wild man with bells alluding to the king's music-making related to his authorship of the Psalms. These subjects appear in a mid-twelfth-century psalter from Winchcombe, now in Trinity College, Dublin, MS 53, fol. 151r (fig. 99).[34] They include the seated king at the center, bell ringers, and a somersaulting dancing figure to illustrate the Ark episode, each enclosed within a medallion-like

armature like the Green Court gate sculptures and forming a composite image.[35]

David's inclusion in the context of the Gatehouse would be plausible for two reasons. To prove the legitimacy of his dynasty, he ordered a census of Israel and Judah, a model of judicial ordering. And to express his remorse for his adultery with Bathsheba and the murder of her husband Uriah, he penned the seven penitential Psalms (6, 31, 37, 50, 101, 127, 142). Within monastic circles, Cassiodorus in the sixth century stressed the penitential Psalms as the means of obtaining forgiveness. Judgments made in the prior's court demanded penance from those determined guilty.

In addition to the figural subjects, many of the entry archivolts display foliage enclosed in alternating round and lozenge frames. They are composed of four-petaled leaf forms with central beaded stems which radiate outwards from a core with their ends turned back towards the center. Similar examples appear in Wibert's architectural detailing in the Precinct. Deborah Kahn connects this kind of foliage to "Winchester acanthus" (Kahn 1991, 128–31), known in manuscript painting from the same period, and associates it with Channel School work at the abbey of St.-Bertin in St.-Omer.[36] This important monastery less than twenty miles from Calais enjoyed close ties to Christ Church, providing the home for Archbishop Theobald and his household during their exile (1148–52) imposed by King Stephen and, again, for the exile from 1207 to 1213 of Archbishop Langton imposed by King John (Saltman 1956, 25–28).

The same decorative motifs appear in manuscript painting, notably in early *Decreta*. A surviving page with an initial to illustrate *Causa* I shows the letter Q (fig. 100) composed of interwoven heart-shaped forms from which extend dense sprays of foliate ornament with beaded leaves, a decorative composition similar to those carved on the archivolts of the Green Court Gatehouse (see fig. 97B). That a *Decretum* was in the curia of the archbishop (and probably also in the Priory's library) in the 1150s when the Gatehouse was under construction can be assumed. Archbishop Theobald played a central role in the revival of Roman law and the emergence of canon law in England. As early as 1143 (the year before Becket entered his household), Theobald had imported from Bologna the precocious young law magister Vacarius to provide him with top-rank legal backing in his struggle to wrest the papal legateship from the bishop of Winchester, Henry of Blois, and to enforce canon law in England. Vacarius would have brought with him a *Decretum* for use in his work and also

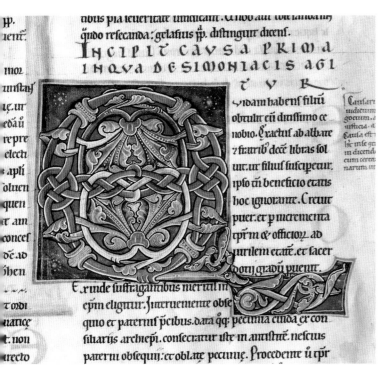

100   Gratian, *Decretum*, initial Q, Cleveland Museum, 1954.598 (courtesy Cleveland Museum). Detail from manuscript used by Becket in 1164.

perhaps his teaching. While in Canterbury, Vacarius wrote his treatise on marriage, *Summa de matrimonio*, which reflected Gratian's influence and appeared at the same time as the start of work on the Gatehouse (Maitland 1897, 133–43 and 270–87). Also written at Canterbury in the 1150s was his most influential work, the *Liber pauperum*, which included excerpts from the *Decretum* and from Justinian's *Codex* and *Digesta*. Vacarius remained at Canterbury for fifteen years, probably teaching law there (his pupils possibly including the young Becket and the rising star within the Priory, Wibert), before relocating to York in 1159 in the service of Archbishop Roger Pont L'Evêque (1154–81), formerly archdeacon of Canterbury; he then spent the next forty years in Yorkshire (Southern 1976, 257–86).

Another source for possession of a *Decretum* was Thomas Becket. Sent in the early 1150s to Bologna to attend the law school, Becket's studies would have included the *Decretum* (Duggan 2007, 11). He continued his law studies at Auxerre, twelve miles from the Cistercian mother house of Pontigny. When he was recalled by Archbishop Theobald to Canterbury in 1154 to take up his appointment as Archdeacon and as an ecclesiastical advisor to Henry II, it would be very surprising had he not carried back with him a *Decretum* because his new responsibilities would have entailed constant consultation of its contents. A further connection can be established. Within the Cistercian order *Decreta* are recorded in the late 1150s at Cîteaux in Burgundy and at Clairvaux in Champagne (Bock 1951, 7–31). After Becket became archbishop in 1162 and was exiled by Henry II, he spent two years (1164–66) at Pontigny, and while there his secretary, Herbert of Bosham, recorded in a marginal note in a *Decretum* that Becket and he studied the manuscript together (Cahn, 1975a, 56). It was from this manuscript that the surviving page now in Cleveland comes.

At Canterbury the identified subjects carved on the Gatehouse's entry arch are hard to organize into a single program. They make reference to legal matters and to the law's Old Testament's antecedents epitomized in exemplary Davidic themes of humility and atonement. Illustrations in manuscripts connected to the establishment of canon law such as the *Decretum* including marginal finding-aids to identify relevant text passages offer sources for some scenes. Together the subjects showcased the Priory's legal responsibility as the Liberty of Christ Church. Some parallel the Eadwine Psalter being written in the adjacent scriptorium where Old Testament exemplars prefigure New Testament ones, with David appearing in Psalm 1 with a cruciform halo as Christ (see fig. 17B). Once inside the Precinct, biblical exemplars are similarly cited, such as in the Norman Staircase leading to the prior's Court Hall where Solomonic references recall the Judaic king's judgment hall and serve as an appropriate prototype for the prior's Court Hall.

Monastic culture at mid-century was dominated by the revival of Roman law and the emergence of canon law. During the same years as Prior Wibert was constructing the entry complex, Theobald's curia included four important Italian law school magisters such as the already mentioned Vacarius. In the 1150s he was joined by Master Lombard of Piacenza, Becket's canon law mentor at Canterbury and his champion in the 1160s within the papal court, where he later became cardinal and archbishop of Benevento. The two others were Magister Reginald FitzJocelin, known as the Lombard, and Magister Humbert the Lombard, later archbishop of Bourges and then, from 1185 to 1187, Pope Urban III (Knowles 1971, 57, 108; Duggan 2007, 10–19). These four high-powered legal figures from centers connected with the revival of jurisprudence and their association with Becket provide strong support for a plausible linkage of architectural and sculptural forms which otherwise have no history of use in England.

The new legal climate was not limited to Canterbury. In York as noted above, Archbishop Theobald's protégé, Roger Pont L'Evêque, was in office as archbishop after serving as Archdeacon at Christ Church, and it was there Vacarius moved in 1159. At Bury St. Edmunds the legal innovations described in *The Chronicle of Jocelin of Brakelond*, written ca. 1201, detail the early years of Abbot Samson's rule (1188–1211). Bury had three courts, like Canterbury: the sacrist's, the cellarer's, and the abbot's (Butler, 1949, 33–34, 77–81, 105–6). All had notary clerks, a clear sign of tighter judicial procedures requiring reference to written texts. Brakelond does not specify the texts used, although Gratian's Bologna compilation was likely. He does mention Abbot Samson's efforts to get instruction in canon law, however (Butler 1949, 34). Bury St. Edmunds was also a Liberty, though its architectural development occurred about twenty years earlier than Canterbury. It lacked the adjacent buildings distinctive of Canterbury such as a court hall, tower, and prison clustered around the principal entry, and no contact is recorded to link it to the burgeoning jurisprudence in Italy.[37] Dating to the generation before Canterbury, the Bury buildings provide a means of grasping the speed of developments at mid-century and the unique way in which the Priory's contacts enabled it to embark on this new departure in monastic architecture.

BEYOND THE ENTRY COMPLEX

Moving into the Green Court a visitor passed a range of service buildings – the Bakehouse, Brewhouse, and Granary – framing the northern side of the open court and then, turning south, encountered an unnamed building and the Bath House. These will be discussed next.

Pistrinum, Bracinum, Granarium,
and *Novum Stabulum Prioris*

The importance of the *Pistrinum* (Bakehouse) for the functioning of the Priory is illustrated by the responsibility of the master baker who was required to deliver daily five different kinds of bread; for the monks, corrodians, visitors, servants, and kitchen staff (Woodruff 1936, 75–77). *Drawing I* shows the Bakehouse and Brewhouse buildings as a unified 200-foot-long building.

The former was supplied with dual faucets, the latter with one. A tower at the west end and a second tower about halfway down the length of the building indicate ovens. At what period the building was divided into two separate structures is unclear. Updatings at intervals continued until the suppression in 1540. Remodeled for the use of the King's School, they form the northern boundary of the Green Court. The long history of use and successive renovations make reading out a history difficult. Exteriors and interiors of both buildings contain scattered, fragmentary medieval building features. In its divided form the Bakehouse was three bays in length with an oven in the north wall of the west bay, which contains part of a molded hood.

The *Granarium* (Granary) lay to the east as a separate building with the *Novum Stabulum Prioris* (Prior's New Stables) lying behind it (Sparks 2007, 60–63). No trace survives of the Granary. For the Stables, documentary evidence provides some minimum information. They housed the prior's horses – he was permitted twenty-six – and those of senior officials such as the cellarer. In addition, they provided for the horses belonging to the distinguished visitors to the Guesthouse and the prior's *Nova Camera* (Smith 1943, 220–21). A forge would also have been necessary.

Domestic buildings cluttered the site until the 1150s when Prior Wibert purchased and demolished them. Most likely the Stables stretched along much of the new priory wall parallel to Queningate Lane. A reference under Prior Chillenden's *Repairs to the Curia* (1399–1411) mentions them (Willis 1868, 150). Stables remained in this part of the Precinct until the 1920s.

Unlabeled Building

Turning south, where the precinct wall forms an L-shaped angle, *Drawing I* shows a stone building. The artist supplies no *titulus* and the building's identity remains a mystery. As drawn, the building is windowless except at the gable end. It was probably two stories to judge by the north-facing gable, with low walls and a high-pitched roof. A document of ca. 1200 refers to its use on occasion as an overflow prison when the one in the *Aula Nova* was filled (Smith 1943, 96). Mention is made that it was constructed of stone ashlars.

The unnamed building's purpose has never been agreed. Willis connected it to Eastry's list and saw it as the "magna grangia ad fenum" (Willis, 1868, 114). Urry favored it as the tailor's shop (Urry 1986, 54). A barn for the storage of grain is also plausible. Under Prior

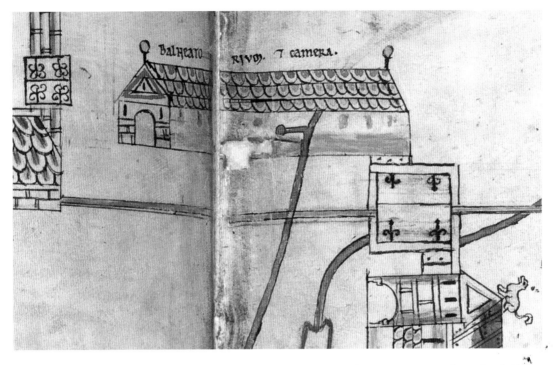

101   Eadwine Psalter, *Drawing I*, detail with image rotated showing Bath House, Trinity College, Cambridge (courtesy the Master and Fellows, Trinity College Library).

Goldstone (1495–1517) a document refers to his conversion of the building and the adjacent Bath House into a guesthouse for the top rank of visitor. They would thus have become an annex to the prior's *Nova Camera*.

Balneatorium et Camera

Placed on the east boundary of the Green Court on *Drawing I* was a large building labeled *Balneatorium et Camera*: Bath House and Room (fig. 101). Known only through this image, the Bath House is the least known of the thirty buildings depicted on *Drawing I*.[38] Consistent with its purpose, the artist shows a tap to supply the baths in the lower story. It is drawn as a two-story structure without windows on the ground floor, their omission probably explained by the baths. The upper floor, presumably the *camera*, was lit by eight windows. Use of the singular rather than the more expected *camerae* is unexplained (see Sparks 2007, 57). The entry shows a door rising into the upper story and indicates a monumental façade. The façade lay adjacent to the gate which led from the Green Court into a pie-shaped area of land within the Roman city wall.

Nearly all traces of Wibert's Bath House have vanished. Frequent changes by the Priory's late medieval priors and, after the suppression, by Canterbury's powerful deans have obliterated the medieval original. Willis identified only a remaining fragment in a vaulted passage 4 feet under the room in the northwest angle of the dean's house (Willis 1868, 112). Documents mention a bath under the paved chamber in a structure adjacent to the Prior's Gatehouse Tower (at the south end of the Deanery) and in part of the dean's wash house (Sparks 2007, 149–50). Modern examination indicates a building about 90 feet long and 27 feet wide, about half the size of the present day dean's residence.

The choice of a hall type for the Bath House connected it to other buildings raised by Prior Wibert in the Green Court such as the *Aula Nova* or the Guesthouse in the Cellarer's Court. At the same time it distances the building from the elaborate structures, multiple functions, and intricate plans associated with public baths (*thermae*), at least in the sense of Roman classical and post-classical times, of which remains of two have been found within the city of Canterbury.[39] Sparks draws parallels with a similar but slightly larger building at Dover Priory (Sparks 2007, 57). Documents from the mid-twelfth century name four men as staff, all secular servants: Pagan, Milo, Richard, and Cole (Urry 1967, 16, 18, 159).

The Bath House's placement in the Green Court indicates functions related to the Priory's guest accommodation. Three of the four areas for guest hospitality have a frontage to the Green Court. For the highest class of visitor such as royalty, aristocracy, and church dignitaries who resided with the prior in his *Nova Camera*, a separate bath and cistern are shown on *Drawing I* (see Chapter 7). Whether the Bath House also served the monks is an unresolved question. No bath house for them is shown on *Drawing I*, apart from the small one for the use of the Infirmary. The omission is hard to explain unless the monks constituted a second group of users. Every monastery required a bath house. All are of modest scale compared to Canterbury: for instance, the approximately 13 foot by 13 foot structure shown at Cluny III, which served a community three times larger in size than the Priory's (Conant 1968, fig. 6, and p. 40).

The Priory's Bath House lay outside the strict enclosure, and this raises the issue of how the monks gained access if they were, in fact, among the users. One clue is provided by the Prior's Gatehouse, which shows connecting corridors on each flank lit by small round windows. On the west the connection is made with the monks' *Necessarium*, on the east with the Bath House. A sharing of the Bath House between the monks and visitors is not impossible.[40] Dual use does not imply joint use, and designated times would have kept each group separate. Other spaces at Canterbury were shared; the Great Cloister's west range, for instance, provided for guest accommodation under Archbishop Lanfranc (1070–89).

In the *Rule* of St. Benedict and in monastic *Customaries*, baths for monks are ordained twice yearly before Christmas and Easter. The commonly held belief about the taboo on baths, however, is moderated in patristic writings from Jerome and Gregory the Great, and more flexible conditions are indicated in Cassiodorius' description of the curative waters at Vivarium (Squatriti 1998, 48–65) (see fig. 20). Monastic baths needed to be separated from urban bath houses, and monks who patronized the latter were severely disciplined. Lanfranc's *Constitutions* list a bath house to which the brethren "have to be conducted," a detail that indicates a location outside the cloister enclosure (Knowles and Brooke 2002, 15–17, 41). Most of what Lanfranc has to say concerned deportment and modes of undressing. He insisted on the maintenance of silence during baths and the need for "seemly and orderly" procedures, and he ordered the provision of individual tubs with curtained screens for privacy. Lanfranc's preoccupation with

modesty surfaces elsewhere a century later. Among the Cistercians, the ca. 1175 *Ecclesiastica Officia* contains a reference to the care a monk should take at the weekly *mandatum fratrum*: "When [the monks] have removed their shoes, let them be careful, as far as they are able, not to show their bare feet, but to hide them under their cowls."[41]

The difference between the tiny bath house at Cluny and the major scale given to the Canterbury structure involved a fundamental change in thinking (rather than a straightforward development). Writer-physicians such as Avicenna (d. 1037) argued that baths of varying temperatures helped readjust the body's four humors and thus cured ailments ranging from depression to digestive disorders. Treatises in preventative medicine such as the *Regimen sanitatis* from the famous medical school in Salerno increased the popularity of baths in southern Italy (Caskey 2004, 102). This work was probably known in England through the students with medical training from Salerno (the pre-eminent center for the study of medicine in the eleventh century) who practiced medicine in England.[42] About fifty years after the construction of the Canterbury Bath House, literary accounts provide fuller information about bath culture, notably Pietro da Eboli's popular poem *De Balneis Puteolanis*, written ca. 1211–20 and dedicated to Frederick II.[43] The poem describes the medicinal baths (thirty-five are mentioned) at Pozzuoli near Naples, which had flourished since classical times. The curative function of baths has, therefore, to be considered, although the steps by which these views were assimilated into monastic life remain to be shown.

A second explanation centers on multicultural contacts resulting from the intersection of western and Islamic cultures in Norman areas of Sicily and around Amalfi. Twelfth-century bath houses still surviving at Amalfi, such as the Ruffolo House with its domed bath house, suggest the assimilation of Islamic ideas (Caskey 2004, 97–103). However, these structures are small. Their scale is domestic and they were often elaborately decorated. A third explanation points to specific episcopal and papal precedents. Episcopal bath structures are best known in the mid-twelfth century from Italian examples in Lombardy, the Po Valley, and Rome (Squatriti 1998, 48–65; Caskey 2004, 97–103). They reflect changes in conceptions of health and hygiene. In Rome, the papal court at the Lateran Palace with its English pontiff, Adrian IV, contained a sizable *Balneatorium*.[44] Adrian's biographer, Cardinal Boso, mentions the pope's interest in water systems and his construction of "a very necessary and extremely large cistern" at the Lateran Palace (Bolton and Duggan 2003, 230–31). Presumably, the work supplied water for the bath house and the cloister. This would have been well known to members of Archbishop Theobald's court from their visits to the Lateran in 1144 and 1152. As noted in previous chapters, Theobald's entourage included Thomas Becket, and his role in the appearance of the Bath House at the Priory remains an open question. Contemporaries record Becket's chronic stomach ailments, which caused him continuous discomfort and made him short-tempered (Barlow 1976, 25–26, and n. 2). To alleviate this gastric ailment doctors prescribed special diets. Another standard remedy mentioned by Avicenna would have been warm baths. Comprehensive curative properties were associated with hydrotherapy (Daston, Park 1998, 138–44). Becket's contemporary, Ailred of Rievaulx (1147–67), underwent as many as a dozen baths a day to treat his gout and urinary problems in the 1160s. Becket's knowledge of contemporary treatment for such illnesses could plausibly have been gained from his travels to Italy, including Rome and the papal palace at the Lateran.

The construction of the Bath House at the Priory counters the myth about the waterless Middle Ages. Suggestions of change in hygiene occur in contemporary castle construction, where the great tower at Rochester in the 1130s was constructed with well water on all four floors, as was the case in the 1180s at Dover Castle.[45] More importantly, it suggests another, entirely different way in which Canterbury and Italy were connected in the mid-twelfth century. Water featured in many of the Priory's customs and rituals. The Bath House takes its place in the context of the laving culture of these years embodied also in the five fountains provided as part of Prior Wibert's installation of the water system, the separate baths for the most distinguished category of visitor in the prior's *Nova Camera*, and the commitment of the community to foot washing in the rites of the *mandatum hospitum* and the *mandatum fratrum*. To see these laving interests in terms of hygiene alone addresses only one aspect of the matter. They did, of course, provide for laving as indicated in St. Mark's Gospel, where four verses address the issues of the cleansing of the body and of food (Mark 7:2–5). These verses move freely from the literal to the spiritual aspect of cleansing. But these words had been around for hundreds of years without triggering the changes that followed at the Priory.

Part of the interest of the Priory's Bath House involves recognition that it continued in use for a relatively brief period. By ca. 1400 and possibly earlier, the Bath House had fallen into disrepair. As seen above, Prior Goldstone at the end of the fourteenth century remodeled the Bath House as an annex to the prior's *Nova Camera* for the highest class of visitor. Like the fountains and the water system in general at the Priory, which were noted in a state of neglect a century earlier, the interest in water and laving seems to have peaked in the mid-twelfth century. Equally unclear is the lack of influence of the Bath House on other institutions. No similar buildings are recorded.

Seen broadly, Prior Wibert's development of the Green Court constitutes a remarkable example of monastic planning in mid-twelfth-century England. In scale it rivals urban planning at the same period. The source for ideas most likely lay in the work at Bury St. Edmunds in the preceding generation, where the arrangement of buildings and the open area of the court suggest a model for the Priory (compare figs. 61 and 67). Even if this could be proved, Wibert's integration of infrastructure, range of architectural types, clarity in the separations of function, elegance of forms, concern for the welfare of visitors, and curative interests directed to body and mind made possible by the new water system stand out as distinctive contributions. They also argue for the Green Court as the prior's most ambitious architectural undertaking and one of his most notable achievements.

7

CARE OF THE SICK AND AGED

The Infirmary and Related Buildings

The placement of the infirmary in the eastern part of monastic precincts has an ancient history. Classical authors such as Hippocrates in his *Airs, Waters, and Places* extolled the health benefits of an eastern location (Bell 1998, 212–20). His advice was noted by monastic planners; "The Plan of St. Gall" (ca. 820) placed the infirmary east of the church. The tradition continued into the twelfth century, and well beyond it. Related to the infirmary and usually adjacent was the community's cemetery, a juxtaposition explained by its association with resurrection and rebirth at death.

Infirmaries included much more than the infirmary hall. A cloister was essential for air and exercise for the sick and for those recovering from the six times yearly ordeal of blood-letting.[1] Space had to be provided for the infirmary master and his *herbarium* (medieval medicine was based largely on pharmacological treatment), baths (allowed the sick in the *Rule* of St. Benedict), toilets, kitchen (patients were permitted to eat meat), and a chapel with related buildings to accommodate clergy and often choristers as well. One further feature

was a connection to the residence of the abbot or prior, who in keeping with his responsibility to provide for the monastery's top social class of visitor utilized the infirmary's kitchen, toilets, and baths for their hospitality.

Care of the sick was an obligation taken with the utmost seriousness by every monastic community. Encapsulated in the words of Christ in the Gospels, this obligation was repeated in the *Rule* of St. Benedict: "Before all things and above all things care must be taken of the sick, so that they may be served in very deed as Christ himself; for He said 'I was sick and you visited me; and what you did to one of the least ones, you did unto me'.... But let the sick on their part consider that they are being served for the honor of God, and not provoke their brethren who are serving them by their unreasonable demands" (McCann 1952, 90–91). The *Rule*'s words reveal St. Benedict's perception of care as a spiritual discipline directed to some extent to the benefit of the care-giver as well as to the care-receiver. The dual benefits outlined by St. Benedict were

102 Canterbury Cathedral Priory, Infirmary Chapel and Hall, photograph by Fisk Moore, 1935 (courtesy Canterbury Cathedral Archives and Library © Dean and Chapter).

reflected in the shift from the domestic-scale wards known from "The Plan of St. Gall" to the monumental hall designs of the eleventh and twelfth centuries.[2] The hall-type infirmary facilitated the monastic preoccupation with supervision and organizational control, but it also dignified the role of the care-givers. Just as important, the hall encouraged ventilation and countered corrupted air, which prevailing opinion viewed as the cause of illness, a notion originating with Hippocrates and Galen (Bell 1998, 229–30).

The development from domestic room to institutional hall is well illustrated in France in the eleventh century. At Cluny a series of infirmary rebuildings allows the process to be tracked at about fifty-year intervals. In the early eleventh century, Abbot Odilo (994–1048) constructed a rectangular infirmary divided into domestic-scale rooms, each containing eight beds (for a community of seventy monks).[3] Replaced in the early 1080s by St. Hugh (1049–1109), the new infirmary took the form of a two-story hall with twenty-four beds in the upper story (for a community of around 200 monks). In turn it was replaced after about fifty years by Abbot Peter the Venerable (1122–56) with a larger building consisting of five bays organized in three aisles and measuring 176 feet by 83 feet. A gallery surmounted the aisles, leaving the interior to soar 85 feet to the roof ridge. Estimates suggest about fifty beds (Conant 1968, 110–11, also pl. xxxiv, figs. 60–61) for a community of over 400 monks.

At Canterbury, Lanfranc's arrival as archbishop in 1070 heralded a burst of hospital construction in the city and the Priory. St. John's Northgate (1080–84), close by the monastery, was built on St. Hugh's Cluny design. Lanfranc raised an aisleless hall 200 feet in length which Eadmer characterized as "handsome and ample . . . and of stone." Eadmer also included the information that it was adjoined by several little buildings (habitacula) which Lanfranc added for the infirmary's various requirements along with a spacious court (Livett 1929, 280–84). Attendants and guardians were provided, and across the road Lanfranc raised a chapel in honor of Gregory the Great, which was staffed with clerks who were to administer to the sick in spiritual matters. The wealth of information about Lanfranc's city hospitals makes it all the more frustrating that nothing is known about the infirmary at the Priory which he provided as part of his rebuilding. It is likely that it took the form of a hall, although distinct differences in layout, support functions, and services set the monastic infirmary apart from the urban hospital.

Lanfranc's infirmary was located in the general area of the Infirmary Cloister and probably lay parallel to the Dormitory. The sole clue to the location comes from the Camera Vetus Prioris, the prior's old residence. Drawing I shows the Camera Vetus lying close to the Prior's Gatehouse on its west side, and this suggests an infirmary building covering the eastern half of the Infirmary Cloister. In turn, Lanfranc's infirmary was replaced by his successor, Archbishop Anselm. He acquired additional land by purchase or gift in the area of the Queningate to accommodate his huge extension of the Cathedral. Urry suggested this land also allowed for the development of the infirmary and monastic cemetery (Urry 1967, 27–28).[4]

By the mid-twelfth century, the shortcomings of the Priory's infirmary buildings prompted Prior Wibert to institute major changes as one of his first steps in the renewal of the monastery. Infirmary development enjoyed a building boom in these years that continued into the early thirteenth century. Construction is documented at Bury St. Edmunds, Abingdon, Rochester, St. Albans, Peterborough, Rievaulx, Norwich, and St. Augustine's Canterbury. The last was raised by Abbot Hugh of Trottescliffe (1126–51) with an eight-bay hall on a north–south axis and a single aisle to the east. The building measured 104 feet by 40 feet (A. H. Thompson 1934, 185–87). As suggested in Chapter 5 (see note 6), Queen Matilda's preference for St. Augustine's as the location for her prolonged stay in 1148–49 may have been swayed by her knowledge of its up-to-date infirmary.

Extensive infrastructure was needed before the start of construction. The Necessarium, Infirmary Fountain House, Water Tower, Bath House, Nova Camera with its cistern and bath, and the connection to the Piscina all lay in the east part of the Infirmary Cloister (fig. 103). Their close proximity to each other suggests a unified campaign. All these undertakings are shown prominently on Drawing I (fig. 104), although the artist's compression of features led him into numerous muddles with alignment and adjacency.[5] Work on the Infirmary Cloister walks would have followed. They were formed on the south by the supporting arches of Archbishop Anselm's raised night entry from the Dormitory into the Cathedral's choir and were extended a further six bays from the Water Tower to the Infirmary Hall. On the north, the long cloister walk ran parallel to the Necessarium, and on the east the walk extended from the Prior's Gatehouse to the Infirmary Hall. At the southeast angle of the Infirmary Cloister, Wibert built the Treasury (labeled

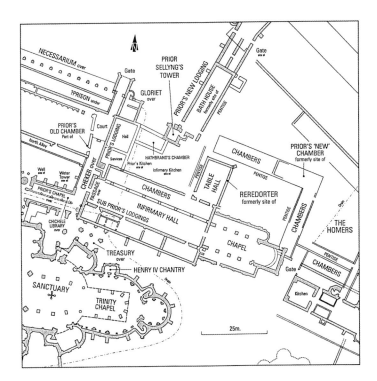

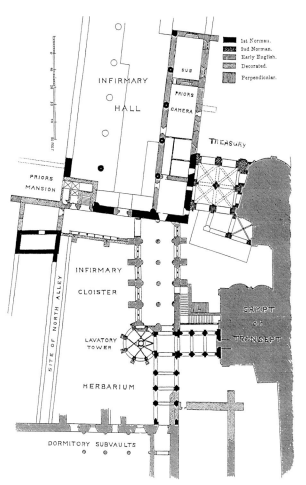

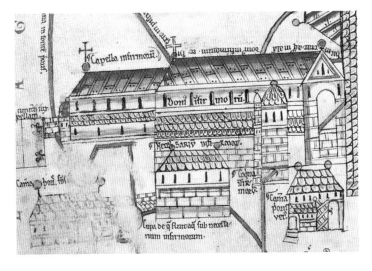

(Above left) 103 Canterbury Cathedral Priory, plan of east precincts (Sparks 2007, p. 38).

(Left) 104 Eadwine Psalter, *Drawing I*, detail showing Infirmary buildings, Trinity College, Cambridge (courtesy the Master and Fellows, Trinity College, Cambridge).

(Above) 105 Canterbury Cathedral Priory, Infirmary Cloister, Hall, and Treasury, plan (Willis 1868, facing p. 48, fig. 5).

Vestiarium on *Drawing I*) between St. Andrew's Chapel and the Infirmary Hall (discussed in the next chapter).

An examination of the principal axes of this new work suggests a common setting-out scheme (fig. 105). The northern wall of the Infirmary Cloister and the northern wall of the Infirmary Hall were constructed on the same alignment. Likewise, the west wall of the Infirmary Hall and the northern walk of the Infirmary Cloister are set at right angles to each other. Both axes indicate a single setting-out scheme and depart from those of the Great Cloister and Dormitory and the Cathedral, all Lanfranc constructions. In contrast to the

Infirmary Hall, the axis of the Infirmary Chapel was shifted some degrees to the north and the Treasury some degrees to the south (Willis 1868, 74–80 and figs. 5, 6) (fig. 103). Each suggests a separate development from that of the Infirmary Cloister and the Infirmary Hall.[6]

Mention of the Infirmary Hall opens the important question of whether it should also be attributed to Prior Wibert. The areas east of the Great Cloister remain the least agreed on parts of his renewal. Widely different dates are assigned to the Infirmary Hall and in turn to its related buildings such as the Infirmary Kitchen, Bath House, *Necessarium Infirmorum*, and the *Nova Camera*.

106　Canterbury Cathedral Priory, Infirmary Cloister arcade, looking south (courtesy Stuart Harrison).

Some specialists assign the Infirmary Hall to 1080; others put it as late as 1160.[7] By contrast, there is widespread agreement that the Infirmary Chapel dates to ca. 1155. Kahn convincingly demonstrated links between its capitals and those on the Green Court Gatehouse and Treasury, both Wibert's work (Kahn 1991, 177). The stylistic differences between the two buildings are admittedly puzzling, although these also mark other buildings from Wibert's years such as the *Aula Nova* and the Norman Staircase. The most plausible explanation has to do with the different modes appropriate to the Infirmary Hall and Chapel.

Examination of the various buildings follows. It shows them, I believe, to belong to Prior Wibert's renewal.

INFIRMARY CLOISTER

Drawing I shows the Priory's Infirmary Cloister as rectangular with three sides framed by arcaded walks (omitted next to the Dormitory) with the open center divided into two parts by a wooden trellis. The western part of the cloister is labeled *herbarium*, indicating medicinal plants used by the infirmary master, and this suggests a location for his office in the undercroft of Lanfranc's Dormitory. The east walk of the Infirmary Cloister retains six bays of original mid-twelfth-century arcading (fig. 106), a survival which ranks as the sole *in situ* cloister arcading standing in Great Britain (Tatton-Brown 2006, 97). Its preservation was the consequence of Prior Eastry's 1288–90 construction of the Counting House (or Checker), the western part of which was built over the east cloister walk. To spread the weight of the new west wall, Eastry employed two wide relieving arches supported on rectangular piers, which enclosed six bays of Wibert's east cloister arcading. When the Checker was demolished in 1868, the mid-twelfth-century arcading was spared, although it was left open to the weather as a ruin for almost a century, this decision accounting for most of its damaged condition. In 1964–66 a new brick building, the Wolfson Library, was erected in part over the cloister walk.[8]

107 Canterbury Cathedral Priory, Infirmary Cloister arcade, onyx column (courtesy Stuart Harrison).

108 Canterbury Cathedral Priory, Infirmary Cloister arcade, Purbeck marble column (courtesy Stuart Harrison).

The six surviving Infirmary Cloister arches are each 6 feet high internally and have a bay spacing of about 4 feet. Two pier types – double and single shafted – support the arches (Tatton-Brown 2006, 95). The double shaft type is composed of Purbeck marble, the single shaft type of fatter, monolithic onyx marble. At the north end of the arcade, the two types go out of step, as Tatton-Brown showed, presumably because the pier in the northeast corner was built last and was intended to support quadruple shafts (although today only three Purbeck marble shafts survive). The shafts (fig. 107) mix Caen stone (also used for the base, capital, and abacus) with calc-sinter for the columns (see Appendix C), whereas the Purbeck marble piers (fig. 108) use Purbeck for all four main elements (a double base with deeply undercut moldings, spirally cut shafts of various types, waterleaf capitals, and abaci). He also noted that the Infirmary Cloister is among the first places in England where Purbeck marble is used monumentally. The taste for semi-precious materials, a distinctive feature of Wibert's work, occurs at the same

time in the Norman Staircase, the *Aula Nova* (see Chapter 6), the Water Tower, the entry doorway to the crypt, and the Treasury.[9] The capitals mix foliate and waterleaf decoration (fig. 109).

109 Canterbury Cathedral Priory, Infirmary Cloister arcade, foliate capital (photograph author).

At the entry to the Infirmary Hall, Wibert constructed a Fountain House. It has not been archaeologically investigated. *Drawing I* depicts the fountain in the southeast corner of the Infirmary Cloister standing free from the arcades, and for compositional reasons it does not line up with the entry to the Infirmary Hall.

The Fountain House projected as a porch-like, western extension from the cloister arcade, as it is shown on the Hill plan of the 1680s (see fig. 5). The artist draws it as a slim, aedicular structure closed by a conical roof covered with lead with a ball finial at the apex (fig. 110A). The extension is confirmed by the survival of two column bases immured *in situ* in the east walk of the Infirmary Cloister. They indicate a three-arcaded entry.

Standing at the entry to the massive Infirmary Hall, the Fountain House served both mundane and metaphysical needs.[10] It addressed Hebrew practice for hand washing (Mark 7:2–4), and as such cleansed, refreshed, and delighted visitors as well as dignifying the threshold of the Infirmary Hall. It should be understood, as well, to reflect the spiritual healing powers of water, as numerous references in the Bible make clear. In Revelation, the evangelist's vision of the Lord reveals him surrounded by a multitude of witnesses who have come out of the great ordeal and no longer experience hunger, thirst, or heat "for the Lord will ... guide them to the springs of the water of life" (7:17). In Jerusalem, close to the Temple Mount, the famous pools of Siloam and Bethsaida were renowned for their healing properties. To spiritual and thaumatergic regeneration need to be added the medieval view of the *fons vitae* as cleansing and healing in a manner allegorized with the wounds of Christ.[11] Such references would have come readily to mind for visitors, monastic and other, to the Canterbury Infirmary.

Adjacent to the Infirmary Fountain House, the artist of *Drawing I* draws a column and well.[12] A *titulus* identifies both service elements: "column into which, when the waters of the source fail, water raised from the well may be poured and it will be distributed to all the offices" (*columna in quam ductu acque deficiente, potest haurire aqua de puteo et administrabitur ominibus officinis*). Physically, a standpipe is a straightforward back-up water device, and to shape it as a column raises a question about wider associations. Spiritually, by association, King Solomon's Temple in Jerusalem was adorned with sculpture made for him by Hiram of Tyre, which included in the vestibule "two pillars of bronze," each named and provided with bronze capitals (1 Kings 7:13–22). Exegetical texts

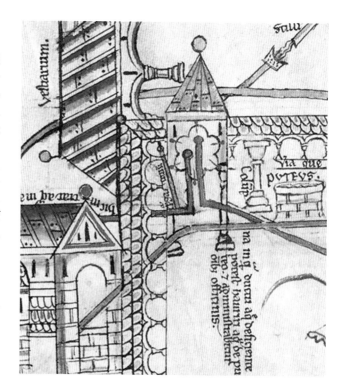

110A Eadwine Psalter, *Drawing I*, detail showing Infirmary Hall, Fountain House, Trinity College, Cambridge (courtesy the Master and Fellows, Trinity College, Cambridge).

on these verses, such as Bede's *De Templo*, contain fifteen heavily allegorized chapters devoted to the Temple's lavers (20.1–15). In chapter 20.9 Bede explains that "the laver was at the top of the capital to teach that the way to the heavenly kingdom had been open to us through baptism."[13] Wibert also renewed the wellhead now removed to St. Martin's Church, Canterbury (fig. 110B). Three registers of decoration – beaded interlace, intersecting arcading with beading, and alternating plain and v-shaped ornament – enrich what must earlier have been a plain wellhead (Tatton-Brown 2000, 19–20).

Memory and meaning are time-bounded concepts. The bearer of meaning for one generation loses focus for later ones. As much is suggested by the documented loss of regard for Wibert's fountain indicated by an entry in the *Registers* of Archbishop Winchelsey (1294–1313). The *Registers* record the laver's poor condition and the archbishop's enjoinder to the monks to keep it clean and not to spit or blow their noses into it.[14] A sharper record of loss comes a century later when Prior Chillenden could refer to parts of the Priory's water system, the pride of Wibert's generation, as "ancient, ruined and forgotten" and in need of repair (Willis 1868, 188).

110B   Canterbury, St Martin's Church, font, former wellhead from Priory (?) (from Kahn 1991, fig. 207).

NECESSARIUM

The *Necessarium* (Rere-Dorter, Garderobe, Privy, or Toilet Building), known to the monks as "the third dormitory," was placed perpendicular to the northeast corner of Lanfranc's Dormitory (fig. 111). It formed much of the south side of the Green Court, occupying the area from the Prior's Gatehouse to the Great Kitchen in the Cellarer's Court on *Drawing I*. The artist shows the *Necessarium* erroneously as a free-standing structure abutting the north range of the Infirmary Cloister. He also shows the piping and sewer connections as lying on the Green Court side of the building (rather than underneath it), presumably to ensure their display. The double channel with its painted links prompted Urry to suggest that the artist intended it to indicate vaulting (Urry 1986, 58).

In all monastic institutions the *Necessarium* needed to provide for two sets of toilet facilities: for day use (and thus accessible from ground level) and for night use (and thus accessible from the sleeping area). Accordingly, the

building was two stories high. No details are known of its form or waste disposal system in the years before Wibert's water system was installed.

The present remains are dated by Sparks and Tatton-Brown to ca. 1100 and therefore to Archbishop Anselm's rule (Sparks and Tatton-Brown 1989, 23; also Tatton-Brown 2006, 91). However, the axis of the surviving *Necessarium* (see fig. 103) lies parallel with the north walk of the Infirmary Cloister (and is continuous with the Infirmary Hall) and strongly suggests a unified build. For Sparks and Tatton-Brown's proposed date to work, the sewer tunnel and pipework (shown on *Drawing I*) would need to have been a retrofit. The scale of the infrastructure work can be established by the chance discovery in 1948 of a section of tunnel 4 feet high on the southeast side of the Cathedral. It had a paved floor with the lower wall constructed of Caen stone and the upper with Kentish ragstone. It was closed with chalk vaults.[15] Retrofitting this under an existing building would constitute a massive engineering feat. The tunnel's impressive scale features in a well-known episode in the Priory's history, the sensational escape from enforced confinement of Roger Norris in January 1188. Norris had been imposed on the monks as prior by Archbishop Baldwin (1184–90) as part of his long-running struggle with them over the establishment of a secular college at Hackington. No sooner was Norris in office than trouble erupted, and he was seized by the monks and imprisoned in the Infirmary. He shrewdly realized that the Infirmary sewer tunnel connected to that of the *Necessarium* (at its east end adjacent to the Prior's Gatehouse), crossed under the Green Court and exited into the city ditch just beyond the *Aula Nova*, and, accordingly, Norris effected his escape through it (Stubbs 1879, vol. II, lxi).

Only the night use arrangements of the *Necessarium* can be reconstructed. They were identified by Willis, who recognized that the north jamb led into a rectangular vestibule against the building's southwest end. The building took the form of a long, narrow, two-story hall. The external measurements are impressive (Willis favored the adjective "portentous"): 172 feet in length, 30 feet in width, and 30 feet in height (Willis 1868, 82; Sparks and Tatton-Brown 1989, 23). It rivalled Lanfranc's cathedral nave in length. The undercroft was groin vaulted on the south with a series of fifty-three arched openings on the north side to support the seats. The great drain ran east to west under the building and took the form of a tunnel flushed by water coming down from the fishpond by way of the Infirmary and supplemented by rainwater from the Cathedral's roofs. The fifty-three

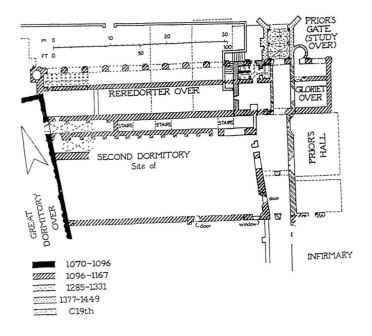

(Above) 111   Canterbury Cathedral Priory, *Necessarium*, plan (Sparks and Tatton-Brown 1989, 25, fig. 2).

(Right) 112   Canterbury Cathedral Priory, *Necessarium*, interior vaults (courtesy Courtauld Institute of Art).

seats on the upper floor were carried on slender (8-inch) arches with measurements from seat-center to seat-center of 2 feet 7 inches. Each seat was screened. A generously scaled corridor ran in front of the partitions. No provision is shown for hand washing.

At the west end at the junction with the Dormitory, the drain and parts of its north wall still stand to gable height. Reading out a clear chronology of work is complicated by raised ground levels, and there has been no attempt to clear or to maintain the remaining parts. At the west end, Sparks and Tatton-Brown reported that the north basement room of the present house contains the roof and walls of the drain; its south wall is also that of the *Necessarium* and stands to full height. About halfway down the range, five arches (for the seats) survive (fig. 112), and at the east end at No. 19 The Precincts a further six arches form the present utility room.

The prior's *Camera Vetus* (Old Residence), shown as an independent structure on *Drawing I*, was connected to the east end of the *Necessarium*. In fact, as already seen in Chapter 6, it is likely the *Necessarium* was linked also to the Prior's Gatehouse and thence to the Bath House.

The surviving parts of the structure have close constructional similarities to those at Cistercian Kirkstall

Abbey (Yorkshire) from ca. 1170, and to thirteenth-century examples at the abbeys of Royaumont (Val d'Oise) from ca. 1230 (fig. 113) and Maubuisson in France (both identified by Willis 1868, 87, n. 1 for Maubuisson).[16] The Priory's *Necessarium* was eclipsed by that at St. Augustine's, whose dimensions were recorded in the abbey's *Customary* as being 192 feet in length but a narrow 24 feet in width (E. M. Thompson 1902, 32).[17] This has disappeared and its relation to the Priory is thus denied us.

The generosity of facilities – 53 toilet seats for ca. 130 monks – far outstrips modern requirements, as has been pointed out by Horn and others (Horn and Born 1979, vol. I, 305–9). Even considering the strict regimentation of monastic life, such provision for high-peak demand and the time when it might be anticipated is puzzling. Similarly hard to understand is the absence of any other toilet facilities on *Drawing I* (excepting the small-scale *Necessarium Infirmorum*). This omission suggests either a license on the part of the artist or, rather less likely, the possibility that the Priory favored a single building for multiple use including servants and visitors, such as the one proposed for the Bath House (see Chapter 6).

At the suppression the *Necessarium* was transformed into a series of separate residences. These are shown on

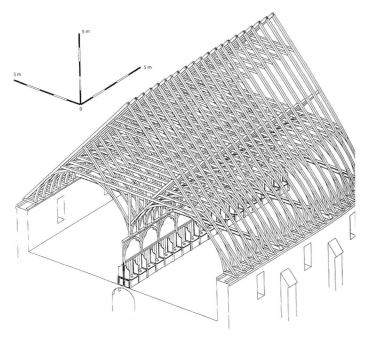

(Above) 113   Abbey of Royaumont, Val d'Oise, Toilet House, ca. 1230 (Epaud 2007, fig. 156).

(Right) 114   Canterbury Cathedral Priory, Infirmary Hall, west bays, south elevation (photograph author).

Thomas Hill's plan (see fig. 5) and remained until the Dean and Chapter ordered their demolition in 1852–54. Willis had studied them five years earlier, and much of what is known about the building depends on his careful notes and plan (Willis 1868, 82–93).

INFIRMARY HALL

Work on the Priory's huge Infirmary Hall, *Domus Infirmorum* on *Drawing I*, began shortly after 1155. It remains the largest monastic infirmary known from twelfth-century England and was the biggest single building raised by Prior Wibert in his far-reaching renewal at the Priory (see fig. 102). It measured 250 feet west to east including Hall and Chapel. The total floor area of the Infirmary Hall eclipsed even that of Lanfranc's Dormitory. Five round columns of the south aisle arcade survive. They carry scalloped capitals and arcades composed of two plain square orders with a shallow plain sunk fillet on the face. There is no trace of the clerestory, although it is shown prominently on

Drawing I, and its height can be estimated from the surviving west end (fig. 114). In section, therefore, the Infirmary Hall resembled a church, with a high central area and lower flanking aisles. Of the north arcade only a few traces remain (Willis 1868, 55–59): some masonry of the west bay without its aisle was left as a support for the west wall which stands just below gable height, and the same for the north aisle of which parts survive at the east end immured in the post-suppression choir house.

On the southwest side, the Infirmary Hall shares the two western bays with the Treasury. The wall is heavily scarred from successive rebuildings, most notably those connected with Prior Chillenden's construction of the sub-prior's two-story chamber in the early fifteenth century. The second story of the Treasury retains two units of original medallion ornament identical to that of the top stringcourse on the east and west façades, and confirms that the upper parts of the wall are original and were exposed to view. Furthermore, the Treasury's angle buttresses extend around the north side at both ends of the building. These features suggest a brief

115 Canterbury Cathedral Priory, Infirmary Hall, watercolor by L. L. Razé, 1865 (courtesy King's School Library).

Razé's watercolor captures three phases in the history of the Infirmary. The original twelfth-century Hall and Chapel are visible with a column from the Hall in the right middle ground and the entry to the Chapel in the foreground. The Post-Suppression modifications are revealed in the demolition in progress of the domestic residences built into the medieval structures. The creation of the ensuing mid-nineteenth century "ruin" is shown emerging.

period when the Treasury was free-standing, as it is shown on *Drawing I*.

The Infirmary Hall provided beds for the sick, for monks recovering from blood-letting, and for the infirm old (called *stationarii* because they had completed the *stagium* of fifty years within the Priory and were presumably in their seventies). Also eligible for care were secular clergy with connections to the prior, benefactors and advisors, and corrodians (Sparks 2007, 45). Beds were placed in the aisles, perhaps two or three per bay, with the bays most likely screened. A count of about thirty

beds would be plausible (for a population of around 130 monks). This estimate would compare with the same provision at a contemporary monastery such as Rievaulx with a population of 140 monks in the 1160s (Fergusson and Harrison 1999, 111–15). The center space would have been filled with chests for bedding, medicines, and equipment, and allowed for the circulation of staff. Some provision for fireplaces can be assumed. More difficult to understand was the construction of a floor-to-roof wall entirely separating the Hall from the Chapel except for an entry door in the center (of which traces remain on the south). The same arrangement occurred at Ely, as Willis was the first to note (1868, 53). The Infirmary Kitchen, Bath House, and *Necessarium* were placed against the north aisle, as also was the connection of the prior's *Nova Camera* to the northeast.

To provide for the care of those in the Infirmary, documents mention the names of doctors from outside the community. A Peter "medicus" is recorded in 1166, and the more famous Feramin in 1169, who is described by the titles "magister," "physicus," and "medicus." He is also credited with administering to "the medical affairs of the brethren" (Urry 1967, 158).

The Infirmary Hall survived the great fire of 1174 that consumed the adjacent "glorious choir" of St. Anselm. The chronicler Gervase, writing sixteen years later, singled out "the Infirmary with the chapel of St. Mary" as being heavily damaged (Willis 1845, 34). Ample evidence of the blaze remains even today on the piers which show areas of "blushing" of the limestone caused by the heat of the fire. At the suppression the Hall bore the name Long Hall (rather than the puzzling term *domus* used on *Drawing I*), indicating that it had probably been appropriated into the residence of the last medieval priors. With the monks gone, the entire north side of the Infirmary was dismantled, the nave serving as a street for the southern side residences which were formed by walling in the arcades and using them to provide structural support for the separate prebendal houses (fig. 115). This condition continued into the mid-nineteenth century. Despite this, in 1846–47 Willis was able to work out the general disposition of the medieval hall and to use it to compare with the same building type at Ely (ca. 1160 forward), which formerly had been thought to be a Saxon church and convent (Willis 1868, 53, n. 1). In the mid-nineteenth century Parliament decreed reductions in the size of cathedral chapters, and at Canterbury this led to the dismantlement in 1864 of the prebendal buildings constructed within the southern walls at the suppression, which Willis referred to as "the parasitic

116 Canterbury Cathedral Priory, Infirmary Chapel (courtesy Stuart Harrison).

additions" (1868, 53). Since then, the Infirmary Hall and Chapel have stood as picturesque ruins, a period taste associated with Romanticism, a circumstance which accounts for most of the loss of twelfth-century stone-work that has occurred in the past 150 years (fig. 116).

exposure to the weather, a few are known from draw-ings by the gifted antiquarian John Carter, published in *The Ancient Architecture of England* (1795–1807, pl. xxix). At the suppression the south side of the Chapel was turned into prebendal residences like the Hall. They

INFIRMARY CHAPEL

The Infirmary Chapel, noted as *Capella Sanctae Mariae* on *Drawing I*, stood at the east end of the Infirmary Hall. The south arcade survives for its full five-bay length with parts of the clerestory windows (fig. 117). The elevation repeated that of the Hall, a high-rising center space with a clerestory and lower flanking aisles. The severe and massive vocabulary used in the Hall was replaced by lighter-scale forms, more richly articulated piers (with cruciform cores and round shafts occupying the re-entrant angles with semicircular responds facing east and west), and windows with chevron moldings. Capitals featured wild beasts and richly carved, stylized leaves with interlacing bands (figs. 118A–C). Kahn relates the capitals to those on the Green Court Gatehouse and draws attention to their resemblance to the capitals in Anselm's crypt (fig. 119). Now much deteriorated by

117 Canterbury Cathedral Priory, Infirmary Chapel, south arcade from aisle (courtesy David Robinson).

118   Canterbury Cathedral Priory, capitals from south arcade, Infirmary Chapel (courtesy Stuart Harrison).

(Above left: A)   Conjoined monsters

(Above: B)   Dragon-tailed dog

(Left: C)   Foliate capital

were similarly freed in 1864, and thus the lower parts of the south aisle have remained exposed as ruins since. Numerous pieces of loose and now crumbling stonework litter the south side and have found their way into the gardens of neighboring houses to satisfy the taste for rockeries.

The Chapel's east termination is controversial. On *Drawing I* the artist shows the building with a semicircular apse, of which Kahn detected traces on the north side in the form of a pilaster capital which supported "the springing of the barrel vault of this apse" (Kahn 1991, 177). Caröe had made the same observation in 1909 when clearing ivy from the wall tops, discovering remains of a barrel vault "in recesses just east of the chancel arch which had been covered with new masonry

in the 1330s" (Caröe 1912, 41–56). None of this is visible today. What survive are the eastern archivolts of the twelfth-century chancel arch (replaced in the early fourteenth century). Both Kahn and Caröe assumed a semicircular apse. They justified this feature in part by a literal reading of *Drawing I*, which shows such a termination. Based on this evidence, Tatton-Brown and others have deduced a two-part development for the Infirmary Chapel: an original semicircular termination from ca. 1155–60 replaced by a flat end before the 1174 fire. However, reliance on *Drawing I* for this detail is debatable. The artist often resorts to abbreviation or other shorthand for compositional reasons, as seen in Chapter 3. At the south end of the Guesthouse he shows a semicircular end instead of the still surviving straight end (see Chapter 5). There is ample reason to believe that the Infirmary Chapel retains the original straight-ended east termination, as Urry realized (Urry 1986, 53). On the north and south exterior sides the clerestory windows show remains of chevron decoration, capitals with pellet decoration, and external angle quoins similar to those in Wibert's eastern towers.

119 Canterbury Cathedral Priory, Cathedral, crypt looking east (courtesy Stuart Harrison).

One major difficulty in accepting a date for the Chapel close to that for the Hall is reconciling the differences in style between them. In the Hall the master mason preferred utilitarian, mid-twelfth-century forms. By contrast, when faced with building the Chapel he opted for lighter, richer forms and favored a more articulated architecture with multiform piers and carved capitals. Did the choice hinge on the building type and use? Or does it reflect a change of master mason? In favor of the first is the example of the *Aula Nova*, as Willis noted, where similar contrasts distinguish the more serviceable Court Hall from the sumptuous lighter architecture used for the ceremonial Norman Staircase. The Treasury also displays a discernible shift between the earlier, small-scale, richly decorated undercroft and the austere monumental upper chamber.

Later changes to the Chapel can be followed in the east wall and north wall windows where tracery from the mid-1330s appears. The split-cusped and sub-cusped trefoils are identical to the window inserted in St.

Anselm's Chapel of the same date, indicating they are additions made by Prior Hathbrand (1338–70), who also built the hall titled "Mensa Magistri Infirmatorii," or Table Hall as it was called at the suppression (Willis 1868, 193). It stood at the east end of the north aisle of the Infirmary Hall. Hathbrand is credited as well with the construction of seven chambers for the infirm on the north side of the Hall, referred to in 1376 in Archbishop Sudbury's visitation. In addition, he appointed a full-time doctor and apothecary (Sparks 2007, 41).

Hathbrand's changes mark the rejection of the hall concept which had dominated infirmary design since the mid-eleventh century. In its place he substituted domestic-scale rooms for patient care. The change reflects different concepts of care, as well as falling numbers in the size of the community. The same development can be followed elsewhere in the infirmaries of the reform orders such as the Cistercian Fountains Abbey. At Benedictine Westminster Abbey, the community went a step further, demolishing their infirmary hall altogether and substituting a cloister with independent chambers around it. At Canterbury a more dramatic remodeling of the Infirmary Hall occurred under Prior Chillenden in the early 1400s. He oversaw the incorporation of the five southwest bays to form a lodging for the sub-prior, variously referred to as the Hostry or *Camera* (Willis 1868, 56, n. 2). This impressive residence drew the admiration of Willis, who was moved to call it "a beautiful specimen of the domestic architecture of the Chillenden period" (Willis 1868, 58). Like Chillenden's other work, the remodeling dramatically increased the size of window openings and incorporated period fitments such as Perpendicular fireplaces.

ANCILLARY INFIRMARY STRUCTURES

Coquina Infirmorum, Necessarium Infirmorum and Infirmary Bath House

Drawing I shows three buildings abutting the north aisle of the Hall: the *Coquina Infirmorum* (Kitchen of the Infirmary), the *Necessarium Infirmorum*, and the *Cupa de quam fluit aqua sub necessarium infirmorum* (the tub, or bath house, from which the water flows under the *Necessarium Infirmorum*). The kitchen is shown as a multistory tower with a single east-facing attached tall chimney, a small compact building of surprising height with a clerestory range and tiled bell-shaped roof. A comparison of the Infirmary Kitchen with the Great Kitchen in the Cellarer's Court shows use of the same graphic formula of tall chimneyed angle to indicate a chimney flue (cf. fig. 38).

All were demolished in the post-suppression period at the same time as the northern half of the Infirmary Hall. No traces remain above ground.

Camera Vetus Prioris

On *Drawing I* the prior's *Camera Vetus* (Old Residence) stood between the Prior's Gatehouse and the Infirmary Cloister, more or less on the site of the Checker or Counting House (for the keeping of accounts). This building was demolished in 1868. Following bomb damage in World War II the site was redeveloped as the Wolfson Library.

Until the late eleventh century the abbot (or prior) of a Benedictine house slept in the dormitory with the community (Knowles 1963, 190). Just when the Canterbury prior moved into a separate residence is not known,

and thus it is hard to date the *Camera Vetus* and specifically to know if the change originated with Lanfranc or Anselm.[18] The nobility lodged with the prior, and for convenience his house was connected to the Infirmary Hall to take advantage of its superior facilities (for kitchen, baths, and toilets).

On *Drawing I* the *Camera Vetus* is shown as detached, although this was probably a device necessitated by the artist's composition. The building was entered by a flight of steps, with a trellis drawn next to a large door which presumably gave entry to the Infirmary Cloister. The *Camera Vetus* was two-storied with seven clerestory windows. Willis reported that "remains and traces of Norman chambers are still to be seen" (Willis 1868, 94–95, 100–2) on the site, although it is not possible to identify these today.

Nova Camera Prioris

The building lying to the northeast of the Infirmary Hall is now covered by the school's Linacre House. It is shown on *Drawing I*, although it is only faintly legible being heavily rubbed and water-stained. It is labeled *Nova Camera Prioris et fons ejus* (Prior's New Residence and cistern).[19] Just to the east is a large circular bath. As drawn, the *Nova Camera* was a large two-story building with an impressive double-story entry. It was connected at the west end to the *Necessarium Infirmorum*. It is not shown as connected to the Infirmary Chapel, although it was doubtless linked to it by a passageway for the convenience of the prior and his guests.

The sole remains are parts of the north side of the ground floor immured in Linacre House (Sparks 2007, 139). To the south of the house the artist of *Drawing I* shows a large cistern (a circle colored green) and to the west the *cupa* or bath (in a smaller circle also colored green).

The *Nova Camera* and accompanying water arrangements were part of Wibert's renewal. Since the *Camera Vetus* lay to the west, adjacent to the Prior's Gatehouse and in the general area of the Checker, the relatively small distance between the old and new residences raises the question of why a rebuilding was thought necessary. The most plausible explanation is that the *Camera Vetus* lay adjacent to or even within the monastic enclosure, whereas the *Nova Camera* lay outside it. Removal from the strict enclosure made the coming and going of guests of the top social rank more flexible. Similar developments can be traced at other major monastic houses at the same time such as Bury St. Edmunds (Whittingham 1971,

16–17 and 23–24). In each case the impulse was to lessen the disruption to communal life caused by distinguished visitors. At Canterbury the *Nova Camera*'s adjacency to the Prior's Gatehouse to the west (from the Green Court) and to the Queningate Gate to the east suggests that access and circulation were impulses behind the rebuilding, along with the provision of bath facilities.

Prior Wibert's construction of the Infirmary Hall and its related buildings coincided with similar developments elsewhere in mid-twelfth-century England. The scale of the Infirmary Hall and the Infirmary Cloister placed the Priory in the first rank of monastic establishments. Likewise, the surrounding buildings and their linkage to the new water system indicate attention to ancillary needs and up-to-date hygiene. The same applies to the provision of medical specialists from outside the community to treat illness or supervise healing. On the other hand, the choice of structure and form is fairly standard, at least as far as the chronology of infirmary halls is understood at present. Prior Wibert's acceptance of prevailing infirmary types and even of the limited degree of ornamentation that came with them contrasts with his more characteristic openness to new ideas evident in his other building work. Only with the addition of the Infirmary Chapel did he employ new architectural forms.

8

CATHEDRAL ENHANCEMENTS AND RELATED BUILDINGS

Prior Wibert's renewal included work on the Cathedral and on buildings related and mostly connected directly to it. Although they are viewed today as piecemeal, relatively small scale, and thus minor undertakings, contemporaries considered them otherwise. Prior Wibert's *obit* details first and foremost his gifts of vestments and furniture to the cathedral. His building additions pale by comparison unless the generality "...like the many more things he made to happen" applies to them. Archbishop Anselm's "glorious choir" raised and furnished ca. 1100–30 and the most celebrated building of its age had over time revealed deficiencies. It was to remedy them that Wibert undertook ambitious building and renovation as well as the outlay of large sums of money for the furnishings.

Included in the undertakings to the Cathedral are two of the best-known survivals of Wibert's renewal, the Treasury and Water Tower. The Treasury (*Vestiarium* on *Drawing I*) is a confusing term. It came into use with Willis and has proved durable (rather than the more accessible term "sacristy").[1] The building is linked to St. Andrew's Chapel on the north side and is sizable, two-storied, and fully vaulted. It was used for the

storage of liturgical vessels and vestments. Where this function was located before is uncertain. Archbishop Lanfranc's *Constitutions* mentioned the sacrist's responsibility for the twice-weekly washing of liturgical vessels and specified that the water so used "be thrown into the piscine in the sacristy" (Knowles and Brooke 2002, 122, 124). This indicates a space distinct from the chapels with a location on an outside wall.[2] By the mid-twelfth century, sacristies as separate structures begin to be noted in documentary accounts elsewhere. Wibert's Treasury was an early and ambitious example, but site conditions determined a unique combination of functions with the upper story assigned to the sacristy, and the undercroft passage at ground level to rites connected with burial. In adopting a single architectural solution for both needs, the prior displayed ingenuity and imagination.

Wibert's other rebuildings for the Cathedral involved a range of different improvements. They included the provision of a laving building – the novel Water Tower – for the monks when they entered their choir for the night office. In addition, Wibert renovated the chapels of St. Andrew and St. Anselm, adding rib

121   Canterbury Cathedral Priory, Treasury, view from east (photograph author).

The ruins of the Infirmary Hall are on the right, the early Gothic Trinity Chapel on the left. The story above the intersecting arcading was added by Prior Chillenden.

vaulting, upper rooms and (in the case of the latter) fresco paintings, heightening the towers on the exterior adjacent to them, and embellishing roofs with finials and sculpture. He also enhanced with relief decoration both interior entries to Anselm's huge new crypt.

In related developments, Wibert provided new features on the south side of the Cathedral: an enlarged free-standing campanile for the cemetery, an arched entry in the wall that separated the lay from the monks' cemetery, a fountain opposite the south transept, and plans for an improved gatehouse to the Precinct from the city, the Christ Church Gatehouse.

TREASURY

The two-story Treasury straddles the space between the Infirmary Hall and Archbishop Anselm's existing St. Andrew's Chapel, which opened out of the north side of the sanctuary (fig. 121). It stands free from the former

but is connected to the latter. In the upper story the building was linked to the Cathedral with a doorway cut through the Chapel's outer wall. Whether it also served as the location for the security of money is debated. Smith and du Boulay link the building to Prior Wibert's financial reforms that resulted in the creation of the new office of dispensator in the early 1160s (Smith 1943, 14, and du Boulay 1966, 252).

The Treasury is the only building from Wibert's rule which survives with uses still more or less intact, at least for the upper story.[3] At ground level the building served in the Middle Ages as a gateway or passageway connecting the monastic enclosure (at the west) to the monastic cemetery (at the east), and is best explained in the context of burial and perhaps the anniversary liturgies connected with it.[4]

The artist's depiction of the Treasury on *Drawing I* shows a lower building than the present one (fig. 122). Above the dominating arched openings at ground level, a low upper story is depicted. There is no indication of

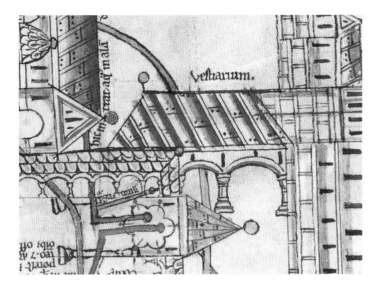

the increased height given to the upper story consequent on the insertion of the vault. The artist magnifies the importance of the ground floor relative to the upper story, the direct opposite of the present view of the building. Either this represents an abbreviation by the artist or it shows the building in the brief period before the introduction of rib vaulting and the subsequent heightening visible in the top story in the intersecting arcades (fig. 123).

The dual orientation for the Treasury is manifest in the unusual provision of two similar façades. The west façade, facing the Infirmary Cloister (fig. 124), is enriched with slightly greater detail, with the two arches at ground level framing low segmental tympanums, a feature missing on the east arches. Explaining the difference is the lower height of the arches of the east façade (the ashlar coursing between the arch heads and the first stringcourse shows three courses on the east side and one on the west). The interior vaults were adjusted accordingly; those on the east descend to the arch heads, and those on the west form recessed segmental tym-

122   Eadwine Psalter, *Drawing I*, detail (rotated) showing the Treasury (*Vestiarium*), Trinity College, Cambridge (courtesy the Master and Fellows, Trinity College, Cambridge).

123   Canterbury Cathedral Priory, Treasury, east façade (courtesy Stuart Harrison).

The Treasury is the most complete of Prior Wibert's buildings to survive. The upper story comprising the triplet windows and intersecting arcading retains many of its intended functions as a sacristy.

124   Canterbury Cathedral Priory, Treasury, west façade (photograph author).

125   Canterbury Cathedral Priory, Treasury, under story, interior, southwest bay (photograph author).

panums. The suspicion is thus raised that the interior vaults are insertions, the change made while construction was in progress (probably to replace groin vaults). Jogged abaci confirm this idea, as do the cut-back vault springers to accommodate them (fig. 125). The segmental tympanums at the west play no part in the door design or help to facilitate closure; there are no rebates against which the doors would close and no marks of closure on the archivolts of the segmental tympanum. Moreover, had this been the case, the door-leaves for such a doorway would have opened outward, departing from the traditional medieval technique of bar-bracing behind the leaves. Today, the door jambs show iron hinges whose date cannot be fixed. They are most likely secondary, as, too, are those flanking the crypt window in the southeast bay that offered access into the Holy Innocents Chapel in the crypt and those of the adjacent openings to the cloister walk.

The arches on the east and west sides of the building are decorated differently. A downward-facing chevron marks the east side, and a bolder outward-facing chevron elaborated with beading is on the west side (on the northern arch). By contrast, a Greek key motif (giving the carvers problems in its adjustment to the archivolts – fig. 126) ornaments the inner arch on the west side, embellished with drilled circular pellets and a billet on the edge, a motif used again on the stringcourse above. Both western arches are framed by hood moldings (omitted on the east arches) consisting of roundels overlaid with interlinked diagonal crosses and pellets. The inner faces of these arches reverse the order of decoration, perhaps reflecting an in-and-out circulation. Shafts *en délit* support the arches; those on the east are slim and made of limestone, those on the west bulkier with sumptuous polished calc-sinter columns, a luxurious, semi-precious stone not normally used on exteriors (see Appendix C).

Above the doorways, a central wall buttress separated the elevation into two bays, each with a splayed window flanked by lower blind arches. The resulting triple

126 Canterbury Cathedral Priory, Treasury, west façade, southwest arch (photograph author).

arrangement (low-high-low/narrow-wide-narrow) is articulated by plain limestone shafts *en délit* topped with scalloped capitals. The window arches have a twisted foliate molding surmounted by billet hoods. Heavy bars secured the windows; those on the eastern side survive, but those on the west are now reduced to iron stumps.

The elevation displays arched compositions in ascending number. The single arched opening at ground level is topped by triple openings to bring light to the interior, and then crowned in the attic story by a band of intersecting arches. As already mentioned, this last register corresponds to the increase in height of the rib vault in the interior (see below). To close the overall elevation, the master mason used a stringcourse (rather than a cornice) composed of a band of decorated medallions. Originally, a pitched roof with lead sheeting covered the building, as shown in *Drawing I*, and was decorated with a finial at the northern gable end.

The elevation's rich decorative motifs reveal a varied lineage. Many resemble those used fifty years earlier in Anselm's east extension to the Cathedral. Intersecting arcading appears on the exterior of the eastern transept towers; and beaded strapwork, fretwork arches, scallop decoration, and columns with scaling can all be found in the crypt, such as the Holy Innocents Chapel. Citations from Anselm's work suggest a desire to adjust the Treasury to the deceased archbishop's adjacent building and constitute a lithic genuflection to a venerated figure from Canterbury's recent past. They also indicate an impulse to harmony and reflect his pervasive influence

during the period when the Priory was making strenuous efforts to advance his canonization. An active lay guild furthered this process which culminated in his *translatio* to the south chapel of the east transepts in 1163 (Urry 1959, 571–93). At the same time, Prior Wibert incorporated new forms, such as the up-to-date shield designs enriching the scalloped capitals, as Kahn has noted (1991, 187–88). A further allusion may be discerned in the use of saltire (or diagonal) crosses, the symbol of St. Andrew, on the hood moldings (fig. 126), and abacii of the center pier (fig. 127B). They signal the immediate adjacency of the chapel dedicated to him, as well as the space's function (see below).

The passageway or undercroft was rib vaulted in four bays, the vaults springing from a central compound pier with scallop capitals ornamented with shield designs. Roll-molded vault ribs intersect with animal-headed keystones cut from blue lias marble. Each carries an iron ring to support a hanging lamp. The rings have to be original features because there is no possible way of inserting them after the keystones were set. Elsewhere, rich carving marks the capitals, abaci, and wall shafts. For the capitals, scallop along with early foliate designs predominate (figs. 127A–C), and drew the attention of Austin to serve as models for his *Aula Nova* renewal (fig. 128). The wall shafts against the west openings are adorned with palmette patterns (on the north) and scale patterns (on the south) like those on the axial pier in the adjacent Holy Innocents Chapel. Adding to the decorative splendor, the walls of the passageway were originally painted with star and crescent decoration, some areas of which may still be discerned.[5]

Turning to the first-floor interior, the Treasury was linked to the Cathedral by a low doorway driven through the west bay of St. Andrew's Chapel (fig. 129). The Treasury's height made it necessary to block two of the Chapel's windows; their heads are visible through the limewash on the interior. The Treasury's interior is revealed as a single, dramatic, high-rising, fully vaulted space, 20 feet in height on a plan measuring 22 feet 9 inches east and west, 23 feet north and south, and thus a near cube.[6] Adjustment to the trapezoidal floor area resulting from the oddly swung Anselm Chapel meant that the bay widths varied; the vault formerets do not line up with the four splayed windows. The choice was to favor consistency in window placement on the exterior where it was easier to disguise the fan shape of the ground plan.

Dominating the space is the imposing octopartite rib vault (32 feet long on the diagonal), as shown in John

127   Canterbury Cathedral Priory, Treasury, under-story capitals.

(Above left: A)   Capital with foliate leaf extended from side to front (courtesy Stuart Harrison).

(Above: B)   Capitals with scallop variations with abacus showing beaded saltire crosses (courtesy Stuart Harrison).

(Left: C)   Capital with trumpet scallop with foliate mouths and beaded circular discs (courtesy Stuart Harrison).

(Below left) 128   Treasury, drawing from the Austins' *Sketchbook*, n.d., unpaginated (Canterbury Cathedral Archives and Library, © Dean and Chapter).

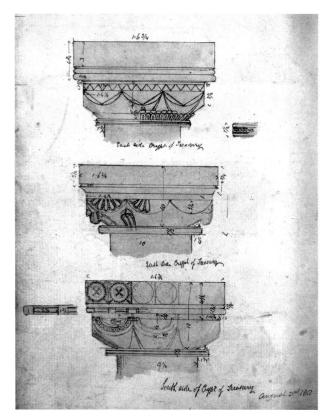

Bilson's cleverly devised diagram (fig. 130). The single-span vault intersects at a keystone carved with the heads of four lions inscribed within a broad framing molding which is decorated with abstracted lions' manes rendered as alternating semicircular and triangular strigillated tufts (fig. 131). The vault is supported on the outer walls by semicircular shafts of coursed ashlar with scallop capitals enriched with beading (these are omitted in the corners where the vaults die into the abaci). The last feature led Bilson to realize that the vault was an insertion made during the course of construction like those in the under story. The original intention was probably to vault from a central support, as was done in the story below. The substitution of the single octopartite vault occasioned an increase in height of 9 feet. It also resulted on the exterior in the addition of the intersecting arcading.[7]

Overall, the interior of the upper story conveys an effect markedly more austere than the undercroft. Decoration shows little of the richness and exuberant

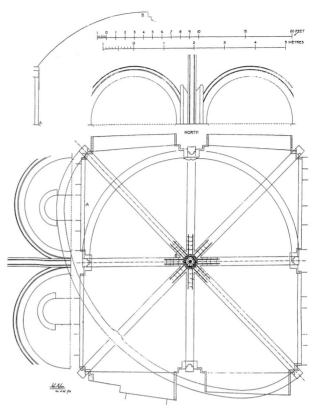

(Above) 129   Canterbury Cathedral, St. Andrew's Chapel, north wall, with entry cut through to Treasury (courtesy Stuart Harrison).

(Above right) 130   John Bilson, diagrammatic drawing of upper-story vault of the Treasury (*Archaeological Journal*, 74, 1917, 26).

(Right) 131   Canterbury Cathedral Priory, Treasury, upper story, keystone with lions' heads (courtesy Conway Library, The Courtauld Institute of Art, London).

accumulation of small-scale features found below. Restraint is palpable and the monumentalizing impression conveyed by the assertive power of the vault predominates. It is conceived, however, not in the historicizing tradition of Romanesque but in the new spatial tradition of Gothic.

Two distinct functions of the building need to be distinguished. As already mentioned, the upper floor served the Cathedral's needs for a treasury, namely a vesting sacristy and liturgical vessel and relic repository. Taking first the upper floor, its functions and topographic placement show a number of correspondences to biblical descriptions, specifically of Solomon's Temple complex.[8] In 1 Kings and Ezekiel we are told that the Temple lay between separate courts, was two stories (with the lower one serving as an underpassage), used semi-precious materials (the calc-sinter columns framing the west doorways), and employed carved lions' heads (on the crowning single annular keystone of the interior vault).[9] Whether the octopartite rib vault might be considered along with the lions' heads as connected to the Temple's bronze stands with lions' heads made of one piece by Hiram of Tyre (see 1 Kings 7:25) is difficult to prove. That Solomonic references could be associated with loggias or galleries, however, is confirmed from a description of the chapel of the castle at Ardres of ca. 1120, where the loggia was "like the Temple of Solomon in its decoration" (Mortet 1911, 185). Earlier, at Canterbury, Anselm had established as specific interests the study of the Old Testament king, patriarch, and Temple builder, leading him, among other things, to adopt Solomonic columns to surround the main crypt altar, and instigating the ordering of the astonishing liturgical cope equipped with 100 tiny silver bells.[10]

The under story, by contrast, is today little more than a support for the upper story. Once a passageway linking parts of the Convent, it is now a fenced enclosure used as storage space for the buildings' works department. Referred to in the literature as a gatehouse, this term is clearly invalid because the façades feature nearly identical back and front designs, and the absence of evidence of closure separates it from other gatehouses at the Priory. The latter point is made emphatic in *Drawing I*, where the artist underlines the Treasury's manifest openness and lack of doors, a striking contrast to the care with which he shows zones of enclosure with doors, locks, and embellished hinges throughout the Precinct. The under story was, I argue, designed to be open. It was thus closer to an archway than a gateway, a framer of space more than a closer of it.

The Treasury's role as gateway and liturgical passageway can only be grasped in the context of twelfth-century monastic practice. A clue to the use of the ground floor of the building comes from the rich decoration. Elaborately carved columns and capitals, painted walls, hanging lamps, and semi-precious stone (on the Convent's side) indicate an importance whose original context is essential to grasp. The building linked monastery to cemetery, providing thereby a monumental setting for each. Lanfranc's *Constitutions* record much about the community's practices when one of its brethren died. A vigil was prescribed before burial, designated for a separate chapel, along with its accompanying service, the Placebo. Where this was conducted in Anselm's extended east end is unknown, although it was likely in the Holy Innocents Chapel in the adjacent crypt. At Durham, *The Rites of Durham* specify the chapel dedicated to St. Andrew, which was solely reserved for this function (Fowler 1902, 51–52). At Canterbury, the Treasury's adjacency to St. Andrew's Chapel suggests the same use as the later one at Durham. Complicating matters, the sole doorway at ground level is the one at the base of Anselm's north transept, corresponding to the crypt. The door's relation to the remains of a vaulting compartment lying at the southwest angle of St. Andrew's Chapel and directly adjacent to the Treasury is unclear. Willis identified it as an "ancient vestibule" related to the thoroughfare to the cemetery (Willis 1845, 80–81, also fig. 5). The adjacency of these spaces to the cemetery is obscured today because William of Sens's extended choir and Trinity Chapel occupy much of the old burial ground, distancing in consequence the original connection of archway and cemetery. Unfortunately, Lanfranc's *Constitutions* do not specify the route taken by the funeral procession (Knowles and Brooke 2002, 188–92). The most plausible linkage of burial liturgy with the spaces seems to be for the singing of Psalm 113/114, *In exitu Israel*, traditional for interments, which was directed in the *Constitutions* (Knowles and Brooke, 2002, 188).[11]

Psalm 113/114 shaped much of the concept of death in the Middle Ages. Death was viewed as a transition rather than a termination. The dead had exchanged earthly life for eternal life. In consequence, cemeteries and the departed dead resting in them were seen as part of a living culture, rather than being marginalized from it as in modern cemeteries (Geary 1994, 2, also Paxton 1990). For monks the connection was particularly relevant. The dead were an embedded feature of monastic culture. Every day the community recalled them in chapter, offered them liturgical commemoration in choir,

132 Jerusalem, church of the Holy Sepulchre (photograph James Robertson and Felice Beato, 1857, courtesy Conway Library, The Courtauld Institute of Art, London).

and awaited in anticipation their re-embodied return in visions. For monks, death was seen thus not as an end to be dreaded but as an entry to be celebrated. As a "gateway" to the Eternal City, death called for memorialization. The community also chanted Psalm 118 with verse 19 "...open to me the gates of righteousness that I may enter through them and give thanks to the Lord. Seen in this context, the Treasury's highly decorated archways signified an entryway to the community's burial ground, more richly decorated on the entry (or monastery) side than on the return or east side.

One model with some similarities of purpose to Canterbury can be suggested. The most famous burial site in Christendom, the Holy Sepulchre in Jerusalem, had received a monumental new entrance in the 1150s (a few years before work began at Canterbury) to serve the thousands who flocked to visit the tomb of Christ (fig. 132). Twin entrances lead into a vestibule that carries a second story with openings, all elaborately decorated. Folda has suggested a model based on the Golden Gate on the east side of the Haram al-Sharif.[12]

Other models existed in Rome. In the mid-twelfth century visits to cemeteries were particularly noted as a tradition in Rome, as also were memorial arches connected with them.[13] The English author of the *Mirabilia Urbis Romae* (ca. 1150) lists the city's triumphal arches and mentions that "there are, moreover, other arches, which are not triumphal but memorial arches, such as the Arch of Piety in front of Santa Maria Rotundo" (Nichols 1986, 7). These structures survived from the Roman practice of constructing posthumous arches to honor the dead. The tradition extended back to Augustus, and construction required the permission of the Senate of Rome.[14] Memorial arches functioned as portals per se as well as literal and symbolic markers of passage for Roman religious rites, not unlike triumphal arches (Kleiner 1985, 33–37, 41–44; de Maria 1988, 106–8). Returning to *Drawing I*, it is interesting that the building's appearance without the addition to the upper-story vaults adheres to a more traditional arch composition.

Knowledge of such models explains the Treasury's distinctive twin façades and the unusually rich range of decoration with which they were treated.[15] Two motifs carry particular funerary connotations: the circular medallions woven to the saltire crosses over the west-facing entry arches and the abacus of the central supporting pier echo the *paternae* of Roman memorial arches, and the moon and star pattern on the interior walls explicitly recalls the same motif symbolizing the celestial afterlife in Roman funerary reliefs.[16] If these are added to the already mentioned references made by the decoration – the motifs recalling Anselm, the lions' heads King Solomon, the saltire crosses St. Andrew – it is clear that the building's prominent ornament was devised to convey meaning.

An earlier sacristy is recorded under Anselm (Fergusson, 2006, 58) and another at nearby St. Augustine's a little after. The building type comes into vogue in the mid years of the century. At Salisbury Bishop Roger (1107–39) is recorded as having built a treasury early in his career (Montague 2006, 55–56, 63), although no details are known, and at Winchester Henry of Blois (1129–71) modified existing space in the south transept for this purpose (Kusaba 1988, 38–49). Similar interests mark the papal palace at the Lateran, where Prior Bernard is recorded as having adapted between 1139 and 1145 the old chapter house to serve this purpose.[17] A little later than Canterbury, Noyon Cathedral embarked upon the construction of a treasury-sacristy which still stands. At Peterborough in the late 1170s, Abbot Benedict constructed a sacristy on the west side of the south transept, like Winchester, only placing it at ground level.

133   Canterbury Cathedral Priory, Water Tower, view from north (courtesy Stuart Harrison).

Rib vaulted in unusual five-part vaults, it shows connections to the Priory from which Abbot Benedict had come. None of these attempts, however, shows the same interest in the elision of functions that marked Canterbury, and none provides a precedent for its grandeur. For both, the agency and interest of Prior Wibert remain as fundamental.

NIGHT ENTRY WATER TOWER

Archbishop Anselm's decision to double the size of the Cathedral by adding a huge new east termination, to bring the measurements to those of old St. Peter's, Rome, entailed a number of adjustments for its users. For the monks it involved a new night entry for the first office of the day which commenced at 2:30 a.m. Anselm reversed Lanfranc's arrangement of a passageway

across the west end of the Chapter House and then down a circular vice into the northwest transept (Strik 1982, fig. 3; Willis 1868, 17–18). Instead, a doorway was driven through the opposite wall of the Dormitory (in the southeastern bay) at first-floor level and a passageway constructed above the walk leading from the dark entry to the Infirmary Cloister. The passageway was given an L-shaped form (see fig. 105), moving eastwards for four bays before turning at right angles to continue southwards to enter Anselm's newly built transept of the Cathedral, and thence led to the monks' choir. The ensuing passageway's under story doubled as the south arcade of the Infirmary Cloister and was groin vaulted. At the angle where the passageway turned, Prior Wibert inserted an octagonal Water Tower projecting boldly into the Infirmary Cloister.

The Water Tower (figs. 133 and 134) ranks among the most widely illustrated examples of twelfth-century monastic architecture (Carӧe 1929, 25–37). Despite this exposure, the structure has been little studied and remains poorly understood. The importance placed on the building in the mid-twelfth century can be grasped from *Drawing I*, where the artist shows it (see fig. 14A) at exaggerated scale, in considerable detail, and as dominating the Infirmary Cloister. The building's preservation is owed to its continued use after the suppression in 1540, when it became an entry to the Cathedral from the Green Court. Visitors entered from the former Larder Gate, traversed the former Dormitory, and when they reached its southern end chose either a route into the Cathedral along the former night passageway or one to a connecting stair that led down to the Great Cloister and the Chapter House (or Sermon House) (Sparks 2007, 119).

As intended, the Water Tower served the monks for a ritual cleansing after they exited the Dormitory and before they entered their choir. The rite was specified in Archbishop Lanfranc's *Constitutions* (Knowles and Brooke 2002, 20, 22, 40, 60).[18] Where this was performed in Lanfranc's church is unclear, although Strik's identification of a *piscina* in the pier forming the northeast corner of the transept, in the adjacent bay at the base of the monks' stair from their dormitory, suggests a possible placement (Strik 1982, fig. 3). Nothing is known of the same feature in Anselm's extended east end. The remarkable prominence given to the Water Tower by Prior Wibert indicates a much elevated role for the rite.

To house the laver, Prior Wibert adopted an architecture strikingly different from that used elsewhere. It took the form of a pavilion-like solar, somewhat miniaturized, with richly ornamented slender forms articulated with linear supports and rib vaults, and well lit from six windows. Gibson assessed the Water Tower as Wibert's most celebrated achievement, but she was moved to continue that it was "a highly decorated, slightly old-fashioned little edifice" (Gibson 1995, 58–59). Her judgment could hardly be less apt. In its mid-twelfth-century form, the Water Tower stood out as a brilliant and highly visible conceit. Expensive, even flashy, it must have struck visitors as a feature signifying up-to-date extravagance and institutional pride.

Constructed on an octagonal plan, the Water Tower rests on an outer ring of eight columns linked by arches decorated with chevrons filled with simple triangles. From each column an attached shaft rose into the upper story, a feature conveying light buttressing and one that needs to be restored in the mind and separated from the much heavier supports added by Chillenden 250

134   Canterbury Cathedral Priory, Water Tower and connecting upper storey passageway to monks' dormitory (courtesy Stuart Harrison)

years later when he increased the size of the windows (fig. 135).

At ground level, the structure rests on a central columnar, stem-like support constructed of wedge-shaped stones cut with great precision to form the radial core (fig. 136), just as shown on *Drawing I*. The support enclosed as well the pipe and drain for the upper-story laver, all robbed for the value of the lead at the suppression with the space filled by replacement stone. The support stood on a round plinth later enlarged with four piers, with paired attached shafts toward the aisle closely clustered around it. Only the two on the south are original and retain trumpet scallop leaves and an impost of palmettes bordered by beaded frames (fig. 137) (the two on the north are crude, thickened sixteenth- and seventeenth-century replacements).

The central support was encircled by a rib-vaulted ambulatory. Vault compartments alternate square and

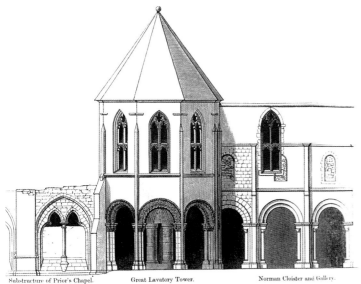

Substructure of Prior's Chapel.   Great Lavatory Tower.   Norman Cloister and Gallery.

Fig. 7.— ELEVATION OF PART OF THE SOUTH SIDE OF THE INFIRMARY CLOISTER.

135 Canterbury Cathedral Priory, Water Tower, Willis's drawing showing Chillenden renovations, and connecting passageway from monks' Dormitory over the Infirmary Cloister arcade with Wibert's twelfth-century blocked windows (Willis 1868, facing p. 50, fig. 7).

136 Canterbury Cathedral Priory, Water Tower, supporting masonry stem for supply, drain pipes, and inspection hatch (blocked) (courtesy Stuart Harrison).

137 Canterbury Cathedral Priory, Water Tower, capital from under story (courtesy Stuart Harrison).

triangular over trapezoidal bays (one for each two arch openings), the ribs with skewed intersections. The ribs have profiles worked with center rolls and flanking rectangular moldings accented with rows of billet, and with carved keystones at their intersections. For the southern bays, the master mason opted for transverse arches and awkwardly shaped cells (without ribs). Throughout, vault adjustments indicate the difficulty of handling rib intersections over turning bays and suggest a series of *ad hoc* solutions. Similar problems were faced in the nearby undercroft vaults in the Treasury (see below).

The upper room forms a delicate octagon. Lit originally by six round-headed windows (fig. 138), three escaped Chillenden's remodeling when taller, two-light transomed windows were inserted. The Wibert windows have chevron ornament both downward-facing and outer-facing, the latter with an unusual superimposed fret motif. Each bay was provided with an inset Purbeck marble seat and back (fig. 139). Although empty now, the room needs to be imagined with the large scalloped-edged laver with eight spigots in the center.[19] *Drawing I* shows the laver's waters with strigillated patterns on their surface, a means of conveying the constant surface motion resulting from the eight jets (but omitted in Willis's line drawing).

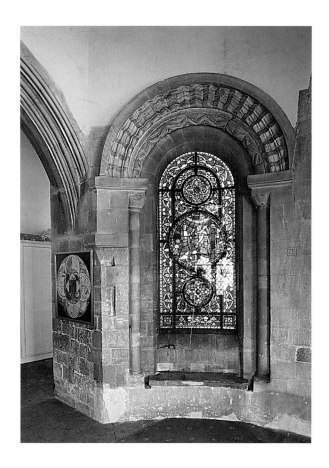

(Left) 138　Canterbury Cathedral Priory, Water Tower, interior, original bay (courtesy Stuart Harrison).

(Above) 139　Canterbury Cathedral Priory, Water Tower, interior, with Purbeck seat and back (photograph author).

The entry was elaborately screened from floor to enclosing arch. Fragments survive on the east jamb and indicate an open-work composition of intersecting arches. Presumably the screen provided an in-and-out entry door system. Even so, the convergence of around 130 monks on the structure within a short period of time must have caused a circulation problem. The screen was dismantled, probably by Chillenden. His intention was to open up the walls with higher tracery windows and to eliminate the screened division of laver from passageway. On the western side the remains of a mid-twelfth-century base built into later walling indicate that the present entry is a contraction of the original one. The lavish decoration applied at small scale to the screen would have given the Water Tower a highly worked, even precious, closed quality.

While the Water Tower functioned as a laver, the provision of the expensive marble seats lacks explanation.[20] The building's octagonal form and the laver's eight foils were clearly intended to evoke the tradition of regeneration carried by this number. These operated across a broad sweep from baptism to resurrection and would have been readily understood in the mid-twelfth century.[21]

The later medieval history of the Water Tower is sketchy. Chillenden's enlargement of the windows and likely removal of the screen around 1400 have been mentioned and probably reflected fashion more than wear or damage. In the early sixteenth century brick and flint buttresses were added to brace the lateral thrusts of the arches. At the suppression in 1540, the laver was destroyed but the building was otherwise spared. In the late eighteenth century, the Water Tower underwent a surprising reincarnation as a baptistery for the Cathedral and enjoyed a century of use as such (see Chapter 1).

ST. ANDREW AND ST. ANSELM CHAPEL RENOVATIONS

Prior Wibert's work on the Cathedral focused first on the chapels of St. Andrew and St. Anselm which flanked the pre-fire east end. Prompting the latter was doubtless the campaign undertaken by a lay guild as well as the monastic community for the beatification of Anselm. Achieved in 1163, it honoured the great figure in the intellectual and spiritual life of Canterbury. An added factor for the renewal may have been structural necessity, as Woodman argues (1981, 83), an observation based on reinforcements visible in the aisles and crypt chapels below them. Just as important was Wibert's decision to construct upper chambers above the chapels.

Wibert's work in the chapels included the insertion of rib vaults (to replace earlier groin vaults), probably beginning with the north chapel. More far-reaching were changes to the south chapel where new capitals were inserted with stylized flowers and beaded interlace, and fresco paintings commissioned.

EAST TRANSEPT TOWERS

Wibert's heightening of the west towers of the east transepts survives as some of his most spectacular work. Constructed ca. 1100, the bases and lower stages up to eaves height are all Anselm's work and recall Lotharingian and Italian tradition for marking eastern complexes (McClendon 1987, 85–90). Whether the towers were left incomplete or were always intended to be low-rising is unknown. Wibert's decision to add to them complemented mid-twelfth-century tastes for multi-towered east ends such as those that survive at the cathedrals of Laon and Tournai.

On both sides Wibert's heightened tower stages are easily distinguished from the plain-walled lower stages of ca. 1100 (figs. 141 and 142). Work began around 1160. *Drawing I* omits the towers. The towers survived the devastating fire of 1174, although the interior and exterior of the upper stages bear signs of scorching.

Different designs and decorative detailing mark each tower.[22] Interpreting this feature is complicated. Did the asymmetry reflect work of slightly different periods? Was variety the intention? Can divergent purposes, as access to the upper galleries, explain the differences, the North Tower serving the convent, the South Tower the laity (and the city)? The towers' vigorous ornament exhibits a delight in rich variations of arch forms festooned by rippling wall patterns and paneled arcading in high relief and sunk relief. These stylistic traits can be traced to the west façade of the cathedral at Rochester and other churches in the southeast, as Kahn and Halsey have shown (Kahn 1991, 114; Halsey 2006, 78–79).

Although the towers typify the second phase of Wibert's renewal, these preferences were short-lived. Within a decade they were superseded and their decorative exuberance subdued by the new aesthetic of William of Sens's Gothic.

East Transept, South Tower

Among the most brilliant examples of Prior Wibert's renewal, the South Tower's mural surfaces vibrate with superimposed arcades and light-catching relief. In the upper stages the decoration expands over the corner buttresses as if to escape the constraints of the architectonic frame and effectively unifies the composition.

The lowest stage displays intersecting arcades enriched with flowers set against a backdrop of speckled black and white lozenge work. If the choice of arcading nods towards the lower stage of Anselm's work, the enclosed paneling asserts Wibert's penchant for decorative enrichment. The stage above deploys chevron for the arcades and pairs two blind arches either side of a single central opening with the dividing pilasters shimmering with chevron. The third stage adopts further variations. Twin openings dominate the center with flanking blind arches all with chevron, and the arcades capped by chip-work. Finally, the top stage features a single opening with rich chevron in two orders framed by blind arcades. Oculi enrich the spandrels of the outer arches and corner buttresses, more easily seen in Britton's 1822 engraving (fig. 140) than in the restored fabric.

140   Canterbury Cathedral, east transept, South Tower, engraving by John Britton of top stage, 1822 (published Britton 1836).

141   Canterbury Cathedral, east transept, South Tower (courtesy Stuart Harrison).

142   Canterbury Cathedral, east transept, South Tower, upper stages (photograph author).

The lower stages of the Tower date from Anselm's church, the Tower's upper stages from Wibert's renewal.

blind arcades with intersecting arches. The top two stages display heavily encrusted registers of raised and sunk relief featuring stacked wave and scale patterns and playfully alternate wider arcades against slimmer, taller arcades and open against blind arcading. Sunk roundels fill the corners giving a distinctive up-and-down quality abandoned on the south tower.

CATHEDRAL CRYPT ENTRANCES

The interior entrances to Anselm's ca. 1100 crypt were located under the principal crossing of the Cathedral but by mid-century were clearly deemed to be in need of embellishment. Prior Wibert provided variant designs for each. On the north (fig. 144) the descending staircase is cut with a diaper pattern with each groove formed of twin strands, one passing over, one passing under, at each intersection. On the south the flight of stairs is ornamented with lozenge pattern. The embellishment included semi-precious jamb shafts (see Appendix C).

143   Canterbury Cathedral, east transept, North Tower (courtesy Conway Library, The Courtauld Institute of Art, London).

East Transept, North Tower

The North Tower is simpler (fig. 143). Openings are fewer and the resulting larger wall areas display a robust variety of small-scale decorative patterns animated by sunk relief.

The lowest stage of tightly spaced arcading with intersecting arcades is topped by a stage with a more broadly spaced center panel with a single opening and

144   Canterbury Cathedral Priory, Cathedral crypt doorway, north entry (courtesy Conway Library, The Courtauld Institute of Art, London).

Middle Gate

A large gateway (fig. 145) separated the monks' cemetery from the lay cemetery and is shown on the Precinct drawing (fig. 146 and 147). Still standing when Wenceslas Hollar drew the Cathedral from the south in 1655 (see Collinson, Ramsay, and Sparks 1995, pl. 32), the wall and gate were disassembled around 1840 and relocated 164 feet further east. It now serves as the entry to the Memorial Garden, referred to on interwar plans as the Harris Gate.

　　With its elaborately carved twin decorative order, the gateway was intended to serve as a monumental marker. Detailing with mixed chevron and medallion ornament clearly places it as part of Prior Wibert's renewal. Not all the carved parts are to be trusted. On the south the

(Right) 145　Middle Gate, formerly cemetery gate, now the entry to the Memorial Garden (photograph author).

(Below) 146　Eadwine Psalter, detail of Cemetery Gate, Campanile, and Entry laver, Trinity College, Cambridge (courtesy The Master and Fellows, Trinity College, Cambridge).

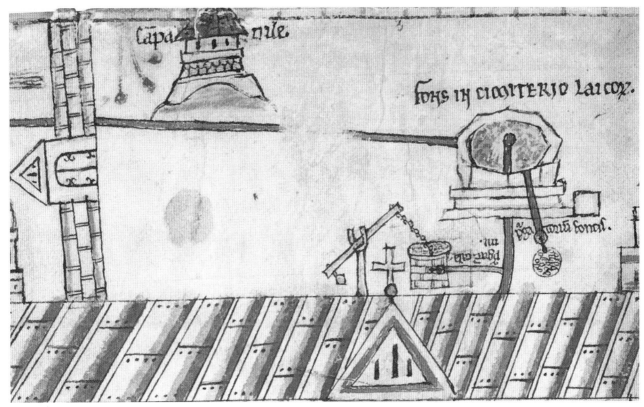

147 Middle Gate, formerly Cemetery Gate, now the Memorial Garden, from the east (courtesy Stuart Harrison).

gate's two springers consist of reused medallion ornament, although where they originated is unclear.

South Transept Fountain

Known only from *Drawing I*, the south transept fountain carries the titulus *fons in cimitero laicos* (fountain in the laypersons' cemetery) (fig. 146). It is drawn between the west and east transepts and would have been placed adjacent to the Cathedral's main public entry through the large porch (rather than the ceremonial entry at the west end). Eadmer records that the "suthdure" was the principal entrance in Archbishop Lanfranc's Cathedral, and it is shown on both the Priory's First and Second Seals (see fig. 16). The fountain was close to the original Christ Church Gatehouse, which gave entry to the Precinct from the city and whose approximate position lay in line with the middle bays of the nave, as is suggested by the artist in the gap he leaves in the precinct wall.

The fountain suggests ritual cleansing, similar to those associated with entry atriums in the southern Mediterranean such as the basilican churches in Rome. It is drawn with an octagonal laver with a single central pipe and an outflow pipe, but unlike other fountains at the Priory, it was not graced with an aedicular covering. The laver rested on a high base; on the west side the artist draws a stone block for the ease of those using it to draw water, indicating thereby one of the fountain's several purposes. Adjacent to the fountain was a well complete with a derrick and counterweight. This suggests a holdover from the earlier water system. A pipe connects the well to the main feeder pipe of the fountain, again pointing to a supplementary function in case of drought or repair.

Although no trace of either the well or the fountain is visible on the ground, the Cathedral's master mason, Heather Newton, informs me that the octagonal outline of the fountain can still be discerned from the Cathedral's high roofs in certain frost conditions and confirms the accuracy of the artist's location.

Campanile

Archbishop Lanfranc constructed a free-standing campanile (fig. 146 and see fig. 3) as part of his additions to the south side of the Cathedral (Sparks 2007, 77). Few details are known beyond the schematic representation in *Drawing I*, where it is labeled as "campanile." It is mentioned in *Rental B.84*, where it is called a "clocarium" (Urry 1967, 233). The campanile belongs to the rich tradition of detached towers which functioned in relation to the adjoining cemetery, a subject recently studied by Stocker and Everson in the context of burial cults (2006, 84–88; also McAleer 2002, 56). At Canterbury, Stocker and Everson point to the tower's connection with St. Michael's Chapel, the southernmost chapel in the Cathedral's west transept. A similar tower was noted at St. Augustine's for its cemetery (Tatton-Brown 1991b, 78–79).

In *Drawing I* the Campanile is shown lying west of the dividing wall that separated the monks' from the laypersons' cemetery. It rises from arches which support a drum decorated with arcading. An upper story contained openings with a covering roof in the form of a dome or spire. Sparks suggests a timber construction (2007, 77), citing fifteenth- and sixteenth-century repairs involving the purchase of wooden shingles (Woodruff 1936, 50–72). Possibly the shingles were for the structure's roof. Among other things the Campanile needed to provide for Prior Wibert's massive bell which took thirty-two men to ring (Appendix A). It joined five others installed by Prior Conrad. On the sixty-eight annual feast days listed in 1273 for the cathedral a total of 93 ringers was required (Woodruff 1936, 77–8) of which only four were regularly employed in the sacrist's household.

Smith established that the sacrist's court assembled in the base of the Campanile (Smith 1943, 68–82). The sacrist was one of the major monastic officials; his household required fifty-six servants in the twelfth century (Urry 1967, 157–61). His residence was located in the southeast corner of the Precinct, making the Campanile a convenient location for his court. A similar campanile was constructed in the 1120s at Bury St. Edmunds which also served as the location of the sacrist's court (Fergusson 2011, 29).

The Campanile featured in one of the best recorded portents of the martyrdom of Thomas Becket. At Pentecost in 1169 William of Canterbury noted the mystic vision of the infirmary doctor, Master Feramin, when the heavens opened and a voice announced the future glory of St. Thomas. This was followed by a vision of the Pentecost procession at the rear of which the saint was seen riding with Henry II through the Precinct of Canterbury (Urry 1967, 204).

The Campanile was demolished in 1540 at the suppression (Sparks 2007, 77).

Christ Church Gatehouse

Drawing I records an opening in the precinct wall opposite the west bays of the nave. Whether this can be interpreted as evidence of Prior Wibert's intention to provide an improved entry from the city to the Cathedral or simply marked existing conditions is debatable.

Narrow and indirectional, the entry in use throughout the twelfth century (about 200 feet east of the present Christ Church Gate) stood at the end of a winding alley leading from the city's marketplace through an area of congested domestic and merchant housing (Urry 1967, 14).

It is plausible that Wibert set his sights on improving the entry as part of his plan to diminish the risk of fire by buying up properties on Burgate Street and to move the parts of it that ran adjacent to the east parts of the Cathedral further to the south. Prescient as this idea was, it got blocked by the merchants with properties on Burgate Street, with the well-documented result of the devastating fire of 1174. At the end of the twelfth century the new entry was constructed at the west end of the Buttermarket; the Treasurer's accounts for 1198–99 record payment "pro nova porta." Payments continued through 1201–2 and indicate a sizable structure. This gatehouse was superseded by the sixteenth-century Christ Church Gatehouse, which serves today as the main entry to the Cathedral.

Piscina

Placement of the *Piscina* (fishpond) close to the east termination of the Cathedral is without precedent in monastic precincts (see fig. 3). The location elevates what was mostly considered a utilitarian necessity (to keep a ready supply of fresh fish, albeit at a surprising distance from the Great Kitchen) to an eye-catching feature just a few feet away from the east end of the Cathedral and adjacent to the buried brethren of the Priory. No trace of it survives in an area known today as the Oaks.

In most monastic plans the *Piscina* was consigned to the outer court. But there was no space at the Priory for an outer court. The decision therefore to enclose the Priory's *Piscina* within a twelve-lobed architectural frame and to place at its center an island adorned with sculpture was remarkable and hard to interpret. Was it an eccentric idea of Prior Wibert as patron of the renewal? Or was the intention to make visible a prized feature of the Priory's technological accomplishment? Favoring the latter was the decision to feature the *Piscina* on one folio of *Drawing II*, again endowing it with an unsuspected prominence. Some hint of the importance given to this element of monastic precincts comes from Bury St. Edmunds, where an elaborate zigzag design, known as the Crankles (see fig. 61), was constructed in the outer court on the east side of the precinct (Whittingham 1971, plan).

Whatever the interpretation, it is relevant to add that the Priory's *Piscina* ran into difficulties. By 1290 mention is made at Horsefold (the source of the water for the Priory's water system) of "vivarii apud Horsfold une" (Hussey 1881, 10), indicating the transfer of the *Piscina* three-quarters of a mile to the north. What caused this is unknown, although an insufficiency of water may be suspected or problems with the containing material in the basin. No remains of the *Piscina* in the Precinct have been sought, and Urry estimated an increase in ground level of at least 9 feet since the twelfth century.

9

MONASTIC AND
ARCHITECTURAL CONTEXT

Architectural historians are accustomed to thinking of the mid-twelfth century in terms of Cistercian reform.[1] Cistercian expansion – from the first settlement in 1128 to forty-five monasteries twenty years later – and the white monks' self-confident critique of the older monastic institutions has obscured another element of these years, Benedictine renewal.[2] What emerges from the evidence of building is a different, less triumphalist narrative. For much of the 1140s and 1150s the energies of the Cistercians focused on the establishment of their lands and economies. Only when these were on a surer footing could the order turn to the development of a distinctive large-scale architecture (Wilson 1986, 86–90). A rival version of these years needs to consider the vigorous Benedictine push-back in the face of the new monastic movements. The process can be followed in architecture, although it is more readily apparent in conventual building than in church building. New guest accommodations, gatehouses, dormitories, refectories, cloisters, treasuries, barns, and kitchens register the process by which the older monastic institutions addressed the outflow of patrons and postulants to the new reform movements.

The Benedictine response is most clearly seen at England's senior metropolitan cathedral priory at Canterbury. The widespread renewal of the precinct buildings involved physical expansion, the adoption of new architectural types, the exploitation of a distinctive up-to-date style, and the utilization of technological innovations. Improved living conditions can be seen as a statement of revitalization as well as an upgrading of facilities. Prior Wibert's installation of the water system transformed hygiene, while his construction of the Infirmary and Almonry tackled issues of health and urban poverty. Likewise, the development of the entry complex around the Green Court Gatehouse devoted to the revival of jurisprudence established the standard for the administration of the Liberty, and the expanded quarters for visitor hospitality reflected the new cultural impulses expressed in travel and travelers' expectations. By no means least the changes to the Cathedral addressed problems with improvements.

Developments in monasticism were paralleled by important shifts in government and royal power. The end of Stephen's reign halted two decades of political and social disruption and outbreaks of civil war.[3] With

145

the shift from Norman to Angevin rule, the accession of Henry II (1154–89) opened prospects of peace, better economic conditions, and access to new ideas resulting from the cosmopolitan contacts of the young king and queen. The euphoria of reconciliation swelled further when news reached England from Rome of the election of Nicholas Breakspear as Pope Adrian IV (1154–59). His attention to the communal movement in Italy and France and the reform of law tackled the major issues of his day and attracted churchmen from England to the papal curia at the Lateran. Canterbury played an important role in these events. Archbishop Theobald moved in the highest circles of national life. Looked to as the preeminent spokesman on ecclesiastical and political matters, he had been appointed papal legate by Eugenius III in 1150, a position renewed by Adrian IV in 1154. His earliest contacts with the twenty-two-year-old king convinced the archbishop that Henry knew little about the English church. To remedy this, Theobald recalled one of his most able clerks, Thomas Becket, from law study in Italy and France to serve as Henry's advisor. The thirty-six-year-old Becket was further elevated within a matter of weeks to royal chancellor of England as his friendship with the young king flowered. Becket's return to Canterbury at the period when the Priory's renewal was launched placed him in a position to influence its development.

The convergence of monastic and historical factors formed the background for the resurgence of the Priory's administration and finances under the leadership of Prior Wibert. At the start of this period the regenerative impulse was widespread. Within a decade, however, the context had changed and the map of patronage and the atmosphere of possibility that underlay the renewal had shifted. Assessments of the king and queen became more cautious. Archbishop Theobald sickened and died. Becket's relationship with Henry II soured after his appointment as archbishop in 1162. Adrian IV died and was replaced on the papal throne by the formidable Alexander III.

An understanding of Prior Wibert's renewal of the Priory has steadily expanded in the last twenty years. Whereas earlier scholarship attributed to the prior the new water system and a limited number of buildings such as the Treasury and the Green Court Gatehouse, present estimates swell that number by more than a

dozen further projects. As the extent of the renewal has come into focus, the corpus of work makes it possible to broaden discussion from building attributions to the consideration of such matters as patronage, sources and prototypes, construction campaigns, and architectural style. For the first of these, Wibert's undertakings can now also be evaluated in terms of planning processes, design preferences, choice of architectural types, iconographic meanings, and the creation of human environments. Despite the absence of biographical material, a picture emerges of the prior as a figure of unusual intelligence and ambition whose wide-ranging interests ran in tandem with his control of resources, a critical component in the realization of the renewal. Wibert's prescient land purchases, for example, depended on his thorough overhaul of the Priory's financial affairs. Combined with the unique spirit of the age when change was in fashion, the stage was set for a brilliant period in the Priory's history.

Reconstructing Wibert's work is made vastly easier by the representation of the precinct buildings bound in at the end of the Eadwine Psalter in Trinity College, Cambridge. Made halfway through Wibert's years in office, shortly after the completion of the first campaign of the renewal around 1158, this extraordinary drawing is central to an understanding of the Priory's condition and the purpose behind the renewal. The standard study remains the one carried out by Robert Willis in the late 1840s and published twenty years later. Willis saw the "waterworks" as the *raison d'être* for the drawing. Further, as an expert engineer himself, he claimed the image to be a unique representation of this major engineering achievement. Following from this, the precinct drawing appeared to him to be unrelated to the Psalter into which it was bound.

Willis's claim, repeated into the present, that the drawing recorded the installation of the water system needs to be reassessed. Doubts about its reliability are raised by notable inconsistencies in what the drawing shows. Misplaced pipework, the omission of water connections to buildings known to have been part of the system, the absence of toilets for everyone except the monks, and the muddled relationships of structures in the most critical area of the water system's mechanism (the eastern part of the Infirmary Cloister) indicate a purpose other than a waterworks' blueprint. Clues to what this might be come from the artist's inclusion of buildings with no connection at all to the water system, his adoption of a distinctive interior viewpoint, and the combination of varied projections uniting visible physical features of the Precinct with invisible, abstract, conceptual elements. The drawing was clearly multilayered, its purposes ranging from inventory to commentary, from record to prophetic symbol.

Placing the drawing in the context of psalter production in northeast France and the Lowlands at this period reveals it as less singular than Willis thought. Other psalters include full-page images of buildings, some with water features and inscriptions. These represent Jerusalem with its sacred monuments (see fig. 22) and show the city partly with observed details alluding to old Jerusalem and partly with evocations of the New Jerusalem whose promised appearance was described by St. John in the Book of Revelation (21:10). The duality reflected St. Augustine's accounts of Jerusalem in his most ambitious theological work, *De civitate Dei*. He argued for a Jerusalem observed under two aspects, the earthly physical city and the metaphorical heavenly city (Meyer 2003, 47–65). His views influenced later thinking and are reflected in Archbishop Anselm's widely admired *Cur Deus Homo* written at Canterbury ca. 1100 (Heslop 2011, 122–26).

The Eadwine Psalter precinct drawing falls within this exegetical and revelatory tradition. It shows a recognizable construct as well as an encompassing ideal. Rendering the monks' material ambiance as ordered, cared for, well watered, and spacious, the artist also abstracts the Precinct from the urban and archepiscopal context of which it was a part. He shows it with gates closed, secured and cut off from its surroundings, and asserts its interiority through the various folded-out projections. As such, the image mirrors the broader meaning of the *civitas Dei* described by Augustine and Anselm (Abulafia 1990, 11–12). Composed of the community of the faithful bound together in their common life and devotions, the City of God was manifested in the Priory's arcaded cloister walks, the disposed order of the Green Court, the expansive volumes of the Infirmary Hall, the varied guest facilities, the new court buildings for its Liberty, the playful delights of the five fountains, and the overpowering presence of the Cathedral. *Drawing I* doubles, then, as a materialized transcription of buildings and spaces and as a prophetic "text" about their purpose. An analogy of this kind of double-think can be made with the image of the psalmist, King David, in Psalm 1 of the same manuscript (see fig. 17B). David is presented as author-musician and pedestalized king of Israel, and also as Christ, haloed with a cross, writing in an open book, flanked by two angels, and enclosed by a baldachin (not unlike those employed for the Priory's fountain houses).

Below, a river god dispenses bountiful waters to nourish the righteous, who are allegorized as living trees. The figure's compounded identity in the manuscript resembles that of the architecture in the Precinct. The Priory's buildings combine, then, material and rememorative meanings, mirroring the multilayered, flexible reality accepted as standard by the twelfth century (Ousterhout 1998, 393–404).

While the renewal was directed first and foremost to the monks, its effects were also clearly calculated to impress the Priory's visitors. To them the new architecture was an unambiguous statement of the vigor of Benedictine renewal, a conscious, constructed response to the critique of monastic tradition mounted by the reform movements. Underlined by the status and authority of the institution in the face of its critics, the Priory presented an exemplar of rational organization to visitors who entered the Green Court, an affirmation of the rule of law after the lawless years of Stephen's reign. Enhanced visibly and audibly by the five fountains and the innovations and buildings the water made possible such as the Bath House, the renewal reflected new health and social standards associated with the wide-ranging Angevin world with its knowledge of Islamic, Mediterranean, and European cultures.

A different message was conveyed by the historical and biblical sources drawn on for the architectural types deployed by Wibert. They convey much about the Priory's contacts. Some were the consequence of physical displacements. The exile of the archbishop and his curia to St.-Omer from 1148 to 1152 exposed important churchmen to architecture then in construction in the Low Countries and the Capetian lands of the Île-de-France. Others resulted from long established contacts such as those with Cologne, or the presence of distinguished foreign scholars in the archbishop's cosmopolitan curia such as the law magisters from Bologna, brought to Canterbury to enact the new legal disciplines of canon law. Along with their books, they came with knowledge of the building types in formation in central Italy for the law's administration. Similarly, the resurgent building under way in Rome was familiar to men such as Becket and John of Salisbury who traveled to the papal court at the Lateran Palace.

Placing Wibert's work in chronological order in these years is possible with the help of *Drawing I*. If the date proposed in this study of 1158 for the image is accepted, the buildings completed then can be separated from those undertaken after the drawing and not included in it. The first campaign of around five years, extending from 1154/55 to 1158/59, began with the installation of the water system, a process involving complex trenching, the placing of pipework and waste channels, and the construction of the mechanisms for the water's control such as cisterns and conduit houses. Integral with the infrastructure were the buildings dependent on it, such as the *Necessarium*, the Bath House, the Infirmary Fountain House and the Water Tower, and the prior's *Nova Camera* with its separate bath and cistern. These formed an interconnected group along with the Treasury and Infirmary Cloister. To imagine their construction outside a single unified campaign stretches credibility. Closely following were three large buildings: the Green Court Gatehouse and the *Aula Nova* (started before the Gatehouse was finished), the huge Infirmary Hall, and the Great Cloister with the sumptuously sculpted Great Laver which dominated the entry to the Refectory, the last alluding to the model in the French royal abbey of St.-Denis (Wilson 2010, 37, n. 57). A later phase of this initial campaign can be discerned in further important undertakings such as the Guesthouse, Treasury, and Infirmary Chapel. Their use of foliate ornament, smaller scale, and elegant detailing sets them apart from Wibert's earlier work where monumental piers, scallop capitals, and restrained moldings dominated. If the calculation of about five to six years is accurate, this first campaign was marked by the willingness of the monks to endure prolonged disruption in the cause of renewal.

A second campaign can be distinguished and dated to ca. 1160–65. None of the work connected with this is shown on *Drawing I*. It included the construction of the Pentice Gatehouse as the entry to the Guesthouse, the adjacent north range, and projects related to the Cathedral, notably the heightening of the Treasury, the renovation of the chapels of St. Andrew and St. Anselm, and the added tower stages to the eastern transepts. To these can be added the energies directed to the design of the projected large chapel referred to in Prior Wibert's *obit* (see Appendix A) but unrealized at his death. Less transformative of the Precinct than those of the first campaign, the undertakings of this second campaign were no less notable for the display of formal invention and the exploitation of rich decorative systems of gleaming color and formal fullness.

Turning to the architecture adopted for these buildings, the first response of a visitor would have been to ask their purpose. With no earlier history of use in England, identification would have been needed for the Treasury, Water Tower, entry buildings for the administration of the Liberty, and the free-standing hospitality centers.

These unfamiliar building types constituted the prior's single most striking contribution to monastic architecture. For their design Wibert showed a distinct preference for the double-story hall. Consisting of a vaulted under story with a timber-roofed hall above, it was used most spectacularly for the *Aula Nova* and the Guesthouse. Displaying an unfamiliar splendor, these two buildings were linked in design. Both were impressively scaled, free-standing, fronted by arcaded porches, elegantly articulated, enriched with sculpture, and lavished with architectural decoration. Each combined several functions. For the *Aula Nova* these included the prior's Court Hall and Prison, the ceremonial Norman Staircase, and the Common Hall and the Servants' Hall. For the Guesthouse, they combined hall and dormitory, and vaulted formal parlor. For the latter, the juxtaposition of the ground-floor hall with surmounting dormitory recall precedents connected to monastic east ranges.

The common elements of the *Aula Nova* and the Guesthouse indicate the work of a single master mason. The double-story hall was familiar from usage in England such as the Norwich Cathedral Hostry (see fig. 35) or, closer in time to Canterbury, at a building such as Lincoln's St. Mary's Guildhall (see fig. 36). Tracking the identity of the master mason responsible for the major part of Prior Wibert's renewal is possible as well through the study of the Priory's decoration. This can be connected to immediately preceding work in London, Lincoln, Rochester, Faversham, Reading, and Bridlington and other sites. Individual motifs at Canterbury such as the accumulation of dense moldings, foliate capitals enriched with pellets, and the adoption of the drill as a work tool were anticipated at St. Bartholomew's Smithfield, Lincoln's St. Mary's Guildhall, the Temple Church London, and Rochester Cathedral.[4] A connection to the last comes from Archbishop Theobald's brother Walter, who was bishop of Rochester (1148–82). The extension of this work, and the taste for a florid lushness in its application, is characteristic of undertakings such as the Treasury and the heightened towers of the Cathedral. For both, prototypes were subjected to a development dazzling in its inventive use of varied arched motifs set against different decorative backdrops. Not everything came from outside Canterbury. The stimulus of Anselm's huge east extension, the "glorious choir," supplied internal inspiration. This is most readily seen in the capitals on the Green Court Gatehouse and the Infirmary Chapel with their fantastic animals and imagined beasts, which suggest an intimate knowledge of those in the surviving crypt of the Cathedral.

These sources were most likely known to both the master mason and Prior Wibert. From the latter would have come the decision to incorporate features with no obvious English antecedents, such as the ceremonial Norman Staircase added to the *Aula Nova* or the tower flanking the entry gatehouse, with ideas drawn from committal halls in France and episcopal residences in Italy. Similarly, it must have been Prior Wibert's penchant for expensive new building materials and the painstaking finishing and polishing that led to their widespread adoption for the major undertakings of the renewal.

Related to the Guesthouse and the *Aula Nova* were four further prominent buildings: the Treasury, the Water Tower, the Norman Staircase, and the Great Cloister. For the first of these, a clear connection exists between the centralized, fully rib-vaulted lower story and the similar design adopted for the Parlor of the Guesthouse. Architectural decoration also links the Norman Staircase, Treasury, and Great Cloister. All broaden an understanding of the work of the master mason and underscore his English background. At the same time, they explain his unfamiliarity with the technical advances in the Île-de-France evident in his uncertain handling of rib vaulting and his conservative attitude to wall structure.

Prior Wibert relied on the work of the same master mason for the Guesthouse and the Infirmary Hall, as Willis recognized in the 1840s. To this can be added the Infirmary Cloister, the Water Tower, the *Necessarium*, and the fountain houses. The demands of each may have differed, but they called on qualities of adaptation and technological resourcefulness. Distinct from these buildings was the Infirmary Chapel. Lighter forms, a more delicate scale, and architectural decoration controlled by a more imaginative sensibility point either to a single figure capable of working in different modes or, plausibly, to a successor master mason.

Seeing the work of the Priory in the wider history of twelfth-century architecture in England raises questions about style. Was the Priory's renewal in the 1150s and 1160s part of Romanesque? Or should the renewal be understood less as mutation than as a distinct development in its own right? Standard medieval periodizations describe this work under a variety of terms such as late Norman or Romanesque (Sauerlander 2008, 40–56), baroque Romanesque, Transitional, proto-Gothic, or *premier art gothique* (Bony 1963, 81–83). All imply developmental processes and impose a teleological apparatus on discussion. What they fail to capture are the distinctive language of forms, the discernment of

intention, and the contingent elements at work in every undertaking.

Alternative names include the term "Channel School" suggested by scholars working in disciplines such as sculpture, ivory carving, metalwork, and manuscript painting in mid-twelfth-century England, northeast France, and the Low Countries (Dodwell 1954, 106ff.; Cahn 1975b, 196–97).[5] As a term it has met resistance in the literature. Yet new interests associated with it such as small scale, weightlessness, denseness, formal inventiveness, and the loss of concerns with the monumental and historicizing tendencies associated with Romanesque are worth isolating and mark a break with preceding work. For architectural sculpture Deborah Kahn demonstrated similarities between Canterbury Cathedral Priory and the abbey of St.-Bertin in St.-Omer (Pas de Calais), less than thirty miles from the Calais crossing to Dover and the monastery where Archbishop Theobald and his household spent their exile at the height of the disruption of Stephen's reign (Saltman 1956, 25–28; Kahn 1991, 128–30).[6] The workshops at both monasteries show sculptors using the drill, animating surface through highly wrought ornament, and pursuing effects at variance with architectonic clarity. Such direct institutional contacts underlie the stylistic shift towards northern France and the Low Countries evident at Canterbury. Similar trends mark manuscripts written for Archbishop Becket and his secretary, Herbert of Bosham, around 1160, notably glossed books of the Bible such as Peter Lombard's on the Pauline Epistles and the Psalms, and early copies of Gratian's *Decretum* (see fig. 100).

Whether similar formulations might explain developments in architecture remain unexplored.[7] The renewal of the Priory, particularly in the second campaign, heralds the emergence of clear preferences with tenuous connection to earlier Romanesque work. These include the use of sumptuous building materials such as polished marble and limestone evident in the Great Cloister, the Norman Staircase, the Water Tower, and the Treasury, and the interest in small-scale and dense architectural decoration, evident as well in the two heightened towers on the choir sides of the east transepts.[8] The separation of this work from earlier architecture in England stands out and establishes a fashion linked to buildings in Hainault, southern Flanders, and the Rhineland. Wibert's exploitation of these motifs becomes a hallmark of this second campaign of his renewal. Such stylistic impulses offer numerous contrasts to Gothic work of the following generation, notably the new choir and

Trinity Chapel of Canterbury Cathedral (1174–84), in which large-scale forms, decorative restraint, structural slimness, mural contraction, and spatial expansion dominate (Draper 2006, 13–33; Wilson 2010, 19–44).

Beyond style, enough has been recovered of Wibert's architecture to extend our understanding of its goals. Several buildings connected to the Priory's renewal, such as the Treasury and the Norman Staircase, feature components which are best explained by conscious reference to biblical description of the archetype building, the Temple in Jerusalem. Monasticism was a text-based culture. The Bible was consciously spread across the Priory's buildings, filling them with associations extending out beyond their geographical confines. Exegetical commentary added to this study, notably Anselm's definition of types (Heslop 2011, 107–09). This mental practice was central to monastic study and involved the discipline of mnemonic recall, as Carruthers has shown (1998, 269; 2008, 202–17).

In the early and mid-twelfth century attention focused on the Old Testament kings, Solomon and David. Solomon stood as a particularly apt model for Wibert for, among other things, he was the wise judge of complex legal cases and the builder of the Temple in Jerusalem. The Victorines in Paris in these years focused attention on the Temple in writings and commentaries, and it is likely that at least one volume of their work would have been in the Christ Church library (Schröder 2000, vol. 2, 132ff.).

Since direct study or experience of these archetypes was impossible because of their destruction many centuries earlier, the Temple archetype had to be imagined through a combination of biblical and historical knowledge. Meditational recollection involved the envisioning of mental constructs connected to memory systems.[9] Archetypes functioned as mnemonic triggers, a procedure singled out for praise by contemporary spiritual figures such as St. Bernard of Clairvaux in his *Vita of Bishop Malachy*, the builder of monasteries in Ireland in the mid-1140s.[10]

Biblical study and exegesis thus conditioned monks to infuse their buildings with associations linked to archetypes. The practice was as common as the recitation of the centuries-old psalms by the monks seven times a day in church. Placing models before monks whose recognition prompted specific associations, Wibert was guided by the conviction articulated by Bernard of Clairvaux: "caelestia exempla sunt terrestrium" (heavenly exempla are the model for the earthly). Although each interpreted the idea differently, the conviction that

heaven begins on earth also justified the massive expenditures involved with the Priory's renewal. Material splendor was a manifestation of the celestial city. Wibert was not alone in this. The same ideas were articulated by Suger in the late 1140s in his anagogical justification for the rebuilding of St.-Denis (Grant 1998, 265–71).

The degree to which Wibert's interests – artistic, curative, hygienic, and iconographic – meshed with those of his far better known and more widely traveled contemporary, Thomas Becket, during his flamboyant years as royal chancellor of England (1154–62) and close advisor to Henry II, remains unresolved. Early in their careers Becket and Wibert resided next door to each other. They worshiped in the same building. Close association is implied in their parallel rise within the hierarchy of the curia and Priory respectively, their shared interests in the new jurisprudence, and, plausibly, their early training in the late 1140s in law in Archbishop Theobald's curia under the tutelage of the Bolognese Master Vacarius. At the least, the two men shared a period taste, a confidence in the new. At the most, their reciprocal interests extended to the discussion of ideas in use elsewhere in Europe for work on manuscript texts and for the utilization of building innovations adapted to the needs of Canterbury.

The influence of Wibert's renewal at the Priory can be discerned in the fifteen or so years before early Gothic swept through England. At the Temple Church in London, the use in the aisle arcade of grotesque heads in the spandrels recalls the laver in the Great Cloister at Canterbury, as Wilson has tentatively suggested (2010, 37, n. 57), and the same for decoration in the Temple Church's west doorway. At Peterborough, the entry buildings serving its Liberty and the sacristy constructed for the monks' vestments and liturgical vessels indicate familiarity with Canterbury prototypes. They were the work of Abbot Benedict (1177–94), who came to Peterborough following two years in office as prior of Christ Church, bringing with him relics of Becket's martyrdom as well as knowledge of its new buildings. The gatehouse survives along with remains of the prison and prior's court to suggest an entry complex analogous to Wibert's. Later examples of the entry complex formula can be traced at Much Wenlock, St. Mary's Abbey in York, Lambeth Palace (Morton's Tower) in London, and Hexham in the archbishop of York's Moot Hall (a late fourteenth-century rebuilding of a likely earlier structure), and of the sacristy in the rebuilding of York Minster. Similarly the ca. 1170 Infirmary at Ely demonstrated links with Canterbury (Holton-Krayenbuhl 1997, 127–35, 166), as also does the somewhat earlier Infirmary at Peterborough (Lindenmann-Merz 2009, 320–25). For hospitality, the buildings designed to meet the different expectations of visitors for accommodation at Canterbury according to their social rank left their mark at Fountains Abbey in the 1160s in the two guesthouses and the large single-aisled building for the common hall. Here Benedictine renewal can be seen as influencing Cistercian reform rather than the other way round.

Influence from Wibert's other undertakings is harder to establish. Gratifying as it would be to see his water system influencing other institutions, surviving information about them is too fragmentary at present to support such claims. Different patrons must have looked with incredulous envy at the prior's fountains, Bath House, the *Nova Camera*'s bath facility, even at his prodigious *Necessarium*, but translating these responses into building works was a different matter. Nothing known of water systems in the second half of the twelfth century indicates the same sophistication as that at Canterbury. Once again, the contingent circumstance of need and the distinctive, even idiosyncratic character of the patron emerge as the most likely explanations and, correspondingly, eliminate replication. For instance, the Water Tower linked to Anselm's new night entry from dormitory to choir set above the south walk of the Infirmary Cloister was a design unique to Canterbury at a time when the rite of laving as a liturgical action peaked in importance.

The status and wealth of Canterbury, its position as the largest Benedictine foundation in England, and its ancient origins extending back more than 500 years fundamentally shaped the Priory's identity. Inasmuch as architecture was designed to fit this identity, many of the mid-twelfth-century undertakings were distinctive to Canterbury. Just as important, they were tied to the discerned interests and empowering personality of their patron, Prior Wibert. His agency as patron reflected his personal interests as well as those of the age in which he ruled. Wibert's contacts, enthusiasms, and pride in the institution led him to promote ideas, while his shrewd use of power and resources enabled him to carry them to completion.

Although books about Romanesque architecture fail to mention his name, Wibert's reputation deserves to be recovered from history. Based on his work at Canterbury, he emerges as a major patron of architecture during an era of important development. The high regard in which contemporaries held his accomplishments is recorded in his *obit*, and, more visibly, given form in the Chapter House, where the "monumentum" located just inside the entry marked the likely site of his burial (Somner 1640, 278). Every member of the convent walked past it daily for nearly 400 years until the suppression, and it was the focus of the anniversary mass celebrated every September 27 complete with the pealing of the great bells specified in the *obit* (Appendix A, n. 6). The contrast between the admiration of the Middle Ages and the neglect since results from the vagaries of time and the inconstancies of taste. That more remains of Wibert's undertakings for us to study today than might be suspected opens a view into a distant past notable as among the most distinguished of Canterbury's varied periods. And they provide us with a glimpse of one of the most enterprising and engaging of its patrons.

Appendix A

PRIOR WIBERT'S *OBIT*

Transcription and translation by Mary Pedley

Prior Wibert's *obit* was written for the Chapter of Christ Church at his death on September 27, 1167. In addition, the *obit* would have been read annually on this anniversary. The *obit* appears in London, Lambeth Palace, MS 20, fol. 225v, a Martyrology complied around 1500 at Canterbury using earlier sources. A shortened version – approximately half – was printed by H. Wharton (ed.), *Anglia Sacra*, v. 1, London, 1691, 138.

All abbreviations are written out [conjectured letters in square brackets].

Item obit bonae memoriae Wibertus prior hic inter multa bona opera quae fecit, isti ecclesiae contulit ornamenta. Scillam unam ma[g]nellum unum. Signum quoque magnum in clocario posuit quod triginti duo homines ad sonandum trahunt. Duo magna tapeta. pallium magnum de melioribus ecclesiae. Curtinam magnam depictam fecit. Duas cappas et duas casulas de pallio. Quinque albas de serico et textam lineam pallio paravit de auro. Amictus duos et stolas totidem de auro. Calicem magnum et duo turribula argentea quidem sed de aurata. textum unum undique argentum de auratum et ornatum et quam plurima habentur. Silvam magnam de Chartham XLta acras habentem quam rustici longo tempore tenuerunt. diratiocinavit. et ecclesiae restituit. Sexaginta et undecim solidatas redditus ecclesiae adquaesivit quos in die anniversarii sui sic instituit expendi. Quadraginta solidos in refectorio ad refectionem fratrum. Viginti solidos vero ad usus pauperum de reliquo autem eleemosynam emendari praecepit: Aquaeductum cum stagnis et lavatoriis. et piscinis suis. quam aquam fere milliario ab urbe intra Curiam. et sic per omnes ipsius curiae officinas mirabiliter transduxit. Ad capp[ell]am faciendam quam facere proposuerat ducentos aureos. et viginti libras reliqui[t]. Item de bosco quem emerat viginti libras dedit. Has et multas alias utilitates Wybertus prior ecclesiae huic utpote bonus pastor contulit. Et tandem in pace quinto kalendis octobris vitam finivit. Pro quo fiet sic servitium ad dirige et ad missam in classis in turribus cum magnellis. missa ad maius altare. cantores duo. Collectae duae. Oratio in el[ee]m[yson]a domine et ffidelium deus. et duo cerei ponentur in cap[u]lo unus ad caput et alius ad pedes. quorum unus ardebit a principio dirige usque in crastinum post collationem.

The translation attempts to stay as close to the original as possible. For clarity it is separated into paragraphs. Added words are placed in square brackets.

Likewise Prior Wibert of blessed memory died. Among the many good works which he did, he provided the ornaments for this very church: one small bell, one ma[g]nellum [bell hammer or clapper].[1] He also placed a large bell in the [free-standing] campanile which thirty-two men pull to ring.[2] [He provided]: two large tapestries, a large pallium[3] for the the convent's superiors, a large embroidered altar cloth, two copes, two chasubles for the pallium, five albs of silk and a woven linen cloth for the pallium of gold, two amices, and as many stoles of gold, a great chalice, and two silver incense burners in the shape of towers and even one of gilt, a cloth woven completely in silver with gilt and decorated, and as many more such things as [he made] happen.

He determined the boundaries of the great forty-acre wood of Chartham, which peasants held for a long time, and restored it to the church. He added seventy-one solidi returned to the church, which he determined to be spent on the day of [the church's] anniversary in this way: forty solidi in the refectory for the meal of the brothers, twenty solidi truly for the use of the poor, of the rest [i.e. eleven], however, he ordered that it be spent on alms.

[He built] a watercourse with its ponds, conduits, and fish pools, which water it carried nearly a mile from the town into the precinct, and thus miraculously through all the offices of the very precinct itself.[4]

For the making of the chapel which he had proposed to make, he left two hundred gold pieces and twenty pounds.[5] Likewise he gave twenty pounds from the wood which he had bought.

These things and many other useful things Prior Wibert as a good pastor contributed to this church. And at last in peace he finished his life on the fifth day before the Kalends of October [i.e. September 27]. For whom a service will be conducted in this way for the funeral and for the mass:[6] in full bell peals in the towers with the magnelli [with hammers or clappers],[7] a mass at the greater altar with two cantors, two collects, an "oratio in eleemosyna, domine" and "fidelium deus,"[8] and two candles will be placed on the raised tomb,[9] one at the head and the other at the feet, of which one will burn from the beginning of the funeral service[10] until the next day after the meal.

Appendix B

ARCHBISHOPS OF CANTERBURY AND PRIORS OF CHRIST CHURCH

LIST OF ARCHBISHOPS FROM LANFRANC TO HUBERT WALTER

Lanfranc	1070–89
Anselm	1093–1109
Ralph d'Escures	1114–22
William de Corbeil	1123–36
Theobald	1139–61
Thomas Becket	1162–70
Richard	1174–84
Baldwin	1184–90
Hubert Walter	1193–1205

LIST OF PRIORS

Henry	ca. 1074–96
Ernulph	1096–1107
Conrad	1108/9–26
Geoffrey I	1126–28
Elmer	1130–37
Jeremiah	1137–43
Walter Durdent	ca. 1143–49
Walter de Mari	1149–52
Wibert	ca. 1153–67
Odo	1168–75
Benedict	1175–77
Herlewin	1177–79
Alan	1179–86
Honorius	1186–88
Roger Norris	1189
Osbern of Bristol	1191
Geoffrey II	1191–1213
Walter	1213–22
John of Sittingbourne	1222–36
John of Chatham	1236–38
Roger of Lee	1239–44
Nicholas of Sandwich	1244–58
Roger of St. Alphege	1258–63
Adam Chillenden	1263–74
Thomas of Ringmere	1274–85
Henry of Eastry	1285–1331
Richard Oxenden	1331–38
Robert Hathbrand	1338–70
Richard Gillingham	1370–76
Stephen Mongeham	1376–77
John Finch	1377–91
Thomas Chillenden	1391–1411

John Wodnesbergh	1411–28	John Oxney	1468–71
William Molashe	1428–38	William Petham	1471–72
John Salisbury	1438–46	William Sellyng	1472–94
John Elham	1446–49	Thomas Goldstone II	1495–1517
Thomas Goldstone I	1449–68	Thomas Goldwell	1517–40

Appendix C

CANTERBURY CATHEDRAL'S MYSTERY 'MARBLE': A DOUBLE IMPOSTURE UNMASKED

Christopher Wilson

Several of Canterbury Cathedral's mid-twelfth-century buildings incorporate a highly distinctive material which has never been identified correctly, although numerous attempts have been made. In 1774 the antiquary William Gostling noted: 'It has so much the appearance of the grain of wood, as to be taken by some for a petrifaction; but when the new pavement of marble was laid [before the high altar in 1732] and many stones of this kind were taken up to make room for it, this notion plainly appeared to be a mistaken one, and many of them were capable of a polish little inferior to that of agate. The edges are in curious *strata* and the tops of many are beautifully clouded [figs A1, A2]. The connoisseurs have called them by different names; some antique alabaster agate, others the Sicilian, and others the Egyptian agate, and the traveller Dr Pocock, late bishop of Meath, diaspro fiorito, the flowered jasper.'[1] In the last two decades of the nineteenth century the favoured term seems to have been 'stalagmite', a guess which, as will emerge below, is not totally wide of the mark. The next attempt at an identification seems to have been in 1981, when Francis Woodman described the shafts in the infirmary cloister as 'jasper from the area of the Red Sea, possibly reused Roman colonnettes'.[2] In the late 1980s and early 1990s several scholars plumped for 'onyx',[3] no doubt meaning 'onyx marble', which, as was explained succinctly in 1995 by Bernard Worssam, is 'not to be confused with onyx, which is a silica material, and as a semi-precious gemstone is related to agate and chalcedony. Onyx marble is a banded crystalline limestone deposited from solution in springs, and so strictly speaking is a variety of travertine. The onyx marble at Rochester probably comes from a Mediterranean source, Italy or perhaps North Africa. Algeria is now one of the largest commercial producers; onyx marble from there was used in ancient Rome and Carthage.'[4] Worssam's identification is by far the most plausible of those which have been advanced but, like its predecessors, it is incorrect.

The identity of this enigmatic material has actually been known for a long time, though not in England. In 1828 a portion of the late first-century Roman aqueduct which brought water from the Eifel hills to the city of Cologne was demolished, and the massive calcium carbonate incrustation of

(Left) A1　Canterbury Cathedral, treasury-cum-gateway, east face, detail of calc-sinter shaft on south arch.

(Above) A2　Canterbury Cathedral, east arm, detail of calc-sinter floor in fourth bay to the east of the east crossing.

the water channel revealed then was recognised as the source of the 'stone' that had been used in the mid-12th century to make shafts for the exterior of the east apse of the Minster at Bonn. The Romans had a marked preference for drinking water with a high mineral content, but that predilection had an unforeseen consequence which was ultimately to render many aqueducts useless. Spring water passing through limestone becomes a solution of calcium bicarbonate which is close to saturation, and any major change in the environmental conditions, for instance in temperature or pressure, causes the water to release its carbon dioxide as gas which in turn causes calcium carbonate to be precipitated as calcite or aragonite. These thick build-ups are termed calx in Latin and Kalksinter in German, and the latter word has for some time been anglicised as calc-sinter. The Eifel aqueduct was built around 80 AD and remained in use for almost two centuries before it was wrecked in a rebellion of Germanic tribes in 260 AD. Some calculations have been done which show that on average three centimetres represent a 40-year build-up. Chemically, there is nothing to choose between calc-sinter and naturally occurring onyx marble. The main difference in their physical structure, and hence in their appearance, is due to the different processes by which they were deposited. Onyx marble generally has concentric zones of striated colour, but most calc-sinter was taken from straight stretches of the aqueduct, where because there was no significant turbulence in the

water, the striations are essentially parallel, albeit with small-scale rippling. The yellowish-brown colouring, which polishing accentuates, is due to the presence of iron compounds (fig. A3).[5] The thickest calc-sinter shafts found in German medieval buildings are 25 centimetres in diameter.[6]

Eighty-three German sites with recycled calc-sinter have so far been identified, thirteen of which are in central Cologne. There are also fourteen sites in the Netherlands and one each in Denmark and Sweden. These figures come from the most comprehensive study of the medieval re-use of calc-sinter from the Eifel aqueduct, that published in 1991 by Klaus Grewe, an archaeologist who has specialised in the history of the management of water resources in antiquity and the Middle Ages.[7] Grewe published an important paper on the waterworks of Prior Wibert, also in 1991, and it is curious that while he was at Canterbury Cathedral, where far more calc-sinter survives than at any of the individual German sites, he noticed only one example, a small shelf incorporated into the outer face of the north wall of the early fourteenth-century choir enclosure.[8] Chronologically, the examples of the exploitation of calc-sinter listed by Grewe range from the early ninth century to the early thirteenth century. There is some evidence indicating that calc-sinter was used in the Palatine Chapel at Aachen alongside the many genuine antique marble shafts brought from Italy by Charlemagne, but nothing of the kind survives in the building today.[9] The material was

A3 Paderborn Cathedral, 'Atrium' porch north of choir, detail of calc-sinter shaft in south wall.

definitely employed in the main apse of the nearby abbey church of Kornelimünster whose patron was Charlemagne's successor Louis the Pious.[10] Clearly a key factor in the initial exploitation of calc-sinter was the proximity of the aqueduct to the power base of rulers willing to bolster their imperial pretensions by using a material which simulated the noblest of building stones, one pre-eminently associated with ancient Rome. The continuing use of calc-sinter as ersatz marble was no doubt due to the nearness of the source of supply to Cologne, the most important city in the German Empire and home to a very large number of rich ecclesiastical corporations. Since the main course of the Eifel aqueduct was 95 kilometres long, it will have seemed to be an inexhaustible quarry.

In the distribution pattern of surviving English examples of calc-sinter Canterbury Cathedral is overwhelmingly preponderant. The only definite instance of its use in the architectural structure of the cathedral church is a single shaft on the south jamb of the northern of the two west entrances to the crypt, to all appearances mid-twelfth-century work.[11] At least three of the numerous buildings erected within the priory precinct during the same period were adorned with shafts of the same material. One of these structures was the infirmary cloister,

whose partly surviving east arcade retains four shafts.[12] The other three arcades of this cloister will no doubt have been similar, and shafts which are almost certainly salvage from the south arcade form the central supports of four windows in the structure which replaced the south walk of the cloister in the early 13th century, the undercroft to the prior's chapel. The second mid-twelfth-century building endowed with calc-sinter shafts is the treasury-cum-gateway attached to the north side of the north-east transept of the cathedral (fig. A1).[13] Its west front is more sheltered and better preserved than the east front, and it is there that the large paired arches of the gateway are flanked by four shafts whose girth is sufficient to impart to them something of the character of classical columns. Two of these shafts are around 24 centimetres in diameter and two 27 centimetres, the latter exceeding by two centimetres the maximum diameter found in the continental examples. It is perhaps surprising to find no calc-sinter shafts on such an ambitious structure as the stair to the Aula Nova, where there is an impressive display of Purbeck and a single shaft of Tournai, the two polishable limestones which became fashionable in the elite ecclesiastical institutions of south-eastern England from the middle decades of the twelfth century onwards. There must be a very good chance that the chapter house, the single most important claustral building, was embellished with calc-sinter shafts in the mid-twelfth century, for there are six such shafts in the two sets of four unglazed windows which flank its entrance from the east cloister walk, and which, like the entrance itself, date from c.1300. The curious undulating 'quatrefoil' section of these shafts is undoubtedly due to the fantasy of the architect of the remodelled chapter house, Michael of Canterbury, and it is interesting that this exceptionally imaginative designer valued an unfamiliar and precious-looking material.[14]

Almost certainly an even more remarkable instance of re-use was the pavement of the cathedral church's presbytery, which was destroyed in stages between the 1730s and the 1870s. In the early 1840s, when Robert Willis saw the calc-sinter paving of the west part of the presbytery, the eastern crossing, he considered that it was probably a survival from St Anselm's early twelfth-century choir.[15] This hypothesis would seem to corroborate the contemporary testimony of William of Malmesbury that at its dedication in 1130 the choir was paved in marble.[16] However, two important objections must be raised. Firstly, any pavement in St Anselm's choir would inevitably have suffered severe damage when the building was gutted by fire in 1174. Secondly, there are no German or other continental parallels for the use of calc-sinter for paving, a fact which would suggest that the material was thought by those who knew it best to be incapable of withstanding heavy usage.[17] Significantly, most of the few slabs of calc-sinter still present today in the floor of the eastern crossing exhibit markedly uneven wear. The importation of calc-sinter into England is not known to have taken place later than the middle decades of the twelfth century, yet on balance it seems likely that the floor of Canterbury Cathedral's presbytery was laid shortly before April 1180, when that part of the post-1174 rebuilding, along with the liturgical choir, first came into use.[18] It is probably safe to assume that during this French-directed building project there will have been no German experts present to counsel against the use of calc-sinter as flooring. All that remains of the presbytery pavement today is to be found in the fourth bay to the east of the eastern crossing, where it was almost certainly installed during the reordering of the presbytery and choir fittings in the 1870s (fig. A2). With an area of approximately 35 square metres it is only around a quarter of the size of the presbytery pavement which survived complete into the early eighteenth century, yet it is still by far the largest extant artefact made from calc-sinter. Its constituent slabs are almost entirely laid in east–west runs, half of them being 58 centimetres wide and nearly all the remainder only slightly less. The largest slab has a length of 130.5 centimetres. The thickness of the slabs cannot be ascertained.[19]

What was the original setting of the calc-sinter in the floor of the late twelfth-century presbytery if it was not recycled from the paving of St Anselm's choir? Among the preliminaries to Gervase's account of the post-1174 reconstruction of the east arm is a description of its predecessor which includes the following account of the enclosing wall or screen running under all 25 arches of the main arcade: 'Ad bases pilariorum murus erat tabulis marmoreis compositus, qui chorum cingens et presbiterium, corpus ecclesie a suis lateribus que ale vocantur dividebat.'[20] The 'marble' slabs making up the choir enclosure would presumably have been fitted into frames of freestone, as in the twelfth-century calc-sinter screen surviving in the choir of the church of St Lebuinus at Deventer,[21] and it is possible that these frames were in turn fitted into the shallow slots which can still be seen in the bases of one of the columnar piers from St Anselm's choir re-used in the crypt in 1178.[22] Canterbury's choir enclosure must have suffered some damage during the fire of 1174, but its position underneath the main arcade arches would have protected it to some extent, and the brunt of any damage would in any case have been borne by the lowest parts of the freestone frames. Use in the choir enclosure of calc-sinter slabs such as those presently making up the floor of the fourth bay from the east crossing would have shown off to very good effect their attractive moiré patterning.

The other examples of calc-sinter in England are not numerous. At St Augustine's Abbey in Canterbury two shafts can be seen built into the buttress in the middle of the south wall of the late medieval chancel of St Pancras's church, and three more are in the wall built in 1542 to enclose Henry VIII's garden at the west end of the nave and cemetery. At Rochester Cathedral, a church linked to Canterbury Cathedral in uniquely strong ways, the outermost shaft on the left jamb of the main portal of the west front is calc-sinter, and no doubt this was true also of the corresponding shaft on the right, now a nineteenth-century freestone replacement. There

is a reference of 1894 to shafts made of 'stalagmite' in the blind arcading above the west portal but nothing of the kind is present in that position now.[23] On the arcading which decorates the lower part of the west wall of the east claustral range at Rochester, and which originally faced into the east cloister walk, there are still two calc-sinter shafts among many more of Caen and Tournai stone.[24] A single example is embedded in the garden wall of the demolished Lord's Place in Lewes, East Sussex, the mansion built on the site of the important Cluniac Priory of Lewes in the sixteenth century. To judge from the scanty fragments which remain, Lewes's mid-twelfth-century buildings were extremely splendid.[25] This pattern of use exclusively by elite ecclesiastical patrons is further reinforced by the final examples known to the present writer, fragments of two small ex-situ shafts from the opulent rebuilding of Wolvesey Castle in Winchester by Henry of Blois.[26]

The sheer quantity of the calc-sinter employed at Canterbury, as well as the material's wide distribution in north-west Europe, is a clear indication that the quarrying of the Eifel aqueduct amounted to something considerably more than a cottage industry. There exists a single crumb of evidence which is capable of being interpreted as an indication that England was participating in a full-blown trade in calc-sinter and that that trade was based on Cologne.[27] This is a charter of 1106 issued by Maurice, Bishop of London, whose witnesses include one 'Girardus marbrarius', Gerard or Gerhard the marbler or marble merchant.[28] It is well known that by the late eleventh century, if not before, the name Gerhard was associated pre-eminently with Cologne and its region, where its popularity was evidently due to the success of the cult of the Cologne-born St Gerard of Toul (died 994, canonised 1050).[29] Girardus the marbler was doubtless in the employ of Bishop Maurice, and in 1106 the latter's grandiose rebuilding of St Paul's Cathedral will have reached the point where the east arm was ready to be fitted out. Girardus's exact role at St Paul's is of course unknown, and it has to be admitted that his designation as a marbler or marble dealer might signify that he was supplying simple opus sectile pavements of the kind widely used in the Rhineland and other parts of northern Germany between the early ninth and early thirteenth centuries.[30] By 1095 a marble pavement of some kind had almost certainly been installed in the east arm of another of England's grandest post-Conquest churches, that of the abbey of Bury St Edmunds.[31] Yet it must still remain a real possibility that Girardus was supplying Bishop Maurice with calc-sinter, conceivably for choir-enclosing screens like that surviving at Deventer and postulated above for Canterbury Cathedral. Commercial links between Cologne and London had been important for some time before 1106, and it is not totally impossible that Girardus was among the German craftsmen and traders known to have emigrated to England in the eleventh century.[32] London's existing trade connections with Cologne might make it seem a more likely bridgehead than Canterbury for the invasion of south-east England's major ecclesiastical building sites by calc-sinter.

Against this, it should be noted that the prior of Canterbury cathedral priory from 1108/9 to 1126 was Conrad, whose name could hardly be more German and less English. Unfortunately, nothing is known for certain about Conrad's origins, but it has been suggested that his patronage of the spectacular paintings and other decorations in St Anselm's choir probably accounts for the sudden appearance of German elements in Kentish manuscript painting in the 1120s.[33] There must be a very good chance that Conrad did indeed hail from northern Germany, and if that was the case it would offer a perfectly adequate explanation for the use of calc-sinter in some of the choir fittings commissioned during his priorate. The very evident contemporary celebrity of those fittings would then account for the spread of one of their most conspicuous innovations to other major centres. Another gap in our understanding of the introduction of calc-sinter into England is the nature of the sales patter employed by the dealers when communicating with their clients. These men were supplying what will undoubtedly have been a costly commodity and it seems reasonable to suppose that they did not go out of their way to advertise the fact that their exotic-looking 'marble' was not even natural stone but recycled industrial waste.

Acknowledgements

I am greatly indebted to those who have helped me in the course of working on calc-sinter in England: Peter Fergusson, who offered this piece an ideal home; Jeff West, who untiringly urged me to publish my findings; John Crook, Richard Halsey and Andrew Rudebeck, who acted on my behalf as spotters of calc-sinter at St Augustine's Abbey, Canterbury and Lewes Priory; Alexandra Gajewski, who took for me the photograph of the calc-sinter shaft at Paderborn Cathedral which is reproduced as figure A3; and Heather Newton, who gave me access to scaffolded parts of the cathedral fabric.

Notes

INTRODUCTION

1   For the case for Theobald's patronage, see Kahn 1991, 95–137.

2   A number of scholars refer to Wibert's building activity in the context of other studies, notably Tim Tatton-Brown (1980), Frank Woodman (1981), William Urry (1986), Deborah Kahn (1991), Margaret Gibson (1992b), and Margaret Sparks (2007). However, no scholarly paper or book has appeared devoted to Prior Wibert's work as such or exploring the reasons for it. I am particularly indebted to Tim Tatton-Brown; he has remained a generous (and tolerant) guide to my efforts to understand Wibert's work as a patron and builder.

3   For Theobald's words, see Saltman 1956, 258–59, Charter 30.

4   A second, much abbreviated version of the water system appears on the following page, fol. 286. It is referred to as *Drawing II*. Both *Drawing I* and *Drawing II* are the subject of Chapter 3.

5   Lanfranc set a goal of 150 monks, although it is doubtful if the community ever achieved this number. Under Archbishop Anselm the numbers reached around 120 monks (Knowles 1963, 714).

6   This assigns to Prior Wibert more buildings than the list presented by Tim Tatton-Brown (2006, 92–93) and accepted by Margaret Sparks (2007). I have attempted to argue the case for the additions to the Wibert canon in the appropriate chapters.

1   ESTABLISHING THE EXTENT OF PRIOR WIBERT'S RENEWAL

1   Denne proved that the Water Tower served as the monks' ceremonial choir laver; see Denne 1794, 108.

2   H. G. Austin's design was published in *The Builder*, May 27, 1854, 278. The evolving design is discussed in Chapter 6.

3   The model was the Congrès archéologique in France founded ten years earlier. Like its French counterpart, the association changes conference sites annually.

4   See Dunkin 1845, 262. For similar uncomplimentary remarks about Austin's rebuilding of the northwest tower of the Cathedral, see p. 241.

5   The transfer of many Canterbury manuscripts to Cambridge colleges is explained by the several masters of colleges who were appinted archbishops of Canterbury. After arriving they shipped the former books of the monastery back to the libraries of the colleges they had headed, see Gameson 2008.

6 Vertue had been at pains to render a sense of color through carefully shaded hatchings. On occasion Willis added color just to the pipe runs, a dramatic way of reinforcing his view of *Drawing I*'s purpose; see reconstruction no. 2 in his loose-leaf insert added to the 1869 book.

7 The state of research on the Cathedral in the Romanesque period is discussed by Fernie 2000, 140–44. For the early Gothic period, see Draper 2006, 13–33.

8 Ironically, the trust's work most important for this study has never been published. This is the excavation of the *Aula Nova*, Almonry Chapel, and Lanfranc's Dormitory which was undertaken in 1977–78. The publication containing it is announced as *Excavations in the Cathedral Precincts, 1* and constitutes volume 3 in *The Archaeology of Canterbury* monograph series. I have not had access to this work. The explanation for the delay of more than thirty years is given as lack of funding. The later work on the precincts, volume 4 of the series, *Excavations in the Cathedral Precincts, 2*, covers work at Meister Omers, Linacre Garden, and St. Gabriel's Chapel, and was published in 1990 (see Driver, Raby, and Sparks 1990, figs. 15–16). For the work on the Cathedral nave, see the trust's series, *The Archaeology of Canterbury*, vol. 1 (Blockley, Sparks, and Tatton-Brown 1997).

9 Accounts of these operations appear in two series of publications. The first is the *Annual Reports of the Canterbury Archaeological Trust*, published yearly since 1976–77. The second, written for a more general readership, the Friends of Canterbury Cathedral, and published now as *Canterbury Cathedral Chronicle*, extends back more than a century.

10 For overviews of the changes, see Gilchrist and Mytum 1989 and 1993; Bond 2004.

2 PRIOR WIBERT

1 The literature on Becket is vast. I have used principally the work of Warren 1973; Barlow 1976; Bolton and Duggan 2003; and Duggan 2007.

2 Greatrex cites variants in the spelling of Wibert, which is sometimes given as Guibert; see Greatrex 1997, 319. Urry 1967 drew attention to the large percentage of the Priory's community who came from Canterbury, implying that Wibert may have been locally born and raised.

3 Based on documents, Urry settled on the middle of the three dates; see Urry 1967, 6, n. 1. Willis also accepted 1153 as the date of Wibert's assumption of office (1868, 4). For Wibert's rule as sub-prior, Tatton-Brown suggests 1140–52 (2006, 92).

4 For the sculpture, see the laver in the Great Cloister, the Guesthouse double tympanums, the Green Court Gatehouse reliefs, the *Piscina*'s aquatic animals on the center island, the symbolic lion on the roof of the Prior's Court Hall in the *Aula Nova*, the giant heads on the Cathedral façade as they appear on the Priory's Second Seal (see fig. 16), and the gilded angel crowning the crossing tower of the Cathedral. For the last, see John of Salisbury's prologue to his *Polycraticus*

where he mentions "angelus e specula totum circumspicit orbem"; see Migne, *Pat. Lat.*, vol. 199, cols. 382ff. For the latter two references, see Heslop 1982, whom I have to thank for kindly drawing my attention to them.

5 Wibert's inclusion can be hypothesized because of his election as sub-prior in 1148 and his involvement in property transactions involving the Priory at about the same time. Furthermore, in his role as prior he would have been responsible for the administration of the "Liberty of Christ Church" in the prior's court in the *Aula Nova* (see Chapter 6).

3 THE EADWINE PSALTER DRAWINGS OF THE PRECINCT

1 The best recent treatments are Urry 1986 and Woodman 1992. Both suggest that the drawing was the work of the famous chronicler Gervase, who at the end of the twelfth century became sacrist of the Cathedral. Urry based his argument on paleographical grounds, noting that the text of the *tituli* is in the same hand as Gervase's account of the 1174 fire and rebuilding of the choir. Woodman based his argument on the artist's grasp of hydraulic and architectural detail, which for Woodman qualified him for the office of sacrist, one of whose responsibilities was the fabric of the Cathedral.

2 Willis believed that the door which opened with difficulty to facilitate Becket's escape from the knights who were to murder him was the one at the northern end of the west cloister alley (see Willis 1868, 116–17). Recent archaeological examination of the palace buildings has shown, however, that Lanfranc's Archbishop's Hall lay to the south of its thirteenth-century replacement. The doorway opened for Becket was more plausibly the center of the three doors at the southern end of the cloister's west range (Sparks 2007, 15). This would make it the same door used minutes later by the knights: see Barlow 1986, 244–45.

3 It is referred to in the literature as the "Small Waterworks Drawing"; see Woodman 1992, 170–71; also Urry 1986, 43–58.

4 The Psalter remained in Canterbury until ca. 1615, when it was removed along with other manuscripts to Cambridge by Thomas Nevile, who for many years had been both master of Trinity College and dean of Canterbury; see McKitterick 1992, 195–96.

5 See Noel 1996. For a facsimile (in black and white), see de Wald 1932.

6 Recognizing the difference between a left to right reading and an orientation by compass points, the artist provides written indications of east, west, and north (but not south) in capital letters placed as borders across both folios.

7 Willis dates the change to ca. 1165 (1868, 4).

8 Lanfranc's *Constitutions* (ch. 90) refers to the "hosteller" who had the responsibility of procuring food for the Guesthouse from the cellarer, a title which suggests a lesser status than seneschal.

9 Not every building is labeled. One building in the northeast area of the Precinct whose purpose remains obscure lies perpendicular to the Granary and is the first through which the new water system passes. The building may well have been a barn or woolhouse; see Chapter 6.

10 This subject is explored by Forsyth 2008.

11 Both might have been expected were *Drawing I* solely a representation of the waterworks. At the least a branch of the water system could have been extended a few feet to service the Archbishop's Palace. It had been Archbishop Theobald who had given the Priory the water source. Such an extension was provided to the Priory of St. Gregory, the foundation of Theobald, as is shown in *Drawing II*. Since the new piped supply passed through St. Gregory's property, an extension was provided.

12 The same tanks and fields appear in *Drawing II* but are unlabeled.

13 Willis's important observations on the projection methods form his Appendix 1 (Willis 1868, 174–81).

14 As pointed out by Givens 2005, quoting Lavedan 1954, 33–35.

15 The literature has expanded beyond Woodman's seminal chapter. The following should be added: Grewe 1991a and 1991b; Paulus et al. 1999; Pressouyre 1999; Magnusson 2001; Bonde and Maines 2004, 357–99. I acknowledge with much gratitude the help of Professor Maines with these additions. See also Fergusson 2009, 83–98.

16 Although some pipes appear to vanish unexpectedly, for instance the main drainage pipe east of the Infirmary, this results from damage to the manuscript rather than from a lapse on the part of the artist.

17 For a useful survey including earlier systems in Europe, see Magnusson 2001, 6–7.

18 See Barlow et al. 1976, 284. For a reconstruction, see Draper 2006, 220.

19 Moorhouse and Wrathmell 1987, 8–11. For Sawley, see Coppack, Hayfield, and Williams, 2002, 22–114.

20 The translation is from Heslop 1992, 180. The image has been the subject of a dissertation at Emory University (2008) by Katherine Baker, to whom I am much indebted for generously sharing her work with me.

21 Baker makes the inscriptional connection, citing Dale 2002, 707–43.

22 Master Hugo appears at the end of Oxford, Bodleian, MS Bodl. 717, fol. 287v, of ca. 1080, although at a much smaller scale. See Alexander 1992, 11. I wish to thank Professor Alexander for drawing this to my attention.

23 A useful analogy is provided by Maines 2006, 5–43. It is no accident that the artist displays the greatest number of specific water details when he shows new architectural features such as in the fountain houses. They are all drawn at exaggerated scale to emphasize what they provided the Priory by way of hygiene and health as well as for their engineering or mechanical qualities. In these instances, both technology and architecture are pridefully displayed.

24 See Abulafia 1990. Jeffrey West kindly drew my attention to this passage.

25 I wish to thank Professor Jeffrey Hamburger for this reference.

26 See Korteweg 2002, 161–65. I owe this reference to the kindness of Lilian Randall.

4 THE GREAT CLOISTER

1 The term "cloister" is complicated and a number of synonyms occur in medieval documents; see Ashbee 2006, 86.

2 Puzzling aspects include use of the plural to describe Lanfranc's Great Cloister and other buildings ("hic etiam claustra, celaria, refectoria, dormitoria caeteraque omnes officinas necessarias et omnia aedificia infra ambitum curiae … aedificavit"); see Lanfranc's *obit* in Wharton 1691, xx–xxi. Use of the plural works, however, if the reference was meant to include the Infirmary Cloister as well as the Great Cloister.

3 The same rites of the *mandatum hospitum* are specified at the monastery of Bec composed during the rule of Lanfranc as prior (1045–70), and they were repeated by him at Canterbury when he became archbishop; see his *Constitutions* (Knowles and Brooke 2002, 49–53).

4 To Lanfranc's details of the provisions made for visitors can be added the even greater detail outlined by Roberta Gilchrist for the Guesthouse at Norwich in the fifteenth and sixteenth centuries; see Gilchrist 2005, 139–42.

5 Uncertainty surrounds the day stair doorway's purpose. Aside from its post-suppression history, it had clearly gone out of use by the thirteenth century when the benching was installed in front of it. Nonetheless, its original intention seems assured when viewed from the back (now the vestibule to the library) and outside from the ruined undercroft of the library. From the latter, the ruined core of the stair turning 90 degrees from the cloister entry is persuasive evidence of its purpose, as, too, is the remaining alcove for the night light.

6 There may be more to add. An argument can be made that Wibert reconstructed the Guesthouse and the Refectory. For the Refectory the accepted sequence is that Lanfranc's ca. 1070 building remained untouched until replaced by Prior John of Sittingbourne between 1226 and 1232 (Sparks, 2007, 21–22). No modern examination of the Refectory, now part of the archdeacon's garden, has been undertaken. For the limited clearance in the late nineteenth century, see Hope 1899, 445–52. The date of Sittingbourne's renewal is sound, but the building's earlier history is unclear. Caröe's survey report in 1898 notes the find of two bays of the undercroft and mentions the observations of his predecessors, Jesse White and George Gilbert, who saw a row of arcading on the western wall which included three shafts of purple or reddish marble. The under story, were it from Lanfranc's time, would be early for the double-story refectory type (see Fergusson 1989, 334–51). Favoring an 1150s rebuild are the structures either side of the Refectory which are indisputably Wibert's: the Cellarer's Court to the north and the galleried walk of the Great Cloister to the south.

7 Tatton-Brown also recognized areas of mid-twelfth-century masonry in areas of the east and south cloister walls, identified infilled parts of the flanking doorways of the Chapter House from the same date, and discovered further Wibert material in the lean-to roof over Chillenden's vaults, along with the remains of the outer molding of the mid-twelfth-century tympanum which served as the processional doorway into the north transept of the Cathedral (Tatton-Brown 2006, 97). Strangely, none of the 100 capitals has yet been found.

8 In fact, the north walk was shifted slightly to the east and each of the arcade-runs varies between 96 and 105 feet in length. The Great Cloister is thus a parallelogram. The column count is only a hypothesis since nothing is known about the treatment of the angles (by a solid pier or, more likely, with quadruple shaft groupings similar to those used at the same time for the Infirmary Cloister – see Chapter 7).

9 Polished limestone was referred to in the Middle Ages as marble, as Tatton-Brown points out, although geologists now define marble as a metamorphosed limestone (see Tatton-Brown 2006, 103, n. 15). For clarification see Appendix C.

10 Over the past years Jeffrey West has generously shared with me his knowledge about the Priory's Great Laver. He also most kindly made available to me a copy of his paper to appear in the British Archaeological Association Canterbury Conference Transactions for 2009 (West 2012, forthcoming), on which I have relied for the discussion which follows.

11 Four reliefs were found in the second bay (third and fourth buttresses) of the west range where they had been reused as masonry with the carved side facing in. In addition to the four panels, the incomplete remains of a fifth panel were found, completely smashed. For details of the finds, see West 2012.

12 See the review by Jill Franklin (1991).

13 Tatton-Brown suggests a circular form (2006, 102).

14 Earlier finds include the well-published "King Canute" relief discovered in 1764 in the *Domus Hospitum*, adjacent to the northwest corner of the Great Cloister (Jessup and Zarnecki, 1953, 1–8), a location only a matter of a few feet from Wibert's Fountain House. The responsibility for upkeep and administration for the Guesthouse, the west and north ranges of the Great Cloister, and the Fountain House lay with the cellarer.

15 The observation was first made by Christopher Wilson, as noted by Jill Franklin in her review (Franklin 1991, 547).

16 Stuart Harrison identified the separate parts as composing a single figure which in turn was attached at the back to an architectural feature.

17 For the Cistercian examples (which lack sculpture), see Stalley 1996, 237–64; Kinder 2002, 85–87, pl. 6; Rüffer 2008, 152–55. Elsewhere see the richly carved double-decker fountain from S. Frediano in Lucca in Decker 1959, pl. 51; also Zarnecki 1973, 1–10. For the Folardusbrünnen in Trier, see Grewe 1991b, 132.

18 For the Stavelot altar, see van Noten 1999, 24–27; for the Malmesbury Ciborium, see Zarnecki 1984, 263–64; for Suger's Great Cross, see Grant 1998, 250.

19 The north range is known from the finds of the late 1960s and 1970s. The case for the west range depends on the Romanesque doorway at the north end, and that for the east rests on the plentiful Wibert fragments reused by Chillenden's masons in the building of the vaults and of the raised inner wall to support them (visible when the inspection covers on the roof are raised). For the last I need to thank Heather Newton, who made it possible for me to see this evidence, and Stuart Harrison for crawling across a number of bays.

20 For the doorway in the west range mentioned in the accounts of Becket, see Chapter. 3 n. 2.

21 Kindly indicated to me by Frank Woodman, who recalls watching repair and reconstruction work in the late 1960s and photographing numerous fragments of Wibert's arcades reused as fill in the wall's core.

22 Little attention has been directed to the dimensions of west ranges, despite their importance and interest. The Canterbury range may be compared with the Norwich Cathedral range (see Gilchrist 2005, 136–42) and with the earliest Cistercian ranges from the 1130s such as Rievaulx (see Fergusson and Harrison 1999, 55).

23 For the Canterbury Cathedral use, see Binski 2004, 3–5.

5   AN ARCHITECTURE OF HOSPITALITY FOR DISTINGUISHED GUESTS

1 Newly founded dioceses such as Norwich illustrate the advantage they enjoyed in this regard. Norwich had the luxury of being able to develop a unified precinct allowing for a full range of monastic and episcopal functions; see Gilchrist 2005, 24–30.

2 The outer court functions for the Priory were provided by the home farm at Barton, a half-mile outside the city's Northgate.

3 In this division the Priory was not a pioneer. A similar separation of the Cellarer's Court marks other Benedictine foundations some years before Canterbury. At Bury St. Edmunds, the Cellarer's Court was separate from the Great Court, forming, like Canterbury, a closed area (see fig. 61). Access from the west was blocked by the placement of the parish church of St. James (Fergusson 2011, 28).

4 It is doubtful whether guest circulation mixed with that of the archbishop in Lanfranc's day. The use of different doors, however, could have solved this. A century later, the door into the south walk of the cloister from the palace had fallen out of use. As much is clear from the eyewitness accounts of Becket's movement from palace to church on December 29, 1170 and the difficulty his servants had in opening the door for him ahead of the pursuing knights; see Barlow 1976, 244. For a plan of the buildings in this area, see Tatton-Brown 1982, 113, fig. 1.

5   The literature on the Guesthouse is unusually thin. The two essential papers are Bowen 1987, 26–27, and Sparks and Tatton-Brown 1987, 36–41. My access to No. 29 The Precincts during the interval between appointments to the office of archdeacon was kindly aided by Heather Newton, the Cathedral's master mason, to whom I remain much indebted.

6   Explaining development of the Guesthouse in strictly practical terms, however, lessens the possibility of historical contingency. A contemporary episode involving King Stephen's queen, Mathilda, may have highlighted the inadequacy of the Priory's accommodations. In 1148–49 the queen spent a number of months in Canterbury. However, she stayed not at the Priory, as might have been expected given her special relationship with Archbishop Theobald, but at St. Augustine's. The appeal of its more up-to-date buildings, specifically the new infirmary where she lodged, has been suggested as the reason for her choice. The infirmary chapel is particularly relevant because St. Augustine's was in these years under Interdict, meaning the imposition of liturgical silence, except for its infirmary chapel. To solve the problem of who was to sing the cycle of services for the queen's devotion, the Priory monks were required to traverse daily the distance between the two monasteries (Kerr 2007, 83 and nn. 182–84). That both the Priory's Guesthouse and Infirmary were rebuilt within a few years suggests recognition of their inferior amenities made painfully clear by the queen's preference of St. Augustine's.

7   See Abou-El-Haj 1991, 3–15.

8   For Gerald of Wales, see Robinson and Platt 2007, 50. The Common Hall provided a different kind of structure and a different range of services from the Guesthouse, most obviously in the separation of hall from dormitory at the latter. At Fountains Abbey resistivity surveying in the mid-1990s showed the remains of the Common Hall in the lawn which presently fronts the abbey's west façade (Coppack 2006, 115–17). Like Christ Church it was twin-aisled and of far larger scale than the guesthouses, but wooden roofed.

9   The provision made for churchmen and religious remains a mystery. Many religious passed through Canterbury whether on business, research, or family visits. Some were doubtless provided for in the Great Dormitory, but this arrangement was less than satisfactory, as is clear from one of Archbishop Winchelsey's *Statutes*, *De Hospitalitate*, of 1298. Winchelsey critically noted that "the hospitality of the house has declined to such a pitch that religious men seeking hospitality . . . are receiving only food and are compelled to lodge in the City"; see Graham 1952–56, vol. 1, 822–23. To correct this, he directed that all such guests with their horses and servants "shall be cheerfully received and lodged for one day and night, and provided with all things necessary." Where this took place is not recorded. It is possible that churchmen and religious were directed to St. Augustine's or to one of the many other religious institutions in the city.

10 Willis 1868, 137 and fig. 27. The capitals now flank the doorway into the residence's lavatory.

11 Built by the North Country mason John Lewyn; see J. Harvey 1987, 181. The reconstruction of the Great Kitchen may well have drawn on the experience of St. Augustine's, where a free-standing octagonal kitchen was constructed 1287–91 for the considerable sum of £414; see Tatton-Brown 1997, 129.

12 See Urry 1967, 161. Lanfranc's *Constitutions*, ch. 90, refer to the "hosteller," who had the responsibility of procuring food for the Guesthouse from the cellarer, a title which suggests a lesser status.

13 The interior of the Guesthouse is presently a walled garden, installed after Willis measured and drew the plans and line drawings of the Guesthouse in 1847 (Willis 1868, 134, n. 3). In the twentieth century a clearance is noted in 1951–52, although no publication followed. The clearance established the ground level of the mid-twelfth-century hall and exposed four of the seven column bases that extended down the center of the building.

14 Unfortunately, the Priory does not possess the wealth of documentary information that Gilchrist cited in her vivid account of the Norwich Hostry. Although much of the material is fifteenth and sixteenth century, some clues about earlier provisions are also included; see Gilchrist 2005, 139–42.

15 The drawing is DCC Printdrawer /2/0/3 in the archives. Margaret Sparks kindly drew my attention to the drawing.

16 Connections between the Priory and Rome were strong during the 1150s and 1160s (see Chapters 2 and 6) and make comparison with north Italian buildings plausible. It should also be mentioned that the pre-Conquest Cathedral at Christ Church had an aisle with a two-story porch. It is illustrated on the First Seal of the Priory; see Heslop 1982, 97.

17 See Verzár Bornstein 1988, 127–34.

18 Sparks 2007, 23–26. In Sparks's 1989 paper co-authored with Tatton-Brown, the authors suggest the increased number of visitors followed Becket's murder in 1170 and the fire of 1174. They also posit Becket as the subject of the standing figure carved over the entry door to the Guesthouse. The fabric of the standing east wall of the Guesthouse is of little help in solving the matter; nineteenth-century rebuildings using flint and rubble walling make it impossible to read campaign breaks.

19 Abbot Anselm's involvement with the inner court comes from his widespread planning of the areas where the monastery and town come together; see Fergusson 2011, 28. The cloister buildings are attributed to Abbot Robert II (1102–7) in the *Gesta Sacristarum*; see James 1895, 118, 153.

20 See Halten-Krayenbuhl 1999, 304. For further examples, see Brakspear 1933, 139–66.

21 With permission, guests were allowed to dine at the prior's table in the Refectory. Again it was the guestmaster who was to "instruct them carefully how to behave in the Refectory; and, after instructing them, when the gong is beaten he shall take them to the parlor, where the abbot, or the

prior if the abbot be away, shall pour water over their hands ... and shall lead them to the abbot's table" (Knowles and Brooke 2002, 131).

22 For the *mandatum fratrum*, see McCann 1952, 88–89; for the *mandatum hospitum*, see McCann 1952, 120–21.

23 E. Searle 1980, 188–91; see also Brühl, 1989, vol. 1, 323–35.

24 On the word "porch" and its different terms, see Ashbee, 2006, 71–90, esp. 86.

25 Neither the Guesthouse nor the Treasury (see Chapter 8) is dated. At the Treasury the ground story was changed during the course of construction and three rib vaults inserted. This modification and the earlier architectural detailing indicate that the Treasury was the model for the Guesthouse Parlor.

6 THE GREEN COURT AND THE PRIORY'S JUDICIAL RESPONSIBILITY AS A LIBERTY

1 The name "Green Court" is not medieval. On *Drawing I* the area is referred to simply as "the court." Other medieval documents use the term "curia monachorum" (the household of the monks). "Green Court" was in use at the time of the Parliamentary Survey of 1650 (see Sparks 2007, 56, 88–89). For help in tracing the early history of the name, I am indebted to Margaret Sparks.

2 Today the Green Court is smaller than in the twelfth century. Walled gardens on the western side connected to the houses of the cathedral clergy inserted after the suppression have encroached into the medieval space and diminished it. Originally, the western boundary was formed by the pentice that led from the Great Gatehouse to the Pentice Gatehouse.

3 The area was indisputably smaller under Lanfranc, as is indicated by the prior's expansion of it. A possible demarcation of Lanfranc's Green Court is suggested on fig. 67, on the east by the shift in the angle of the boundary (now absorbed in the dean's residence), and on the north by a line more or less from the Bakehouse's west end to the Pentice Gatehouse (leading to the Guesthouse).

4 For Durham, see Lowther 1992, 27–119; for Norwich, see Gilchrist 2005, 41–65; for Bury St. Edmunds, see Whittingham 1971, plan (unnumbered, tipped in). Compare with Ely: see Holton-Krayenbuhl 1997 and 1999.

5 Wibert pursued similar property acquisitions elsewhere in the Precinct. On the east side, they included land for the construction of the huge Infirmary Hall (discussed in Chapter 7). Similar plans seem to have been made for expansion on the southern side to reduce fire risk but ran into the opposition of prosperous merchants on Burgate Street. It took the major fire of 1174 to change matters. The blaze began in two Burgate Street properties. Spread by high winds, sparks ignited the roof of Anselm's "glorious choir" of the Cathedral. In the aftermath of the fire, Burgate Street was moved to the south (where it remains), and the new land was absorbed into the Precinct.

6 The gallows were *extra muros*, probably located at Horsefold less than a mile to the northeast, where they are mentioned in the thirteenth century (Urry 1967, 198).

7 Other functions included the upper story of the Green Court Gatehouse, which probably served as document storage for the adjacent Court Hall. The grouping of these functions explains why gatehouses survive in greater number than any other monastic building type, long outliving the suppression and continuing in use into the early nineteenth century (Coppack 2006, 132). The larger the monastery, the larger its estates; hence at Canterbury the need for a court building and prison in addition to a gatehouse.

8 The frames surrounding the crosses are 1843–84 Austin renewals but the roundels are original. For a drawing and details, see Ruprich-Robert 1884–89, vol. II, pl. CXLIV. Similar crosses and chrisms appear on many of the gates of Rome; see Gardner 1987, 199–213; also Giovenale 1929, 183–207.

9 Later restoration of the Gatehouse in 1843–84 by George Austin involved refacing the upper parts of the west façade, the work identifiable by machine cutting of the replacement stone and the use of a different stone. At the same time a number of the foliate archivolts composing the arch were recut, although Austin retained the twelfth-century historiated archivolts.

10 Despite this Willis was able to identify the bays in 1847, before the construction of Galpin's House for the King's School six years later obscured the evidence (Willis 1868, 145). Excavation by the Canterbury Archaeological Trust in 1978 confirmed his findings and added new details about them.

11 Cathedral archives, Add. MS 210. The *Sketchbooks* are a composite of at least two sketchbooks rebound. The inside of the front cover identifies the *Sketchbooks* as containing the work of both George Austin and Frederick Austin, and records that it was "put together" in 1909 by Miss Ethel Austin, who gave it in 1928 to Mr. Caldwell. The volume is unpaginated, and the drawings have only an occasional identifying label. Thanks to a distinctive drawing style, it is clear that the front two-thirds of the *Sketchbooks* are the work of George Austin, the last third that of his grandson, Frederick Austin.

12 The design was reported and illustrated in *The Builder*, May 27, 1854, 278.

13 Today the Norman Staircase leads to an open-air, first-floor platform. In turn, the platform can also be approached from the west by a flight of stairs. The resulting unusual switchback arrangement separates the *Aula Nova* from the school's adjacent Galpin's House.

14 Tatton-Brown accepts the doorway as original. It is constructed from a different material, Wealden/Bethersden marble, rather than from the imported stone used for the arcades (Tatton-Brown 2006, 96 and n. 16).

15 Unlike the ashlar walls of the *Aula Nova*, the Norman Staircase is made of flint rubble which was presumably rendered and painted. To light the space beneath the stairs, the Staircase had a small opening on the south side, shown

clearly in Edward Blore's ca. 1815 drawing (Willis 1868, 147; Sparks 2007, 65). This survives as a small blocked loop with a monolithic round head. The chamber is now filled with rubble.

16 Personal communication. I wish to thank Tim Tatton-Brown for supplying me with this information. In 1993–94 emergency repairs on the staircase's northern side revealed the drainage channel.

17 Sauerlander 1972. However, the same two images appear also on *Drawing I* as roof terminals on the *Necessarium*.

18 The date of the transition from prior to steward may be estimated based on the evidence from *The Chronicle of Jocelin of Brakelond*; see Butler 1949, 33–34, 80.

19 The literature on this subject is very large. I am much indebted to Nigel Ramsay, who helped me with basic bibliography. I have relied on his masterly overview in Ramsay 2008, 250–90. See also Kuttner 1982, 299–323.

20 At the Tower, the king's council chamber derived from models in Normandy such as the *arx palatina* in Rouen (Brown 1970, 66). For Whitehall, see Brown, Colvin, and Taylor 1963, 42–48.

21 For Peterborough, see Gaches 1905; Mellows 1932–33, 29–36. I am much indebted to Dr. Jackie Hall for showing me these buildings.

22 For Lambeth Palace, see Tatton-Brown 2000, 56. I am much indebted to Tim Tatton-Brown for the reference. For Hexham I am grateful to Leslie Milner, who first drew my attention to Hexham at the Canterbury conference in 2009. Subsequently, Christopher Norton and Stuart Harrison provided me with photographs. I need to thank all three for their help. An earlier example of the same architectural type may survive at Much Wenlock, as Stuart Harrison has pointed out.

23 See A. Thompson 2005, 105; see also Radding 1988 and Jones 1997.

24 See Verzár Bornstein 1988; Diemling 1998, 498–513.

25 See the volumes by Natale Rauty with details, and the historical documents in vol. 3 edited by Guido Vannini (Rauty 1981–85).

26 See Radke 1996, 70–74.

27 See Brown 1996, 13, 146–48.

28 See Hubert 1993, 15ff. (also reconstruction figs. 9, 10, 11).

29 Willis was at work on his two important papers in these years but omits all mention of Austin's Gatehouse restoration. Although some authors have suggested that the reliefs were nineteenth-century copies, Kahn correctly saw them as original (1991, 126–32). Examination from scaffolding in 2010 confirms this judgment.

30 For the subject of the wild man, see Husband 1980. It is difficult to track the transformation of the wild man into S. Onuphrius, who by the fifteenth century is, among other things, the patron saint of lawyers (see Stieglecker 2001).

31 For the former, see L'Engle, Gibbs, and Clarke 2001; also Melinkas 1975. Dr. Alixe Bovey kindly drew my attention to a review and wide bibliographical survey of this area of research by Nordenfalk (1980).

32 The *Decretum* is composed of three sections: the *Distinctiones*, the thirty-six *Causae*, and *De Consecratione*. For the illustrations of *Causa* XXXV using architectural settings, see Schadt 1982, 172–80.

33 For comparison with a seated David without a crown, see the embrasure figure at Chartres Cathedral, west portal, ca. 1145–55, in Sauerlander 1970, pl. 14.

34 See Heimann 1965, 86–109.

35 A tympanum with a *Decretum* subject would not be impossible (as was mentioned above) because the artist drew a lintel over the entry gate. For the contemporary tympanum at Notre Dame in Paris with a subject related to secular power, see Cahn 1969, 55–72.

36 See also the mid-twelfth-century Fitzwilliam Museum, Cambridge, MS 83. 1972, fol. 1, illustrated in Alexander 1992, 94. It should be noted that the foliate archivolts on the east-facing archway differ and show greater variety. Only the uniform foliate archivolts on the west are congruent with the source discussed in the text.

37 A building of modest size was identified by Whittingham as the Hall of Common Pleas, located more or less in the middle of the south side of the inner court, close to the entry to the Cellarer's Court. It is difficult to date. Known only from plan, it displayed few architectural features and lacked an external staircase (Whittingham 1971, no. 12 on tipped-in plan).

38 Willis mentions the building only once. It was not listed in his index. On *Drawing II* (where none of the buildings are labeled) the building shown immediately after the water entered the Precinct was probably the Bath House, although the Infirmary Hall would also be possible (see fig. 10).

39 See Yegul 2010.

40 More controversial is whether the monks' *Necessarium* with its fifty-three seats was also a shared building in the same sense of being available at different times for visitors and monks. There is no provision for toilets in the entire Precinct except the monks' *Necessarium* which was located within the strict enclosure.

41 See Choisselet and Vernet 1989, 108.

42 See Flint 1989, 127–45; Getz 1990, 245–83.

43 Maddalo 2003; Kauffmann 1959. I am indebted to Professor Carla Lord, who first drew my attention to the baths at Pozzuoli.

44 Ward-Perkins 1984, 146–49, 254. For a general overview of the Roman baths at this period, see Sagui 1990, including her description of the eleventh-century hypocaust-heated bath complex at the foot of the Palatine (pp. 95–97).

45 For Rochester, see Goodall 2006, 265–99; for Dover, see Goodall 2011, 33–34, 141.

7 CARE OF THE SICK AND AGED

1 For all monastic institutions, bleeding was seen as indispensable for the removal of bodily impurities, the correction of humorial imbalance, and the reduction of sexual appetite

(Knowles 1963, 455–56; Voigts and McVaugh 1984). At Cluny, Peter the Venerable, writing in 1150–51 to a doctor called Bartholomeus, mentioned that his chest illness had forced him to postpone his regular bimonthly blood-letting (Constable 1967, vol. I, 379–83, and vol. II, 247–51). Harvey suggests seven to eight bleedings a year at Westminster Abbey in the thirteenth century (Harvey 1993, 97).

2 At St. Gall provision was made for a separation of the critically ill from the aged infirm, who occupied separate rooms in the area of the northeast devoted to the infirmary. A further separation was made for monks recovering from being bled; see Horn and Born 1979, vol. I, 288–89, 302–8, 313–21, and vol. II, 175–88.

3 The building is described in the *Customs of Farfa*; see Conant 1968, 63–64, pl. iv, fig. 4; Jetter 1978.

4 A more precise understanding of the Priory's eastern boundaries can be gained from the Canterbury Archaeological Trust's excavation in the garden of Linacre House of the King's School in 1990. Among other things, it unearthed the foundations of the earlier precinct wall (Driver, Raby, and Sparks 1990).

5 The artist of *Drawing I* shows both the northern gallery walk and *Necessarium* at exaggerated scale, although this may be due to his need to "fill" the space which he had erroneously assigned between the west transepts of the Cathedral and the eastern towers, rather than further east.

6 The Treasury is shown as free-standing on *Drawing I* with the north wall and gable separate from the Infirmary Hall's south aisle, although the accuracy of this can be argued. The north wall is heavily scarred from successive rebuildings, most particularly the construction of the sub-prior's chamber in the fifteenth century in the southwest bays of the Infirmary Hall.

7 For Woodruff and Danks the building was Archbishop Lanfranc's (Woodruff and Danks 1912, 252); for Tatton-Brown it originated with Anselm around 1100 (Tatton-Brown 2006, 91); for Sparks it is assigned to ca. 1120 (Sparks 2007, 39); and for Willis to Wibert and the 1160s (Willis 1868, 54). Willis's opinion was based on the use of similar forms and heavily scaled components to buildings such as Wibert's *Aula Nova* of the late 1150s. Kahn dismissed Willis's comparison with the debatable observation that the Infirmary Hall's architectural detailing was "common throughout the twelfth century" (Kahn 1991, 174).

8 As Tatton-Brown observed, the arcading remains dirty and was not cleaned in 1966 (2006, 93).

9 The material previously called onyx in the literature has been shown by Christopher Wilson to be calc-sinter imported to Canterbury from Cologne (see Appendix C). Its later appearance in the center of the double openings in the north and south walls of the prior's chapel undercroft and in the chapter house doorway represents a reuse of this highly prized twelfth-century material.

10 The Fountain House should not be confused with the Infirmary Hall's need for water to provide for baths (allowed to the sick in the *Rule* of St. Benedict; see McCann 1952,

90–91). These were met by a separate structure on the north side of the Hall. Similar bath structures for infirmaries can be documented at other contemporary monastic sites, for instance at Cistercian abbeys such as Rievaulx (Yorkshire), Waverley (Surrey), and Fountains (Yorkshire). For Rievaulx, see Fergusson and Harrison 1999, 127–28; for Waverley, see Brakspear 1905, 64; for Fountains, see Coppack 2003, 96.

11 See Underwood 1950, 41–138.

12 The ornament is similar to that on the column jamb to the day stair (see fig. 25).

13 See Connolly 1995, 99.

14 See Graham 1952–56, vol. 1, 819. This reference was kindly drawn to my attention by Margaret Sparks.

15 The tunnel came to light when a mechanical excavator preparing the foundations for a new boiler house for the heating of the Cathedral gouged a hole in the medieval structure. See photo in the *Friends of Canterbury Cathedral, Twenty-Second Annual Report*, 1949. Unfortunately, there was no recording of evidence undertaken.

16 I wish to thank Mr. Stuart Harrison for the Epaud reference.

17 Tatton-Brown suggests that it was drawn in part by William Stukeley (1991b, 69).

18 At Battle Abbey Abbot Odo, who had been prior at Canterbury, was still sleeping in the dormitory in the last quarter of the twelfth century. However, by the end of the century a separate residence had been constructed for him; see Knowles 1963, 406. At Rievaulx, Abbot Ailred withdrew to separate quarters built specially for him with the approval of the General Chapter in 1157; see Fergusson and Harrison 1999, 128–29.

19 For the general development of the abbot's or, in the case of priories, the prior's house, see Robinson 1911, and Brakspear 1933, 139–66. The area is also referred to as the Homors, Meist'omors, or Meister Omers, a term in use at least by the early 1400s (Willis 1868, 96–98).

8 CATHEDRAL ENHANCEMENTS AND RELATED BUILDINGS

1 See Willis 1868, 79–80, where he devotes a page to the discussion of the different names assigned to these purposes. The medieval term "vestiarium" places priority on the Priory's sacred garments and carries strong association with Hebrew texts. There is ample evidence that vessel and relic storage was also part of the building, as Willis notes. The word "vestiarium" on *Drawing I* should be distinguished from the same word on the St. Gall plan of ca. 820, where it described the abbey's storehouse for monastic habits as well as blankets and the like, and was the responsibility of the keeper of the monks' clothing (Horn and Born 1979, vol. I, 281–84). For the relationship to the sacrist, which is relevant for the Priory's Treasury, see ibid., 145.

2 Further references to this space come in 1093 and concern an incident connected with Anselm's installation as arch-

bishop. The ceremony was performed by the archbishop of York, and there came a moment in the ceremony when he realized he was required to accept Anselm as Primate of All England. Since this compromised the independence of the northern province, Thomas returned to what the document calls the "vestiarium" and there removed his vestments. Feelings were calmed down eventually, and Thomas was persuaded to put his vestments back on and return to the altar (see Raine 1879–94, vol. II, 104–5). I am indebted to Christopher Wilson for drawing this document to my attention.

3   In the 1860s the late medieval and post-suppression buildings retrofitted into the adjacent Infirmary Hall were demolished, and at the same time an extensive restoration of the Treasury was undertaken. Although a good deal of twelfth-century ashlar was retained, the exterior stonework and ornament contain many replacements. The façade design was turned around the corner to form faux wall buttresses (easily discerned by the machine-cut stonework and Portland cement joints). Further restoration of the building took place during 1998–99.

4   The area to the west of the building is today carpeted with inscribed tomb slabs relocated in the 1990s from the floor of the nave of the Cathedral, an injudicious displacement.

5   The decorative motif is most likely to be thirteenth century, an observation I owe to David Park. However, it may well have replaced an earlier decorative motif, of which evidence remains in a number of areas on all four sides of the under story. This takes the form of scribed arcs and circles. These seem to have served as a kind of underdrawing, a technique resembling that found in the east chapels of the Cathedral, as pointed out to me by Heather Newton.

6   See John Bilson's justly celebrated paper on the origins of Gothic architecture (Bilson 1917, 1–35). Bilson placed the octopartite vault in a line of descent from a vault of similar form in the lower stage of the crossing tower at the Benedictine nunnery of Montivilliers (Seine-Inférieure), thereby asserting Norman sources over those from the Île-de-France (the reverse of opinion then prevailing in France). Bilson offered no explanation for the change, or for the rebuilding of the vaults in the ground story. He also made no comment about the need to increase the height of the building because of the high-rising single octopartite vault.

7   The present top story to the building was added by Eastry in 1292 (mentioned in his list of works) to provide extra storage for the sacrist (Spark 2011, 21–22). Access to the new story came via a mid-twelfth-century stair in the wall thickness that had originally provided access to the roof over the vault. From the exterior, Eastry's story is uncompromisingly stark, its bleak flint-textured walls contrasting with the richly decorated and carefully cut ashlar of the twelfth-century building on top of which it sits.

8   On the general importance of Solomonic themes in twelfth-century art, see Cahn 1976b (reprinted in his *Studies in Medieval Art and Interpretation*, 2000). For the influence of the Temple, see Dynes 1973, 61–67; Ousterhout 1990, 44–54. For

the impact of Temple imagery on the papal liturgy in the mid-twelfth century, see de Blaauw 1990, 299–316. For continuing Solomonic influence for Gothic buildings, see Weiss 1995, 308–20; Davis 1996–97, 15–30.

9   For lions' masks in general, see Sauerlander 1972.

10 See Fernie 1989, 18–29; Heslop 2000. I am indebted to Sandy Heslop for this reference.

11 See also Rutherford 1975, 391–95.

12 Folda 1998. On the Jerusalem gates, see Steckoll 1968, and, earlier, Morgenstern 1929.

13 Herklotz, 2000, 24–27; see also the mentions in Fabre and Duchesne 1889. These references were kindly drawn to my attention by John Doran.

14 Rose 1997, 19, 234, n. 65; also Richmond 1933, 149–74. For help on these matters I am indebted to Brian Rose.

15 Other examples of elision in a setting with funerary connections with resulting twin façades and not altogether different from the Priory at Canterbury can be mentioned, such as Church Gate at Bury St. Edmunds built by Abbot Anselm (1121–48) (Fergusson 2011a, 25–34) or, much better known, the Lorsch Gatehouse: see Jacobsen 1985, 9–75, who suggests that the building served as a ceremonial arch to mark the entrance to the burial ground of Louis the German and his dynasty.

16 See Bodel 1999, 258–81, esp. 265.

17 The *Ordo Officorum* states "vestiarum id est capitulum vetus"; see de Blaauw 1990, 308.

18 The practice attracted followers after ca. 1150. Four further examples can be traced, all related to the upper entry of choirs: at the cathedrals of Ripon and York, and at two Cistercian houses, Rievaulx and Byland. For Rievaulx, see Fergusson and Harrison 1999, p. 162, fig. 133. I owe these examples to Stuart Harrison.

19 Lavers more or less contemporary with Canterbury survive at a number of sites, such as the Palace of Westminster, Much Wenlock, and Durham Cathedral. See Kahn 1991, 103–5, and n. 12 (p. 193) and n. 23 (p. 194).

20 They cannot have served for the weekly *mandatum fratrum*, which was specified for the Chapter House; see Knowles and Brooke 2002, 4.

21 See Krautheimer 1969; Underwood 1950.

22 The towers differ internally. The north tower has only a wall stair plus a tiny top spiral. In contrast, the south tower contains an extension of the broad spiral stair from below.

9   MONASTIC AND ARCHITECTURAL CONTEXT

1   For the architectural historians' view, see Fergusson 1984, 16–18; for the wider view of the historian of the reform movements, see Constable 1996.

2   See Constable and Smith 1972.

3   See King 1994.

4   For Smithfield, see Webb 1921, vol. 2, 8–10, 42–56; for Lincoln, see Stoker 1991, 29–31; for the Temple Church, see Wilson 2010, 34–43; for Rochester, see McNeill 2006, 181–204.

5 The suggestion has not proved durable. The term has faded and been replaced by broader views of the influence of Louis VII. What is more important than the name is the definition of a style extending ca. 1140–60 with its own distinctive qualities. These resist definition as either Romanesque or Gothic.

6 For the politics, see King 1994, 117–44. When prior of Bec, Theobald attracted from Matilda major gifts of jewelry and plate to the monastery: see Poirée, 1926, vol. I, 292–95, 650–51. The same contacts were suggested by George Zarnecki for the sculpture at the royal abbeys of Reading and Hyde (1984, 172–75).

7 Useful architectural surveys of this period are Branner 1963; Bony 1983; Wilson 1990; Fernie 2000.

8 Binski associates the use of polished marble with the rebuilding of the Trinity Chapel from 1174 (2004, 4) and suggests it as an innovation. The taste may be dated to at least fifteen years earlier. The same interests mark various buildings sponsored by Bishop Henry of Blois (1129–71) at Winchester, and at Glastonbury where Henry also occupied the office of abbot (1126–71). Polished stonework appears in the north of England in the choir of York Minster rebuilt by Archbishop Roger Pont L'Evêque in the 1160s, where the crypt piers display detailing, ornament, and even "boasting" of the stonework similar to Canterbury, as pointed out to me by Christopher Norton and Stuart Harrison. Before moving to York, Roger had been part of Archbishop Theobald's curia at Canterbury. Further north, the distinctive taste for rich, polished materials appears in the Galilee porch at Durham Cathedral ca. 1170 where Purbeck marble was supplemented with polished Blue Lias (Harrison 1993, 219–22) and the refectory lectern at Rievaulx ca. 1175 (Fergusson and Harrison 1999, 143–44). The term marble is used in its medieval sense as a polished stone; see Tatton-Brown 2006, 92, 95, and n. 14, also Appendix C.

9 This has been identified by Richard Krautheimer and subsequently enlarged by Frances Yates and, more recently, by Mary Carruthers, and Robert Ousterhout. See Krautheimer 1969; Yates 1980, 4–13; Carruthers 1993, 881–904; Ousterhout 2010, 153–69.

10 See Rudolph 1997, 401.

APPENDIX A PRIOR WIBERT'S OBIT

1 *Manellum/magnellum* (from *manellus/magnellus*): parallel to classical Latin *librilla*, a heavy stick used in warfare for throwing objects; related to the verb *librare*, to cause something to hang or swing, therefore a kind of hammer or clapper used to vibrate the bell. For citations, see *Lexicon Latinitatis Nederlandicae Medii Aevi*, vol. V, Leiden, 1977, 2802, 2885.

2 See Chapter 8; also Stocker and Everson 2006, 85.

3 "Pallium" may refer not only to a mantel worn by a priest as part of his vestments, but also to a large drapery or tapestry hung along the walls of the church or in the choir or in front of the altar.

4 For discussion of the water system, see Chapter 3 above.

5 The "cappam" in the manuscript has been transcribed as "cappellam." This is the only known mention of the project. The money set aside was considerable. It suggests a substantial chapel, perhaps even an east terminal structure.

6 The reference is both to the prior's funeral in 1167 and to the anniversary masses and celebrations of his life. For an account at Bury St. Edmunds of the anniversary service held in the Chapter House for Abbot Robert, who had died nearly eighty years earlier and which was accompanied by "the ringing of the great bells," see *The Chronicle of Jocelin of Brakelond* (Butler 1949, 90).

7 See note 1 for the translation of "magnellus."

8 Both collects are used in the funeral mass. The first derives from Tobias 12:8: "Bona est oratio cum jejunio, et eleemosyna magis quam thesauros auri recondere." The second is the standard collect: "Fidelium deus omnium Conditor et Redemptor: animabus famulorum" (For all the faithful departed).

9 The noun "caplo" in the manuscript has been corrected to "capulo" from "capulus"; the line over the "o" in the manuscript should probably have been over the "p" to show where the missing letter went. The meaning covers a tomb or sepulchre or funeral bier. The most likely of these is the raised tomb or "monumentum" at the entry to the Chapter House where Wibert was buried. This survived the suppression, and parts of its inscription were noted by Somner 1640; see Chapter 2. "Capsa" was used to describe Anselm's sarcophagus when it was "raised to the altars" in 1163.

10 The "dirige" refers to a service or a mass in general, from the opening line of the introit "dirige nostros actus, domine" (direct our acts, Lord). The reference could equally apply to the anniversary mass.

APPENDIX C CANTERBURY CATHEDRAL'S MYSTERY 'MARBLE'

1 Gostling 1825, 308. Although not cited, Gostling is presumably the source of the recent statement that some of the external nook shafts of the aisle windows of the early twelfth-century choir appear to be made from fossilised wood; Fernie 2000, 143. All of the currently existing nook shafts seem to be of freestone.

2 Routledge, Sheppard and Scott Robinson 1889, 254; Woodman 1981, 80.

3 Tatton-Brown 1989, 25; Tatton-Brown 1990, 74–75; Kahn 1991, 111, 144, 179, 195 n. 29; Caröe 1993, 4; Tatton-Brown 1994, 27.

4 Worssam 1995, 27. Following the publication of Worssam's article most writers adopted 'onyx marble' rather than 'onyx', but not consistently.

5 Shultz 1986, 263–65, 269. The calc-sinter formed in the Eifel aqueduct is of exceptional quality. That from the Pont du Gard, for example, was formed at a far faster rate (ca. 1.15 centimetres per year) but it is porous and useful only for

walling; Grewe and Blackman 2001, 114; Hodge 2002, 228. An Italian publication of 1638 states that the calc-sinter formed in portions of the Claudian aqueduct near Rome had begun to be quarried, polished and used for the decoration of altars in the city's churches; Ashby 1935, 291. A British origin for medieval England's calc-sinter can be ruled out, given the rudimentary character of British aqueduct provision vis-à-vis the rest of the western Empire; Stephens 1985, passim.

6 Haberey 1972, 108–09.

7 Grewe 1991, 341–41.

8 The shelf is immediately west of the north entrance; Grewe 1991, 335–36, 343.

9 Fuchs 1933, 89–90.

10 Grewe 1991, 289.

11 Kahn 1991, 195 n. 29, ill. 183. In his account of the burning and reconstruction of the cathedral's early twelfth-century choir, Gervase stated that the latter contained no marble shafts; Stubbs 1879–80, I, 27; Willis 1845, 59.

12 Tatton-Brown 1996, 93–98, 101.

13 Ferguson 1996, 52.

14 The glazing of the arcade is late nineteenth century. For Michael of Canterbury see Harvey 1984, 45–46; Matthew and Harrison 2002, IX, 945–46.

15 Willis 1845, 108. Willis eschews guesswork about the identity of the material.

16 Lehmann-Brockhaus 1955–60, I, 200 (no. 730). The unique opus sectile pavement west of the shrine of St Thomas is identified as part of the paving of St Anselm's choir in Norton 2002, 13–16.

17 The only extant German opus sectile pavement to include small amounts of calc-sinter seems to be that of ca. 1226–27 in the choir of St Kunibert in Cologne; Kier 1970, 117.

18 Stubbs 1879–80, I, 24; Willis 1845, 55. A similar view regarding the chronological span of the use of calc-sinter at Canterbury is taken in Tatton-Brown 1996, 23. The issue of the evocation of Rome's churches through the use of marble for the choir enclosure and the floor of St Anselm's choir cannot be broached here.

19 The dimensions are well within the maxima noted in Haberey 1972, 109. No doubt the high polish and fine jointing date from the 1870s, when the calc-sinter slabs were probably transferred to their present position. The early 1890s seem to have witnessed the destruction of the cathedral's only other calc-sinter floor, the 'eastern floor' (meaning the floor of the eastern bay?) of the chapel of Our Lady Undercroft in the crypt; Routledge, Sheppard and Scott Robinson 1889, 254. At the time of writing the only slabs of calc-sinter to be seen in this chapel are three small examples just within the north entrance of the western bay.

20 Stubbs 1879–80, I, 13; Willis 1845, 43.

21 Dubbe 1992, 263–64.

22 The divergent widths of the slots in the base of the more southerly of the piers re-used in the crypt (17 cm on the west side, 9 cm on the east side) might be due to the reassembly of the stonework in its present position in 1178.

23 Worssam 1995, 32 n. 21.

24 McNeill 2006, 189.

25 Anderson 1988, passim; Anderson 1992, passim.

26 In 1984 these fragments (catalogue numbers WP 69, WP 519, WP 559) were stored on site at Wolvesey. On Wolvesey see Biddle 1986.

27 Although not concerned with the issue of the medieval trade in calc-sinter, Grewe is emphatic that Cologne must have been the centre for its exploitation; Grewe 1991, 292.

28 Gibbs 1939, 156–58 (no. 198).

29 Schützeichel 1965, 125.

30 Kier 1970, passim. A possible survival from a pavement of ca. 1100 at St Paul's could be the paving of black marble spotted with green noted in the late sixteenth century; Furnivall 1877, book III, chapter IX, 62; Lethaby 1906, 328.

31 Arnold 1890–06, I, 351. For the rather comical attempts of Durham Cathedral Priory to obtain marble for the presbytery floor ca. 1150 see Salzman 1967, 147, 367.

32 For an account of the social, economic and cultural connections between London and Cologne in the eleventh to thirteenth centuries see Huffman 1998. The most important German immigrant craftsman was probably the goldsmith Otto who made the tombs of Edward the Confessor and William the Conqueror; Chibnall 1969–80, IV, 110–11 n. 2; Wilson 2002, 494 n. 188.

33 Heslop 1984, 204.

Bibliography

B. Abou-El-Haj, "The Audience for the Medieval Cult of Saints," *Gesta*, 30, 1991, 3–15

A. S. Abulafia, "St. Anselm and Those Outside the Church," pp. 11–37 in D. Loades and K. Walsh (eds.), *Faith and Unity: Christian Political Experience*, Studies in Church History, Subsidia 6, Oxford, 1990

J. J. G. Alexander, *Medieval Illuminators and their Method of Work*, London, 1992

F. Anderson, "The Tournai Marble Sculptures of the Priory of St. Pancras at Lewes, East Sussex," *Revue belge d'archéologie et d'histoire d'art*, 57, 1988, 23–49

——, "'Uxor Mea:' The First Wife of the First William of Warrenne," *Sussex Archaeological Collections*, 130, 1992, 107–29

T. Arnold ed., *Memorials of St. Edmund's Abbey*, Rolls Series, 96, 3 vols., London, 1890–96

J. Ashbee, "Cloisters in English Palaces in the Twelfth and Thirteenth Centuries," pp. 71–90 in M. Henig and J. McNeill (eds.), *The Medieval Cloister in England and Wales*, special issue of the *Journal of the British Archaeological Association*, 159, Leeds, 2006

K. Baker, "The Appended Images of the Eadwine Psalter: A New Appraisal of their Commemorative, Documentary, and Institutional Functions," PhD thesis, Emory University, Atlanta, 2008 (in course of publication)

F. Barlow, *Thomas Becket*, Berkeley, 1976

F. Barlow et al., *Winchester in the Early Middle Ages*, Oxford, 1976

R. Bartlett, *England under the Norman and Angevin Kings 1075–1225*, Oxford, 2000

D. Bell, "The Siting and Size of Cistercian Infirmaries in England and Wales," *Studies in Cistercian Art and Architecture*, 5, 1998, 211–38

P. Bennett, "Rescue Excavations in the Outer Court of St. Augustine's Abbey," *Archaeologia Cantiana*, 103, 1986, 79–118

M. Berg and H. Jones, *Norman Churches in the Canterbury Diocese*, Stroud, 2009

M. Biddle, *Wolvesey. The Old Bishops Palace, Winchester, Hampshire* (English Heritage Handbook), London, 1986

J. Bilson, "The Norman School and the Beginnings of Gothic Architecture: Two Octopartite Vaults, Montivilliers and Canterbury," *Archaeological Journal*, 74, 1917, 1–35

P. Binski, *Becket's Crown Art and Imagination in Gothic England 1170–1300*, London, 2004

P. Binski and S. Panayotova (eds.), *The Cambridge Illuminations: Ten Centuries of Book Production in the Medieval West*, London, 2005

T. N. Bisson, *The Crisis of the Twelfth Century: Power, Lordship, and the Origins of European Government*, Princeton, 2009

K. Blockley, M. Sparks, and T. Tatton-Brown, *Canterbury Cathedral Nave: Archaeology, History and Architecture*, The Archaeology of Canterbury, New Series, vol. 1, Canterbury, 1997

C. Bock, "Les cisterciens et l'étude du droit," *Analecta Sacri Ordinis Cisterciensis*, 7, 1951, 7–31

J. Bodel, "Death on Display: Looking at Roman Funerals," pp. 258–81 in Bettina Bergman and C. Kondoleon (eds.), *The Art of Ancient Spectacle*, Studies in the History of Art, 56, Center for Advanced Study in the Visual Arts, Symposium Papers 34, Washington, D.C., 1999

B. Bolton and A. Duggan (eds.), *Hadrian IV: The English Pope 1154–59*, Aldershot, 2003

J. Bond, *Monastic Landscapes*, Stroud, 2004

S. Bonde and C. Maines (eds.), *Saint-Jean-des-Vignes in Soissons: Approaches to its Architecture, Archaeology and History*, Bibliotheca Victorina, XV, Turnhout, 2004

A. Bonis and M. Wabont (eds.), *L'hydraulique monastique: milieu, résaux, usages*, Grâne, 1996

J. Bony, "Introduction," pp. 81–91 in M. Meiss (ed.) *Romanesque and Gothic Art: Acts of the Twentieth International Congress of the History of Art*, vol. 1, Princeton, 1963

———, *French Gothic Architecture of the 12th and 13th Centuries*, Berkeley, 1983

J. Bowen, "Domus Hospitum," *Canterbury Archaeological Trust, 11th Annual Report*, Canterbury, 1987, 26–27

———, "Domus Hospitium," *Archaeologia Cantiana*, 106, 1988, 326–27

R. Bowers, "The Almonry Schools of English Monasteries c. 1265–1540," pp. 177–222 in B. J. Thompson (ed.), *Monasteries and Society in Medieval Britain*, Harlaxton Medieval Studies, 6, Stamford, 1999

L. Boyle, "The Beginnings of Legal Studies at Oxford," *Viator*, 14, 1983, 107–31

S. Boynton, *Shaping a Monastic Identity: Liturgy and History at the Imperial Abbey of Farfa, 1000–1125*, Ithaca, 2006

S. Boynton and I. Cochelin (eds.), *From Dead of Night to End of Day: The Medieval Customs of Cluny*, Disciplina Monastica, 3, Turnhout, 2005

H. Brakspear, *Waverley Abbey*, Surrey Archaeological Society, London, 1905

———, "The Abbot's House at Battle," *Archaeologia*, 83, 1933, 139–66

R. Branner, "Gothic Architecture 1160–80 and its Romanesque Sources," pp. 92–104 in M. Meiss (ed.) *Romanesque and Gothic Art: Acts of the Twentieth International Congress of the History of Art*, vol. 1, Princeton, 1963

A. H. Bredero, *Bernard of Clairvaux: Between Cult and History*, Kalamazoo, 1996

J. Britton, *Historical and Descriptive Account of the Metropolitan Cathedrals of Canterbury and York*, vol. 1, London, 1836

P. F. Brown, *Venice and Antiquity*, London, 1996

R. A. Brown, *English Castles*, 2nd ed., London, 1970

R. A. Brown, H. M. Colvin, and A. J. Taylor, *The History of the King's Works*, vol. 1, London, 1963

C. Brühl, "Zur Geschichte der Procuratio canonica vornehmlich im 11. und 12. Jahrhundert," vol. 1, pp. 323–35 in *Aus Mittelalter und Diplomatik*, 2 vols., Hildesheim, 1989

A. C. Buchanan, "Robert Willis (1800–1875) and the Rise of Architectural History," Ph.D. thesis, University College, London, 1995 (in course of publication)

———, "William St. John Hope (1854–1919) and the Historiography of Rochester Cathedral," pp. 218–26 in T. Ayers and T. Tatton-Brown (eds.), *Medieval Art, Architecture and Archaeology at Rochester*, British Archaeological Association Conference Transactions, 28, Leeds, 2006

H. E. Butler (trans.), *The Chronicle of Jocelin of Brakelond*, London, 1949

——— (trans.), *The Autobiography of Giraldus Cambrensis*, London, 1937

F. O. Büttner (ed.), *The Illuminated Psalter: Studies in the Content, Purpose and Placement of its Images*, Turnhout, 2004

W. Cahn, "The Tympanum of the Portal of Ste Anne at Notre Dame de Paris and the Iconography of Powers in the Early Middle Ages," *Journal of the Warburg and Courtauld Institutes*, 33, 1969, 55–72

———, "A Twelfth Century *Decretum* Fragment from Pontigny," *Cleveland Museum of Art Bulletin*, 62, 1975, 47–59 (1975a)

———, "St. Albans and the Channel Style in England," pp. 187–230 in K. Hoffman (ed.), *The Year 1200: A Symposium*, New York, 1975 (1975b)

———, "Architectural Draftsmanship in Twelfth-Century Paris: The Illustrations of Richard of Saint-Victor's Commentary on Ezekiel's Temple Vision," *Gesta*, 1976, 247–54 (1976a)

———, "Solomonic Elements in Romanesque Art," pp. 45–72 in J. Gutman (ed.), *The Temple of Soloman: Archaeological Fact and Medieval Tradition in Christian, Islamic, and Jewish Art*, Missoula, 1976 (1976b)

———, "Images, Text and Context: Medieval Landscape and the Encyclopaedic Tradition," in D. Poirion and N. F. Regalado (eds.), *Contexts: Style and Values in Medieval Art and Literature*, special issue of *Yale French Studies*, 80, New Haven and London, 1991, 11–24

———, "Architecture and Exegesis: Richard of St.-Victor's Ezekiel Commentary and its Illustrations," *Art Bulletin*, 76, 1994, 53–68

———, "Solomonic Elements in Romanesque Art," pp. 157–82 in *Studies in Medieval Art and Interpretation*, London, 2000

———, "The Allegorical Menorah," pp. 117–26 in J. F. Hamburger and A. S. Korteweg (eds.), *Tributes in Honor of James Marrow: Studies in Painting and Manuscript Illuminations of the Late Middle Ages and Northern Renaissance*, Turnhout, 2006

———, "Notes on Illustrations of Ezekiel's Temple Vision in

the Manuscript of Nicolas of Lyra's *Postilla litteralis*," pp. 155–69 in K. Kogman-Appel and M. Meyer (eds.), *Between Judaism and Christianity: Art-Historical Essays in Honor of Elisheva Revel-Naher*, Leiden, 2009

H. Cam, *Liberties and Communities in Medieval England: Collected Studies in Local Administration and Topography*, Cambridge, 1944

M. Caröe, "From the Cathedral Surveyor," *Friends of Rochester Cathedral Report for 1993/4*, 20–28

W. D. Caröe, "The Three Towers of Canterbury Cathedral," *Architectural Review*, 17, 1905, 3–12

———, "Wall Painting in the Infirmary Chapel, Canterbury Cathedral," *Archaeologia*, 2nd series, 63, 1912, 41–56

———, "The Water Tower," *Friends of Canterbury Cathedral*, Jan. 1929, 25–37

M. Carruthers, "The Poet as Master Builder: Composition and Locational Memory in the Middle Ages," *New Literary History*, 24, 1993, 881–904

———, *The Craft of Thought: Meditation, Rhetoric, and the Making of Images 400–1200*, Cambridge, 1998

———, *The Book of Memory: A Study of Memory in Medieval Culture*, 2nd ed., Cambridge, 2008

———, "Ars Oblivionalis, Ars Inveniendi: The Cherub Figure and the Arts of Memory," *Gesta*, 48, no. 2, 2010, 99–117

M. Carruthers and J. Ziolkowski (eds.), *The Medieval Craft of Memory: An Anthology of Texts and Pictures*, Philadelphia, 2002

J. Carter, *The Ancient Architecture of England*, 2 vols., London, 1795–1807

J. Caskey, *Art and Patronage in the Medieval Mediterranean: Merchant Culture in the Region of Amalfi*, Cambridge, 2004

M. Caviness, *The Windows of Christ Church Cathedral, Canterbury*, Corpus Vitrearum Medii Aevi, Great Britain, II, London, 1981

C. Chazelle, "Christ and the Vision of God: The Biblical Diagrams of the Codex Amiatinus," pp. 84–111 in J. Hamburger and A.-M. Bouché (eds.), *The Mind's Eye: Art and Theological Argument in the Middle Ages*, Princeton, 2006

M. Cheney, *Roger, Bishop of Worcester, 1164–1179*, Oxford, 1980

D. Choisselet and P. Vernet, *Les Ecclesiatica Officia: Cisterciens du XIIe siècle*, Reiningue, 1989

P. Collinson, N. Ramsay, and M. Sparks (eds.), *A History of Canterbury Cathedral*, 2nd edn., Canterbury, 2002

K. J. Conant, *Cluny: Les églises et la maison du chef d'ordre*, Mâcon, 1968

S. Connolly (trans.), *Bede: On the Temple*, Liverpool, 1995

G. Constable (ed.), *The Letters of Peter the Venerable*, 2 vols., Cambridge, MA, 1967

———, *The Reformation of the Twelfth Century*, Cambridge, 1996

G. Constable and B. Smith (eds. and trans.), *Libellus de diversis ordinibus et professionibus qui sunt in aecclesia*, Oxford, 1972

G. Coppack, "Free-Standing Cloister Lavabos of the Twelfth and Thirteenth Centuries in England, their Form, Occurrence, and Water Supply," pp. 37–43 in H.-E. Paulus et al.,

Wasser-Lebensquelle und Bedeutungsträger, Regensburger Herbstsymposium sur Kunstgeschichte und Denkmalpflege, vol. 4, Regensburg, 1999

———, *Fountains Abbey: The Cistercians in Northern England*, Stroud, 2003

———, *Abbeys and Priories*, Stroud, 2006

G. Coppack, C. Hayfield, and R. Williams, "Sawley Abbey: The Architecture and Archaeology of a Smaller Cistercian Abbey," *Journal of the British Archaeological Association*, 155, 2002, 22–114

C. Davidson Cragoe, "Reading and Re-reading Gervase of Canterbury," *Journal of the British Archaeological Association*, 154, 2001, 40–53

R. Cristiani, "Integration and Marginalization: Dealing with the Sick in Eleventh-Century Cluny," pp. 287–96 in S. Boynton and I. Cochelin (eds.), *From Dead of Night to End of Day: The Medieval Customs of Cluny*, Disciplina Monastica, 3, Turnhout, 2005

T. E. A. Dale, "The Individual, the Resurrected Body, and Romanesque Portraiture: The Tomb of Rudolph von Schwaben in Merseburg," *Speculum*, 77, 2002, 707–43

P. Dalton and G. White (eds.), *King Stephen's Reign, 1135–54*, Woodbridge, 2008

L. Daston and K. Park, *Wonders and the Order of Nature 1150–1750*, New York, 1998

J. Dart, *The History and Antiquities of the Cathedral Church of Canterbury*, London, 1726

C. Davidson, "Images of Gothic Architecture: Structure or Symbolism," pp. 5–16 in M. Howard (ed.), *The Image of the Building*, Papers from the Annual Symposium of the Society of Architectural Historians of Great Britain, 1995, London, 1996

M. Davis, "The Literal, the Symbolic, and Gothic Architecture," *Avista Forum*, 10, 1996–97, 15–30

S. de Blaauw, "The Solitary Celebration of the Supreme Pontiff: The Lateran Basilica as the New Temple in the Medieval Liturgy of Maundy Thursday," pp. 299–316 in C. Caspers and M. Schneiders (eds.), *Mones Circumadstantes: Contributions towards the History of the Role of the People in the Liturgy Presented to Herman Wigman*, Kampen, 1990

S. de Maria, *Gli Archei onorari di Roma e dell'Italia Romana*, Rome, 1988

F. W. de Wald, *The Illustrations of the Utrecht Psalter*, Princeton, 1932

H. Decker, *Romanesque Art in Italy*, New York, 1959

S. Denne, "Evidence of a Lavatory appertaining to the Benedictine Priory of Canterbury Cathedral and Observations on Fonts," *Archaeologia*, 11, 1794, 106–34

B. Diemling, "Medieval Church Portals and their Importance in the History of Law," in R. Toman and A. Bdnorz (eds.), *Romanesque: Architecture, Sculpture, Painting*, Cologne, 1997

———, "Ad Rufam Ianuam: Die rechtsgeschichtliche Bedeutung von roten Türen im Mittelater," *Zeitschrift der Savigny-Stiftung für Rechtsgeschichte: Germanistische Abteilung*, 1998, 498–513

C. R. Dodwell, *The Canterbury School of Illumination*, Cambridge, 1954

———, *The Pictorial Arts of the West 800–1200*, New Haven and London, 1993

L. Donadono, *La Scala Santa a San Giovanni in Laterano*, Rome, 2000

C. Donahue and N. Adams, *Select Cases from the Ecclesiastical Courts of the Province of Canterbury*, Selden Society, 95, London, 1981

P. Draper, *The Formation of English Gothic: Architecture and Identity*, London, 2006

J. C. Driver, J. Raby, and M. Sparks, *Excavations in the Cathedral Precincts, 2: Linacre Garden, 'Meister Omers' and St. Gabriel's Chapel*, The Archaeology of Canterbury, vol. 4, Maidstone, 1990

B. Dubbe, "Interieur en Inventaris tot 1800," in A. J. J. Mekking ed., *De Grote of Lebuinuskerk te Deventer*, Utrecht, 1992

F. R. H. du Boulay, *The Lordship of Canterbury: An Essay on Medieval Society*, London, 1966

C. Dudley, "The Transept Towers of Canterbury: a Reappraisal," *Canterbury Cathedral Chronicle*, 71, 1977, 22–34

A. Duggan, "Thomas Becket's Italian Network," pp. 1–21 in *Thomas Becket: Friends, Networks, Texts and Cult*, Aldershot, 2007

A. Dunkin (ed.), *A Report of the Proceedings of the British Archaeological Association at the First General Meeting held at Canterbury in September 1844*, London, 1845

W. Dynes, "The Medieval Cloister as Temple of Solomon," *Gesta*, 12, 1973, 61–67

F. Epaud, *De la charpente romane à la charpente gothique en Normandie*, Caen, 2007

P. Fabre and L. Duchesne, *Liber Censuum de l'église romaine*, Paris, 1889

C. Fabricius, "Die 'litterae formatae' im Frühmittelalter," *Archiv für Urkundenforschung*, 9, 1926, 39–86, 168–94

P. A. Faulkner, "Some Medieval Archepiscopal Palaces," *Archaeological Journal*, 127, 1970, 130–46

P. Fergusson, *Architecture of Solitude: Cistercian Abbeys in Twelfth Century England*, Princeton, 1984

———, "The Refectory at Easby Abbey: Form and Iconography," *Art Bulletin*, 71, 1989, 334–51

———, "The Green Court Gate at the Cathedral Monastery of Christ Church, Canterbury," pp. 87–97 in W. Boehm (ed.), *Das Bauwerk und die Stadt: Aufsatze für Eduard Sekler*, Vienna, 1994

———, "Modernization and Mnemonics at Christ Church, Canterbury: The Treasury Building," *Journal of the Society of Architectural Historians*, 65, 2006, 50–67

———, "Prior Wibert's Fountain Houses: Service and Symbolism at Christ Church, Canterbury," pp. 83–98 in E. S. Lane, E. C. Paston, and E. M. Shortell (eds.), *The Four Modes of Seeing: Approaches to Medieval Imagery in Honor of Madeline Caviness*, Farnham, 2009

———, "Abbot Anselm's Gate Tower at Bury St Edmunds,"

pp. 25–34 in Z. Opacic and A. Timmerman (eds.), *Architecture, Liturgy, Identity: Liber Amicorum Paul Crossley*, Turnhout, 2011

———, "The Entry Complex at the Cathedral Priory," in A. Bovey (ed.), *British Archaeological Association Canterbury Conference Transactions*, 35, Leeds, 2012 (forthcoming)

P. Fergusson and S. Harrison, *Rievaulx Abbey: Community, Architecture, Memory*, New Haven and London, 1999

E. Fernie, "Archaeology and Iconography: Recent Developments in the Study of English Medieval Architecture," *Architectural History*, 32, 1989, 18–29

———, *The Architecture of Norman England*, Oxford, 2000

———, *Architecture and Sculpture of Ely Cathedral*, Woodbridge, 2003

V. J. Flint, "The Early Medieval Medicus: The Saint and the Enchanter," *Social History of Medicine*, 2, 1989, 127–45

J. Folda, "The South Transept Façade of the Church of the Holy Sepulchre in Jerusalem: An Aspect of 'Rebuilding Jerusalem'," pp. 239–54 in John France and W. Zajac (eds.), *The Crusades and their Sources: Essays Presented to Bernard Hamilton*, Aldershot, 1998

S. Foot, *Monastic Life in Anglo-Saxon England, c. 600–900*, Cambridge, 2006

I. Forsyth, "Word Play in the Cloister at Moissac," pp. 154–78 in C. Hourihane (ed.), *Romanesque Art and Thought in the Twelfth Century: Essays in Honor of Walter Cahn*, University Park, PA, 2008

J. T. Fowler (ed.), *The Rites of Durham*, Surtees Society, 108, Durham, 1902

J. Franklin, "Review of D. Kahn, *Canterbury Cathedral and its Romanesque Sculpture, 1991*", *Burlington Magazine*, 133, no. 2, 1991, 547

A. Fuchs, "Der Kanalsinter als Werkstoff," *Westfalen*, 18, 1933, 87–90

L. B. Gaches, *History of the Liberty of Peterborough*, Peterborough, 1905

R. Gameson, *The Earliest Books of Canterbury Cathedral: Manuscripts and Fragments to c. 1200*, London, 2008

F. Gandolfo, "La façade romane et les rapports avec le protiro, l'atrium et le quadriportico," *Cahiers de civilisation médiévale*, 34, 1991, 309–19

J. Gardelles, "Les palais dans l'Europe occidentale chrétienne du xe au xiie siècle," *Cahiers de civilisation médiévale*, 19, 1976, 115–34

J. Gardner, "An Introduction to the Iconography of the Medieval Italian City Gate," *Dumbarton Oaks Papers*, 41, 1987, 199–213

P. Geary, *Living with the Dead in the Middle Ages*, Ithaca, 1994

R. Gem, "The Significance of the 11th Century Rebuilding of Christ Church and St. Augustine's Abbey, Canterbury in the Development of Romanesque Architecture," pp. 1–17 in N. Coldstream and P. Draper (eds.), *Medieval Art and Architecture at Canterbury before 1200*, British Archaeological Association Conference Transactions, 5, Leeds, 1982

———, "Canterbury and the Cushion Capital: A Commentary on Passages from Goscelin's 'De Miraculis Sancti Augustini'," pp. 83–101 in N. Stratford (ed.), *Romanesque and Gothic: Essays for George Zarnecki*, Woodbridge, 1987

———, "England and the Resistance to Romanesque Architecture," pp. 129–40 in L. A. S. Butler and R. Morris (eds.), *Studies in Medieval History Presented to R. Allen Brown*, Woodbridge, 1989

F. Getz, "Medical Practitioners in Medieval England," *Social History of Medicine*, 3, 1990, 245–83

M. Gibbs, *Early Charters of the Cathedral Church of St. Paul, London*, Camden Society, 3rd series, 58, 1939

M. Gibson, *Lanfranc of Bec*, Oxford, 1978

———, "Who Designed the Eadwine Psalter?" pp. 71–76 in S. Macready and F. H. Thompson (eds.), *Art and Patronage in the English Romanesque*, London, 1986

———, "The Latin Apparatus," pp. 108–22 in M. Gibson, T. A. Heslop, and R. Pfaff (eds.), *The Eadwine Psalter: Text, Image, and Monastic Culture in Twelfth-Century Canterbury*, London, 1992 (1992a)

———, "Conclusions: The Eadwine Psalter in Context," pp. 209–13 in M. Gibson, T. A. Heslop, and R. Pfaff (eds.), *The Eadwine Psalter: Text, Image, and Monastic Culture in Twelfth-Century Canterbury*, London, 1992 (1992b)

———, "Normans and Angevins, 1070–1220," pp. 38–68 in P. Collinson, N. Ramsay, and M. Sparks (eds.), *A History of Canterbury Cathedral*, Oxford, 1995

M. Gibson, T. A. Heslop, and R. Pfaff (eds.), *The Eadwine Psalter: Text, Image, and Monastic Culture in Twelfth-Century Canterbury*, London, 1992

R. Gilchrist, *Norwich Cathedral Close: The Evolution of the English Cathedral Landscape*, Woodbridge, 2005

R. Gilchrist and H. Mytum (eds.), *The Archaeology of Rural Monasteries*, British Archaeological Reports, Oxford, 1989

———, *Advances in Monastic Archaeology*, British Archaeological Reports, Oxford, 1993

G. B. Giovenale, "Simboli tutelari su porte del recinto urbano ed altri monumenti dell'anchità," *Bulletino della Commissione Archeologica Comunale Roma*, 57, 1929, 183–207

J. Givens, *Observation and Image-Making in Gothic Art*, Cambridge, 2005

W. H. Godfrey, "English Cloister Lavatories as Independent Structures," *Archaeological Journal*, 66, 1949, 91–97

J. Goodall, "The Great Tower of Rochester Castle," pp. 265–99 in T. Ayers and T. Tatton-Brown (eds.), *Medieval Art, Architecture and Archaeology at Rochester*, British Archaeological Association Conference Transactions, 28, Leeds, 2006

———, *The English Castle*, New Haven and London, 2011

W. Gostling, *A Walk in and around the City of Canterbury with many Observations not to be found in any Description hitherto Published*, Canterbury, 1774

J. Gould, "The Twelfth-Century Water-Supply to Lichfield Close," *Antiquaries Journal*, 46, 1976, 75–79

R. Graham (ed.), *Registrum Roberti Winchelsey*, 2 vols., Canterbury and York Society, 52, Oxford, 1952–56

A. Gransden, "Realistic Observation in Twelfth Century England," *Speculum*, 47, 1972, 29–51

———, *History of the Abbey of Bury St Edmunds, 1180–1256*, Woodbridge, 2007

L. Grant, "Architectural Relations between England and Normandy, 1100–1204," pp. 117–29 in D. Bates and A. Curry (eds.), *England and Normandy in the Middle Ages*, London, 1994

———, *Abbot Suger of St.-Denis: Church and State in Early Twelfth-Century France*, London, 1998

———, *Architecture and Society in Normandy 1120–1270*, London, 2005

J. Greatrex, *Biographical Register of the English Cathedral Priories of the Province of Canterbury c. 1066–1540*, Oxford, 1997

K. Grewe, "Der Wasserversorgungsplan des Klosters Christchurch in Canterbury (12. Jahrhundert)," pp. 229–36 in K. Grewe (ed.), *Die Wasserversorgung im Mittelalter*, Geschichte der Wasserversorgung, vol. 4, Mainz am Rhein, 1991 (1991a)

———, "Le monastère de Christchurch á Cantorbéry (Kent, Grande-Bretagne): interprétation et signification du plan du réseau hydraulique (XIIe siècle)," pp. 123–34 in K. Grewe (ed.), *Die Wasserversorgung im Mittelalter*, Geschichte der Wasserversorgung, vol. 4, Mainz am Rhein, 1991 (1991b)

———, "Aquädukt-Marmor. Kalksinter der römischen Eifelwasserleitung als Baustoff des Mittelalters," *Bonner Jahrbuch*, 191, 1991, 277–343 (1991c)

W. Haberey, *Die römischen Wasserleitungen nach Köln. Die Technik der Wasserversorgung einer antiker Stadt*, 2nd edn. Bonn, 1972

R. Halsey, "The Twelfth Century Nave of Rochester Cathedral," pp. 61–84 in T. Ayers and T. Tatton-Brown (eds.), *Medieval Art, Architecture and Archaeology at Rochester*, British Archaeological Association Conference Transactions, 28, Leeds, 2006

S. Harrison, "Observations on the Architecture of the Galilee Chapel," pp. 213–34 in D. Rollason et al. (eds.), *Anglo-Norman Durham 1093–1993*, Woodbridge, 1993

———, "Benedictine and Augustinian Cloister Arcades of the Twelfth and Thirteenth Centuries in England, Wales and Scotland," pp. 105–30 in M. Henig and J. McNeill (eds.), *The Medieval Cloister in England and Wales*, special issue of the *Journal of the British Archaeological Association*, 159, Leeds, 2006

S. Harrison and C. Norton, "Reconstructing a Lost Cathedral: York Minster in the Eleventh and Twelfth Centuries," *Journal of the Ecclesiological Society, Ecclesiology Today*, 40, 2008, 53–59

J. B. Hartley and D. Woodward, *The History of Cartography: Cartography in Prehistoric, Ancient, and Medieval Europe and the Mediterranean*, Chicago, 1987

B. Harvey, *Living and Dying in England, 1100–1540: The Monastic Experience*, Oxford, 1993

J. Harvey, *English Mediaeval Architects*, rev. edn., Gloucester, 1987

J. Hayes, "Prior Wibert's Waterworks," *Canterbury Chronicle*, 71, 1977, 17–26

M. F. Hearn, "Canterbury Cathedral and the Cult of Becket," *Art Bulletin*, 76, 1994, 19–52

A. Heimann, "A Twelfth Century Manuscript from Winchecombe and its Illustrations: Dublin, Trinity College, Ms. 53," *Journal of the Warburg and Courtauld Institutes*, 28, 1965, 86–109

I. Herklotz, *Gli eredi di Costantino: il papato, il Laterano e la propaganda visiva nel XII secolo*, Rome, 2000

T. A. Heslop, "The Conventual Seals of Canterbury Cathedral: 1066–1232," pp. 94–100 in N. Coldstream and P. Draper (eds.), *Medieval Art and Architecture at Canterbury before 1200*, British Archaeological Association Conference Transactions, 5, Leeds, 1982

———, "'Dunstanus Archiepiscopus' and painting in Kent around 1120," *Burlington Magazine*, 126, 1984, 195–204

———, "Eadwine and his Portrait," pp. 178–85 in M. Gibson, T. A. Heslop, and R. Pfaff (eds.), *The Eadwine Psalter: Text, Image, and Monastic Culture in Twelfth-Century Canterbury*, London, 1992

———, "Contemplating Chimera in Medieval Imagination: St. Anselm's Crypt at Canterbury," pp. 153–63 in L. Golden (ed.), *Raising the Eyebrow: John Onians and World Art Studies*, BAR International Series, 996, Oxford, 2000

———, "St Anselm, Church Reform, and the Politics of Art," *Anglo Norman Studies*, 33, 2011, 103–26

———, "St Anselm and the Visual Arts at Canterbury, 1093–1109," *British Archaeological Association Canterbury Conference Transactions*, 35, Leeds, 2012 (forthcoming)

L. R. Hoey, "Style, Patronage, and Artistic Creativity in Kent Parish Church Architecture c.1180–1260," *Archaeologia Cantiana*, 115, 1995, 45–70

A. Holton-Krayenbuhl, "The Infirmary Complex at Ely," *Archaeological Journal*, 154, 1997, 118–73

———, "The Prior's Lodging at Ely," *Archaeological Journal*, 156, 1999, 294–341

W. Holtzmann, *Papsturkunden in England*, 3 vols., Berlin, 1930

W. H. St. J. Hope, "Inventories of the Priors of Canterbury," *Archaeological Journal*, 53, 1896, 258–83

———, "An Excavation in the Frater," *Proceedings of the Society of Antiquaries*, 2nd series, 17, 1899, 445–52

W. Horn and E. Born, *The Plan of St. Gall*, 3 vols., Berkeley, 1979

C. Hourihane (ed.), *Romanesque Art and Thought in the Twelfth Century, Essays in Honor of Walter Cahn*, University Park, PA, 2008

H. Hubert, *Der Palazzo communale von Bologna*, Vienna, 1993

J. P. Huffman, *Family, Commerce and Religion in London and Cologne: Anglo-German Emigrants c. 1000–c. 1300*, Cambridge, 1998

T. Husband, *The Wildman: Medieval Myth and Symbolism*, New York, 1980

R. C. Hussey, *Extracts from Ancient Documents Relating to the Cathedral and Precincts of Canterbury*, London, 1881

R. Jacob, *Images de la justice: essai sur l'iconographie judiciaire du Moyen Age à l'âge classique*, Paris, 1994

W. Jacobsen, "Die Lorscher Torhalle: Zum Problem ihrer Datierung und Deutung," *Jahrbuch des Zentralinstituts für Kunstgeschichte*, 1, 1985, 9–75

M. R. James, *On the Abbey of S. Edmund at Bury*, Publications of the Cambridge Antiquarian Society, vol. 28, Cambridge, 1895

———, *The Ancient Libraries of Canterbury and Dover*, Cambridge, 1903

———, *The Canterbury Psalter*, 1935

R. Jessup and G. Zarnecki, "The Fausett Pavillion," *Archaeologia Cantiana*, 66, 1953, 1–8

D. Jetter, "Klosterhospitaler: St Gall, Cluny, Escorial," *Archiv für Geschichte der Medizin*, 62, 1978, 313–38

D. Johnson and M. Wyss, "St Denis II, Sculptures Gothiques récement découvertes," *Bulletin Monumental*, 150, 1992, 355–81

P. Jones, *The Italian City State from Commune to Signoria*, Oxford, 1997

D. Kahn, "The Structural Evidence for the Dating of the St Gabriel Chapel Wall-Paintings at Christ Church, Canterbury," *Burlington Magazine*, 126, 1984, 225–29

———, *Canterbury Cathedral and its Romanesque Sculpture*, London, 1991

C. M. Kauffmann, *The Baths of Pozzuoli: A Study of the Medieval Illuminations of Peter of Eboli's Poem*, Oxford, 1959

———, *Romanesque Manuscripts, 1066–1190*, London, 1975

———, "English Romanesque Book Illumination: Changes in the Field 1974–1984," pp. 61–70 in S. Macready and F. H. Thompson (eds.), *Art and Patronage in the English Romanesque*, London, 1986

———, *Biblical Imagery in Medieval England 700–1550*, London, 2003

J. Kerr, *Monastic Hospitality: The Benedictines in England, c. 1070–c. 1230*, Studies in the History of Religion, 32, Woodbridge, 2007

H. Kessler, *Spiritual Seeing: Picturing God's Invisible World*, Philadelphia, 2000

H. Kier, *Der mittelalterliche Schmuckfussboden unter besonderer Berücksichtigung des Rheinlandes*, Düsseldorf, 1970

T. Kinder, *Cistercian Europe*, Grand Rapids, 2002

E. King, *The Anarchy of King Stephen's Reign*, Oxford, 1994

P. Klein (ed.), *Der mittelalterliche Kreuzgang: Architektur, Funktion, und Programm*, Regensburg, 2004

F. Kleiner, *The Arch of Nero in Rome: A Study of the Roman Honorary Arch before and under Nero*, Rome, 1985

D. Knowles, *The Historian and Character*, Cambridge, 1955

———, *The Religious Orders in England*, 3 vols., 2nd ed., Cambridge, 1959

———, *The Monastic Order in England from the Times of St Dunstan to the Fourth Lateran Council*, 2nd ed., Cambridge, 1963

———, *Thomas Becket*, Stanford, 1971

—, *The Religious Orders in England*, 3 vols., Cambridge, 1976

D. Knowles and C. N. L. Brooke, *The Monastic Constitutions of Lanfranc*, Oxford, rev. ed., 2002

A. Korteweg, *Splendour, Gravity, and Emotion: French Medieval Manuscripts in Dutch Collections*, The Hague, 2002

R. Krautheimer, "An Introduction to an 'Iconography of Medieval Architecture'," pp. 115–50 in *Studies in Early Christian, Medieval and Renaissance Art*, New York, 1969

—, *Rome: Profile of a City, 312–1308*, Princeton, 1980

K. Krüger, "Monastic Customs and Liturgy in the Light of the Architectural Evidence: A Case Study on Processions (Eleventh–Twelfth Centuries)," pp. 191–220 in S. Boynton and I. Cochelin (eds.), *From Dead of Night to End of Day: The Medieval Customs of Cluny*, Disciplina Monastica, 3, Turnhout, 2005

M. Kupfer, "Review of Gibson et al., *The Eadwine Psalter: Text, Image, and Monastic Culture in Twelfth-Century Canterbury*," *Speculum*, 69, no. 4, 1994, 1168–71

P. Kurmann, "Architecture, vitrail, et orfèvrerie: à propos des premiers dessins d'édifices gothiques," pp. 33–41 in *Représentations architecturales dans les vitraux*, Liège, 2002

Y. Kusaba, "The Function, Date, and Stylistic Sources of the Treasury of Henry of Blois in the South Transept of Winchester Cathedral," *Winchester Cathedral Record*, 57, 1988, 38–49

—, "Henry of Blois, Winchester, and the Twelfth-Century Renaissance," pp. 69–80 in J. Crook (ed.), *Winchester Cathedral: Nine Hundred Years*, Guildford, 1993

S. Kuttner, "The Revival of Jurisprudence," pp. 299–323 in R. L. Benson and G. Constable (eds.), *Renaissance and Renewal in the Twelfth Century*, Cambridge, 1982

P. Lavedan, *Représentation des villes dans l'art du Moyen Age*, Paris, 1954

C. H. Lawrence, *Medieval Monasticism: Forms of Religious Life in Western Europe in the Middle Ages*, 2nd ed., London, 1989

J. W. Legg and W. H. St. John Hope, *Inventories of Christchurch Canterbury: With Historical and Topographical Introductions and Illustrative Documents*, London, 1902

S. L'Engle, R. Gibbs, and P. Clarke, *Illuminating the Law: Legal Manuscripts in Cambridge Collections*, London, 2001

W. R. Lethaby, *Westminster Abbey and the King's Craftsmen*, London, 1906

M. Lillich, "Cleanliness and Godliness: A Discussion of Medieval Monastic Plumbing," pp. 123–49 in B. Chauvin (ed.), *Mélanges à la mémoire du père Anselme Dimier*, vol. 3, Arbois, 1982

G. Lindenmann-Merz, *Infirmarien-Kranken-und Sterbёhäuser der Mönche Eine architekturhistorische Betrachtung der Infirmariekomplexe nordenglischer Zisterzienserklöster*, Munich, 2009

G. M. Livett, "Hospital of St John in Northgate, Canterbury," *Archaeological Journal*, 86, 1929, 280–84

P. Lowther, "The City of Durham: An Archaeological Survey," *Durham Archaeological Journal*, 9, 1992, 27–119

H. C. G. Matthew and B. Harrison eds., *Oxford Dictionary of National Biography*, 60 vols. Oxford, 2002

J. P. McAleer, "The Tradition of Detached Bell Towers at Cathedral and Monastic Churches in Medieval England and Scotland (1066–1539)," *Journal of the British Archaeological Association*, 154, 2002, 54–83

J. McCann, *The Rule of St Benedict*, London, 1952

C. McClendon, *The Imperial Abbey of Farfa: Architectural Currents of the Early Middle Ages*, New Haven and London, 1987

D. McKitterick, "The Eadwine Psalter Rediscovered," pp. 195–208 in M. Gibson, T. A. Heslop, and R. Pfaff (eds.) *The Eadwine Psalter: Text, Image, and Monastic Culture in Twelfth-Century Canterbury*, London 1992

J. McNeill, "The Continental Context," pp. 1–71 in M. Henig and J. McNeill (eds.), *The Medieval Cloister in England and Wales*, special issue of the *Journal of the British Archaeological Association*, 159, Leeds, 2006 (2006a)

—, "The East Cloister Range of Rochester Cathedral," pp. 181–204 in T. Ayers and T. Tatton-Brown (eds.), *Medieval Art, Architecture and Archaeology at Rochester*, British Archaeological Association Conference Transactions, 28, Leeds, 2006 (2006b)

J. McNeill and E. Fernie, "Cluny en Angleterre," pp. 370–79 in N. Stratford et al, *Corpus de la sculpture de Cluny*, 2 vols, Paris, 2011

S. Macready and F. H. Thompson (eds.), *Art and Patronage in the English Romanesque*, London, 1986

S. Maddalo, *Il De Balneis Puteolanis de Pietro da Eboli*, Vatican City, 2003

R. Magnusson, *Water Technology in the Middle Ages: Cities, Monasteries, and Waterworks after the Roman Empire*, Baltimore, 2001

C. Maines, "Word and Image – Meaning and Function: The Aque Ductus Relief at Santa Maria de Alcobaça," *Cîteaux Commentarii Cistercienses*, 57, 2006, 5–43

F. W. Maitland, "Magistri Vacarii Summa de Matrimonio," *Law Quarterly Review*, 12, 1897, 133–43, 270–87

P. Meadows and N. Ramsay (eds.), *A History of Ely Cathedral*, Woodbridge, 2003

A. Melinkas, *The Corpus of Miniatures in the Manuscripts of the Decretum Gratiani*, 3 vols., Rome, 1975

W. T. Mellows, "The King's Lodging at Peterborough," *Peterborough Natural History, Scientific and Archaeological Association Annual Report*, 1932–33, 29–36

A. Meyer, *Medieval Allegory and the Building of the New Jerusalem*, Brewer, 2003

M. Miller, "From Episcopal to Communal Palaces: Places and Power in Northern Italy," *Journal of the Society of Architectural Historians*, 54, 1995, 175–85

—, *The Bishop's Palace: Architecture and Authority in Medieval Italy*, Ithaca, 2000

J. Montague, "The Cloister and Bishop's Palace at Old Sarum with Some Thoughts on the Origins and Meaning of Secular Cathedral Cloisters," pp. 48–70 in M. Henig and J.

McNeill (eds.), *The Medieval Cloister in England and Wales*, special issue of the *Journal of the British Archaeological Association*, 159, Leeds, 2006

S. Moorhouse and S. Wrathmell, *Kirkstall Abbey, Volume 1: The 1950–64 Excavations, a Reassessment*, Wakefield and Leeds, 1987

J. Morgenstern, *The Gates of Righteousness*, Cincinnati, 1929

C. Morris, *The Sepulchre of Christ and the Medieval West*, Oxford, 2005

V. Mortet, *Recueil des texts relatifs à l'histoire de l'architecture en France*, vol. 1, Paris, 1911

J. Newman, *The Buildings of England: North East and East Kent*, London, 1969

F. M. Nichols (ed. and trans.), *The Marvels of Rome, Mirabilia Urbis Romae*, New York, 1986

U. Nilgen, "Thomas Becket as a Patron of the Arts," *Art History*, 3, 1980, 357–74

———, "Intellectuality and Splendor: Thomas Becket as Patron of the Arts," pp. 145–58 in S. Macready and F. H. Thompson (eds.), *Art and Patronage in the English Romanesque*, London, 1986

———, "Psalter für Gelehrte und Ungelehrte im höhen Mittelalter," pp. 239–47 in F. O. Büttner (ed.), *The Illuminated Psalter: Studies in the Content, Purpose and Placement of its Images*, Turnhout, 2004

W. Noel, "The Utrecht Psalter in England: Continuity and Experiment," pp. 120–65 in K. van der Horst et al. (eds.), *The Utrecht Psalter in Medieval Art: Picturing the Psalms of David*, Tuurdijk, 1996

C. Nordenfalk, "The Corpus of the Miniatures in the Manuscripts of the Decretum Gratiani by Anthony Melnikas," *Zeitschrift für Kunstgeschichte*, 43, 1980, 318–37

C. Norton, "The Luxury Pavement in England before Westminster," in L. Grant and R. Mortimer eds., *Westminster Abbey: The Cosmati Pavements, London*, 2002, 7–36

R. Ousterhout, "The Church of Santo Stefano: A 'Jerusalem' in Bologna," *Gesta*, 20, 1981, 311–21

———, "The Temple, the Sepulchre, and the Martyrion of the Saviour," *Gesta*, 29, 1990, 44–54

———, "Jerusalem Elsewhere: Flexible Geography and Transportable Topography," pp. 393–404 in B. Kühnel (ed.), *The Real and Ideal Jerusalem in Jewish, Christian, and Islamic Art: Studies in Honor of Bezalel Narkiss on the Occasion of his Seventieth Birthday*, Jerusalem, 1998

———, "Architecture as Relic and the Construction of the Sanctity: The Stones of the Holy Sepulchre," *Journal of the Society of Architectural Historians*, 62, 2003, 4–23

———, " 'Sweetly Refreshed in Imagination': Remembering Jerusalem in Words and Images," *Gesta*, 48, no. 2, 2010, 153–69

D. Park and R. Griffith-Jones (eds.), *The Temple Church in London: History, Architecture, Art*, Woodbridge, 2010

J. Paul, *Der Palazzo Vecchio in Florenz: Ursprung und Bedutung seiner Form*, Florence, 1969

H.-E. Paulus, H. Reidel, and P. W. Winkler, *Wasser-Lebensquelle und Bedeutungsträger*, Regensburger Herbstsymposium sur Kunstgeschichte und Denkmalpflege, vol. 4, Regensburg, 1999

F. Paxton, *Christanized Death: The Creation of Ritual*, Ithaca, 1990

N. Pickwoad, "Codicology," pp. 4–12 in M. Gibson, T. A. Heslop, and R. Pfaff (eds.), *The Eadwine Psalter: Text, Image, and Monastic Culture in Twelfth-Century Canterbury*, London, 1992

A. I. Pini, "Le piazza medievale di Bologna," *Annali di architettura*, 4–5, 1992–93, 122–33

A. A. Poirée, *Histoire de l'abbaye du Bec*, 2 vols., Evreux, 1926

S. Pratt, "The Campanile," *Canterbury Archaeological Reports*, 26, 2001–2, 7–10

L. Pressouyre, "Did Suger Build the Cloister of Saint-Denis?" pp. 256–68 in P. Gerson (ed.), *Abbot Suger and Saint-Denis: A Symposium*, New York, 1986

———, "Les Cisterciens et la signalization de l'eau au moyen âge," vol. 1, pp. 159–62 in A. Cadei (ed.), *Arte d'Occidente, termi e metodi: Studi in onore de Angiola Maria Romanini*, 3 vols., Rome, 1999

L. Pressouyre and P. Benoit, *L'hydraulique monastique; milieux, réseaux, usages*, Paris, 1996

B. Pugh, *Imprisonment in Medieval England*, Cambridge, 1970

C. M. Radding, *The Origins of Medieval Jurisprudence: Pavia and Bologna 850–1150*, New Haven and London, 1988

G. Radke, *Viterbo: Profile of a Thirteenth Century Papal Palace*, Cambridge, 1996

J. Rady, T. Tatton-Brown, and J. A. Bowen, "The Archbishop's Palace, Canterbury," *Journal of the British Archaeological Association*, 144, 1991, 1–60

I. Ragusa, "Terror Demonum and Terror Inimicorum: The Two Lions of the Throne of Solomon and the Open Doors of Paradise," *Zeitschrift für Kunstgeschichte*, 40, 1977, 93–114

J. Raine (ed.), *The Historians of the Church of York and its Archbishops*, 3 vols., Rolls Series, 71, London, 1879–94

N. Ramsay, "The Manuscripts Flew about like Butterflies: The Break-up of English Libraries in the Sixteenth Century," in J. Raven (ed.), *Lost Libraries: The Destruction of Great Book Collections since Antiquity*, London, 2004

———, "Law," pp. 250–90 in N. Morgan and R. Thomson (eds.), *The Cambridge History of the Book in Britain, Volume II: 1100–1400*, Cambridge, 2008

N. Rauty, *L'antico palazzo dei vescovi a Pistoia*, 3 vols., Florence, 1981–85

I. Richmond, "Commemorative Arches and City Gates in the Augustan Age," *Journal of Roman Studies*, 23, 1933, 149–74

D. Robinson and C. Platt, *Strata Florida Abbey, Talley Abbey*, 3rd ed., Cardiff, 2007

J. A. Robinson, *The Abbot's House at Westminster*, Cambridge, 1911

B. Rose, *Dynastic Commemoration and Imperial Portraiture in the Julio-Claudian Period*, Cambridge, 1997

C. F. Routledge, J. B. Sheppard and W. A. Scott Robinson,

"The Crypt of Canterbury Cathedral," *Archaeologia Cantiana*, 18, 1889, 253–56

C. Rudolph, "Building Miracles as Artistic Justification in the Early and Mid-Twelfth Century," pp. 399–409 in W. Kersten (ed.), *Radical Art History: Internationale Anthologie; Subject O. K. Werckmeister*, Zurich, 1997

———, *"First, I Find the Center Point": Reading the Text of Hugh of Saint Victor's The Mystic Ark*, Philadelphia, 2004

J. Rüffer, *Die Zisterzienser und ihre Klöster: Leben und Bauen für Gott*, Darmstadt, 2008

M. Rule (ed.), *Eadmer Historia Nouorum in Anglia*, Rolls Series, 81, London, 1884

V. Ruprich-Robert, *L'architecture Normande aux XIe et XIIe siècles en Normandie et en Angleterre*, 2 vols., Paris, 1884–89

R. Rutherford, "Psalm 113 (114/115) and Christian Burial," *Studia Patristica*, 13, 1975, 391–95

P. Ryder, "The Moot Hall: The Two Towers of Hexham," *Archaeologia Aeliana*, series 5, 12, 1994, 185–217

L. Sagui, *L'esedra della Crypta Balbi nel medioevo (XI–XV secolo)*, Florence, 1990

A. Saltman, *Theobald, Archbishop of Canterbury*, London, 1956

L. F. Salzman, *Building in England down to 1540: A Documentary History*, 2nd edn., Oxford, 1967

W. Sauerlander, *Gothic Sculpture in France 1140–1270*, London, 1970

———, "Löwen in Lyon," pp. 215–24 in A. Rosenauer and G. Weber (eds.), *Kunsthistorische Forschungen: Otto Pächt zu seinem 70. Geburtstag*, Salzburg, 1972

———, "Romanesque Art 2000: A Worn Out Notion?" pp. 40–56 in C. Hourihane (ed.), *Romanesque Art and Thought in the Twelfth Century: Essays in Honor of Walter Cahn*, University Park, PA, 2008

J. Sayers, "Monastic Archdeacons," pp. 177–203 in C. N. L. Brooke (ed.), *Church and Government in the Middle Ages: Essays Presented to Christopher Cheney on his 70th Birthday*, London, 1976

M. Scelles, "La maison romane de Saint-Antonin-Noble-Val (Tarn-et-Garonne)," *Mémoires de la Société archéologique Midi de la France*, 49, 1989, 45–119

H. Schadt, *Die Darstellungen der Arbores Consanguinitatis und der Arbores Affinitatis*, Tübingen, 1982

R. Schilling, "The *Decretum Gratiani* formerly in the Dyson Perrins Collection: An Enquiry into the Origin of its Text and Illumination," *Journal of the British Archaeological Association*, 3rd series, 23, 1962, 27–39

W. Schöller, "Ritzzeichnungen: Ein Beitrag zur Geschichte der Architekturzeichnung im Mittelalter," *Architectura*, 19, 1989, 31–61

J. Schröder, *Gervasius von Canterbury, Richard von Saint-Victor und die Methodik der Bauerfassung im 12. Jahrhundert*, 2 vols., Cologne, 2000

R. Schützeichel, "Die Kölner Namenlister des Londoner MS Harley 2850," in R. Schützeichel and M. Zender eds., *Namenforschung. Festschrift für Adolf Bach*, Heidelberg, 1965, 96–126

E. Searle (ed.), *The Chronicle of Battle Abbey*, Oxford, 1980

W. G. Searle (ed.), *Christ Church, Canterbury, the Chronicle of John Stone and Lists of Deans, Priors and Monks of Christ Church Monastery*, Cambridge Antiquarian Society, Octavo Series, 34, Cambridge, 1902

L. Serbat, "Quelques églises anciennement détruits du Nord de la France," *Bulletin Monumental*, 88, 1929, 365–435

H. D. Shultz, "Schichtungen im Kalksinter der römischen Wasserleitungen nach Köln – Ein Hilfe zur relativen Datierung," in K. Grewe ed., *Atlas der römischen Wasserleitungen nach Köln*, Cologne, 1986, 263–68

R. A. L. Smith, *Canterbury Cathedral Priory: A Study of Monastic Administration*, Cambridge, 1943

W. Somner, *The Antiquities of Canterbury*, London, 1640

R. W. Southern, "Master Vacarius and the Beginning of an English Academic Tradition," pp. 257–86 in J. J. G. Alexander and M. T. Gibson (eds.), *Medieval Learning and Literature: Essays Presented to R. W. Hunt*, Oxford, 1976

———, (ed. and trans.), *Eadmeri Vita Anselmi: The Life of St Anselm by Eadmer*, London, 1996

M. Sparks, "Lanfranc," *Canterbury Cathedral Chronicle*, 83, 1989, 33–38

———, "Estates," pp. 566–70 in P. Collinson, N. Ramsay, and M. Sparks (eds.), *A History of Canterbury Cathedral*, 2nd. ed., Canterbury, 2002

———, *Canterbury Cathedral Precincts: A Historical Survey*, Canterbury, 2007

———, "The Treasury and the Choir Practice Room," *Canterbury Cathedral Chronicle*, 105, 2011, 20–23

M. Sparks and T. Tatton-Brown, "29 The Precincts," *Canterbury Cathedral Chronicle*, 81, 1987, 36–41

———, "19 The Precincts," *Canterbury Cathedral Chronicle*, 83, 1989, 23–28

P. Squatriti, *Water and Society in Early Medieval Italy*, Cambridge, 1998

R. Stalley, "Decorating the Lavabo: Late Romanesque Sculptures from Mellifont Abbey," *Proceedings of the Royal Irish Academy*, 96, 1996, 237–64

M. M. N. Stansfield, "Recovering the Past: The Aftermath of Canterbury Cathedral's Audit House Fire of 1670," *Archaeologia Cantiana*, 117, 1997, 37–50

S. H. Steckoll, *The Gates of Jerusalem*, New York and Washington, D.C., 1968

P. Stein, "Vacarius and the Civil Law," pp. 119–37 in C. N. L. Brooke (ed.), *Church and Government in the Middle Ages: Essays Presented to C. R. Cheney on his 70th Birthday*, Cambridge, 1976

R. Stieglecker, *Die Renaissance eines Heiligen: Sebastian Brant und Onuphrius eremita*, Wiesbaden, 2001

D. Stocker, *St Mary's Guildhall: The Survey and Excavation of a Medieval Building Complex*, Lincoln, 1991

D. Stocker and P. Everson, *Summoning St Michael: Early Romanesque Towers in Lincolnshire*, Oxford, 2006

N. Stratford, "A Romanesque Ivory from Lichfield Cathedral," *British Museum Yearbook*, 2, 1977, 212–16

_____, "Les bâtiments de l'abbaye de Cluny à l'époque médiévale: état des questions," *Bulletin Monumental*, 150, 1992, 383–411

_____, *Cluny 910–2010: onze siècles de rayonnement*, Paris, 2010

N. Stratford, B. Maurice-Chabard, D. Walsh, *Corpus de la sculpture de Cluny*, 2 vols., Paris, 2011

J. J. A. Strik, "Remains of the Lanfranc Building in the Great Central Tower and the North-West Choir/Transept Area," pp. 20–26 in N. Coldstream and P. Draper (eds.), *Medieval Art and Architecture at Canterbury before 1220*, British Archaeological Association Conference Transactions, 5, 1982

W. Stubbs (ed.), *Gervase of Canterbury: Historical Works, the Chronicle of the Reigns of Stephen, Henry II, and Richard I by Gervase the Monk of Canterbury*, 2 vols., Rolls Series, 73, London, 1879–80

J. Summerson, *Heavenly Mansions*, London, 1949

H. Swarzenski, *Monuments of Romanesque Art: The Art of Church Treasures in North-Western Europe*, 1954

S. Sweetinburgh, "Supporting the Canterbury Hospitals: Benefaction and the Language of Charity in the Twelfth and Thirteenth Centuries," *Archaeologia Cantiana*, 122, 2002, 237–58

T. W. T. Tatton-Brown, "The Font in St. Martin's Church," pp. 19–20 in M. Sparks (ed.), *The Parish of St. Martin and St. Paul, Canterbury: Historical Essays in Memory of James Hobbs*, Canterbury, 1980

———, "The Great Hall of the Archbishop's Palace," pp. 113–19 in N. Coldstream and P. Draper (eds.), *Medieval Art and Architecture at Canterbury before 1220*, British Archaeological Association Conference Transactions, 5, Leeds, 1982

———, "The Precincts' Water Supply," *Canterbury Cathedral Chronicle*, 77, 1983, 45–51

———, "Three Great Benedictine Houses in Kent: Their Buildings and Topography," *Archaeologia Cantiana*, 102, 1985, 171–88

———, "A Decade of Archaeology," *Friends of Rochester Cathedral*, Report for 1988/9, 21–29

———, "Building Stone in Canterbury c. 1070–1525," in D. Parsons ed., *Stone Quarrying and Building in England AD 43–1525*, Chichester, 1990, 70–82

———, "Archbishop's Palace, Canterbury: Excavations and Recording Work from 1981–1986," *Journal of the British Archaeological Association*, 144, 1991, 1–60 (1991a)

———, "The Buildings and Topography of St Augustine's Abbey, Canterbury," *Journal of the British Archaeological Association*, 144, 1991, 61–91 (1991b)

———, "The Abbey Precinct, Liberty and Estate," pp. 123–42 in R. Gem (ed.), *St Augustine's Abbey, Canterbury*, London, 1997

———, *Lambeth Palace: A History of the Archbishops of Canterbury and their Houses*, London, 2000

———, "The Two Mid-Twelfth-Century Cloister Arcades at Canterbury Cathedral Priory," pp. 91–104 in M. Henig and J. McNeill (eds.), *The Medieval Cloister in England and Wales*, special issue of the *Journal of the British Archaeological Association*, 159, Leeds, 2006

T. Tatton-Brown and J. Munby (eds.), *The Archaeology of Cathedrals*, Oxford University Committee for Archaeology, Monograph 42, Oxford, 1996

A. Thompson, *Cities of God: The Religion of the Italian Communes 1125–1325*, University Park, PA, 2005

A. H. Thompson, "A Descriptive Note on Sir W. H. St. John Hope's Plan of the Infirmary of St Austin's Abbey," *Archaeologia Cantiana*, 46, 1934, 183–91

B. J. Thompson (ed.), *Monasteries and Society in Medieval Britain*, Harlaxton Medieval Studies, 6, Stamford, 1999

E. M. Thompson (ed.), *Customary of St. Augustine's Abbey Canterbury*, London, 1902

M. H. Thompson, "Robert Willis and Ecclesiastical Architecture in the Middle Ages," pp. 153–64 in T. Tatton-Brown and J. Munby (eds.), *The Archaeology of Cathedrals*, Oxford University Committee for Archaeology, Monograph 42, Oxford, 1996

M. W. Thompson, *The Medieval Hall: The Basis of Secular Domestic Life, 600–1600 AD*, Aldershot, 1995

———, *Medieval Bishops' Houses in England and Wales*, Louth, 1998

P. Underwood, "The Fountains of Life in Manuscripts of the Gospels," *Dumbarton Oaks Papers*, 5, 1950, 41–138

W. Urry, "St Anselm and his Cult at Canterbury," *Spicilegium Beccense*, 1, 1959, 571–93

———, *Canterbury under the Angevin Kings*, London, 1967

———, "A Lost Corner of the Cathedral Precincts at Canterbury: Two Tinted Drawings of 1685 in the Bodleian Library," *Canterbury Cathedral Chronicle*, 72, 1978, 41–50

———, "Canterbury, Kent," pp. 43–58 in R. A. Skelton and P. D. A. Harvey (eds.), *Local Maps and Plans from Medieval England*, Oxford, 1986

K. van der Horst, "The Utrecht Psalter: Picturing the Psalms of David," pp. 23–84 in K. van der Horst et al. (eds.), *The Utrecht Psalter in Medieval Art: Picturing the Psalms of David*, Tuurdijk, 1996

F. van Noten, *La Salle aux Trésors: chef d'oeuvres de l'art roman et mosan*, Turnhout, 1999

C. Verzár Bornstein, *Portals and Politics in the Early Italian City-State: The Sculpture of Nicholaus in Context*, Parma, 1988

L. Voigts and M. R. McVaugh (eds.) *A Latin Technical Phlebotomy and its Middle English Translation*, Transactions of the American Philosophical Society, vol. 74, Philadelphia, 1984

H. Wanley, *Antiquae Literaturae Septentrionalis Liber Alter*, 1705

B. Ward-Perkins, *From Classical Antiquity to the Middle Ages: Urban Public Building in Northern and Central Italy, A.D. 300–850*, Oxford, 1984

W. L. Warren, *Henry II*, London, 1973

E. A. Webb, *The Records of St Bartholomew's Priory and of the Church and Parish of St Bartholomew the Great, West Smithfield*, 2 vols., Oxford, 1921

T. Webber, "Script and Manuscript Production at Christ Church, Canterbury after the Norman Conquest," pp. 145–58 in R. Eales and R. Sharpe (eds.), *Canterbury and the Norman Conquest*, London, 1995

———, "The Bible and its Study: From the Cloisters to the University," pp. 74–117 in P. Binski and S. Panayotova (eds.), *The Cambridge Illuminations: Ten Centuries of Book Production in the Medieval West*, London, 2005

D. Weiss, "Architectural Symbolism and the Decoration of the Ste. Chapelle," *Art Bulletin*, 77, 1995, 308–20

J. West, "The 12th-Century Worked Stones and Romanesque Architecture," pp. 67–74 in L. Keen and P. Ellis (eds.), *Sherborne Abbey and School Excavations 1972–76 and 1990*, Dorset Natural History and Archaeological Society Monograph Series, 16, Dorchester, 2005

———, "A Taste for the Antique? Henry of Blois and the Arts," *Anglo-Norman Studies*, 30, 2008, 213–30

———, "The Romanesque Screen at Canterbury Cathedral Reconsidered," in A. Bovey (ed.), *British Archaeological Association Canterbury Conference Transactions*, 35, Leeds, 2012 (forthcoming)

H. Wharton (ed.), *Anglia Sacra*, 2 vols., London, 1691

A. B. Whittingham, *Bury St Edmunds Abbey*, London, 1971

R. Willis, *The Architectural History of Canterbury Cathedral*, London, 1845

———, "The Architectural History of the Conventual Buildings of the Monastery of Christ Church, Canterbury considered in relation to the Monastic Life and Rules, and drawn up from Personal Surveys and Original Documentary Research," *Archaeologia Cantiana*, 7, 1868, 1–206

C. Wilson, "The Cistercians as 'Missionaries of Gothic' in Northern England," pp. 86–116 in E. C. Norton and D. Park (eds.), *Cistercian Art and Architecture in the British Isles*, Cambridge, 1986

———, *The Gothic Cathedral: The Architecture of the Great Church 1130–1530*, London, 1990

———, "The Medieval Monuments," pp. 451–510 in P. Collinson, N. Ramsay, and M. Sparks (eds.), *A History of Canterbury Cathedral*, Oxford, 1995

———, "The Medieval Monuments," in P. Collinson, N. Ramsay and M. Sparks eds., *A History of Canterbury Cathedral*, 2nd edn., Canterbury, 2002, 451–510

———, "Gothic Architecture Transplanted: The Nave of the Temple Church in London," pp. 19–44 in D. Park and R. Griffith-Jones (eds.), *The Temple Church in London*, Woodbridge, 2010

C. Wilson and J. Burton, *St Mary's Abbey, York*, York, 1988

F. Woodman, *The Architectural History of Canterbury Cathedral*, London, 1981

———, "The Waterworks Drawings of the Eadwine Psalter," pp. 168–85 in M. Gibson, T. A. Heslop, and R. Pfaff (eds.), *The Eadwine Psalter: Text, Image, and Monastic Culture in Twelfth-Century Canterbury*, London, 1992

C. E. Woodruff (ed.), "A Monastic Chronicle Lately Discovered at Christ Church, Canterbury; with Introduction and Notes," *Archaeologia Cantiana*, 29, 1911, 47–84

———, "The Sacrist's Rolls of Christ Church, Canterbury," *Archaeologia Cantiana*, 48, 1936, 38–80

———, "The Parliamentary Survey of the Precincts of Canterbury Cathedral in the Time of the Commonwealth," *Archaeologia Cantiana*, 50, 1938, 195–222

C. E. Woodruff and W. Danks, *Memorials of the Cathedral and Priory of Christ in Canterbury*, London, 1912

B. C. Worssam, "A Guide to the Building Stones of Rochester Cathedral," *Friends of Rochester Cathedral, Report for 1993/4*, 23–34

S. Wrathmell, *Kirkstall Abbey: The Guest House*, 2nd ed., Wakefield, 1987

F. Yates, "Architecture and the Art of Memory," *Architectural Association Quarterly*, 12, no. 4, 1980, 4–13

F. Yegul, *Bathing in the Roman World*, Cambridge, 2010

G. Zarnecki, "The Faussett Pavilion: The King Canute Relief," *Archaeologia Cantiana*, 68, 1954, 8–14

———, "The Carved Stones from Newark Castle," *Transactions of the Thornton Society of Nottinghamshire*, 40, 1955, 23–35

———, "A Late Romanesque Fountain from Campania," *Minneapolis Institute of Art Bulletin*, 1973, 1–10

———, "English Twelfth-Century Sculpture and its Resistance to St. Denis," pp. 83–92 in F. Emmison and R. Stephens (eds.), *Tribute to an Antiquary: Essays Presented to Marc Fitch*, London 1976

———, "The Eadwine Portrait," pp. 93–98 in S. McK. Crosby et al. (eds.) *Études d'art medieval offertes à Louis Grodecki*, Paris, 1981

———, (ed.), *English Romaneque Art 1066–1200*, London, 1984

———, "Henry of Blois as a Patron of Architecture," pp. 159–72 in S. Macready and F. H. Thompson (eds.), *Art and Patronage in the English Romanesque*, London, 1986

Index

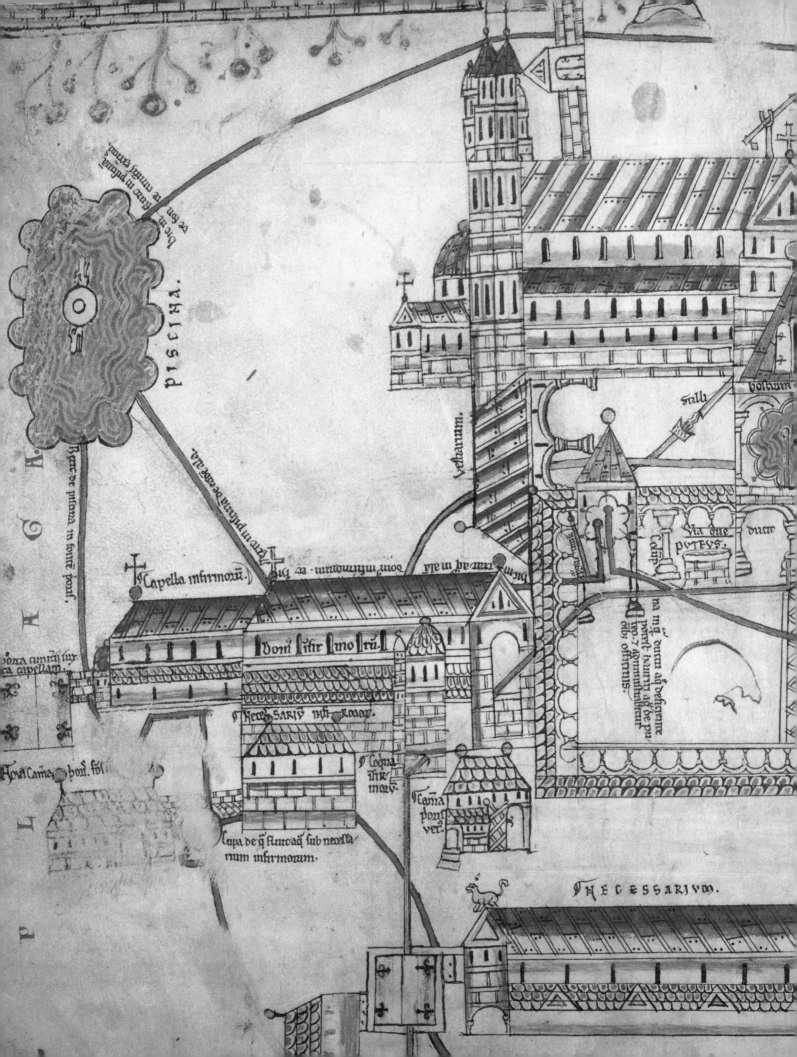

PISCINA.

hc q de prisona in fonce pons.

A GR

PL

na hujusce aque in undis garar.
loq in putheas.

Capella infirmoru.

Pera in piscina de ecce ala.

bona amis sur
ca capellam.

Apud cama hou. sol.

Cupa de q fluicai sub neces la
rium infirmorum.

Necessariu hui loco.

Dom' sier' smo tru.

Cogna
sir mory.

Cama
pons ver.

herbarum.

bic marcai in ala.

pons infirmorum. er.

Caldar

Stall

hostium

via que ducir
PUTEUS.

na ing ducai ab befigente
poterit haurin af de pu
teo. 7 ad omia baltear
cib' officiris.

NECESSARIUM.